# Microsoft
# SQL Server
# Training Volume 2

PUBLISHED BY
Microsoft Press
A Division of Microsoft Corporation
One Microsoft Way
Redmond, Washington 98052-6399

Library of Congress Cataloging-in-Publication Data
Microsoft SQL server training : hands-on self-paced training kit for
    version 6.5 / Microsoft Corporation.
        p.   cm.
    Includes index.
    ISBN 1-55615-930-7
    1. Database management--Programmed instruction.   2. SQL server-
-Programmed instruction.     I. Microsoft Corporation.
QA76.9.D3M5738   1996
005.75'65--dc20                                                          96-18665
                                                                           CIP

Printed and bound in the United States of America.

    2  3  4  5  6  7  8  9   MLML   1  0  9  8  7  6

Distributed to the book trade in Canada by Macmillan of Canada, a division of Canada Publishing
Corporation.

A CIP catalogue record for this book is available from the British Library.

Microsoft Press books are available through booksellers and distributors worldwide. For further
information about international editions, contact your local Microsoft Corporation office. Or contact
Microsoft Press International directly at fax (206) 936-7329.

Vol. 2 -- Part No. 097-0001509

# Contents

# Volume 1

# Volume 2

C H A P T E R   1 3

# Managing SQL Server Security

## About This Chapter

To use a database, each user must have a valid login ID to the server and a valid database username. This chapter addresses the issues in planning how users access a server and database, and implementing server security.

## Before You Begin

To complete the lessons in this chapter, you must have:

- Configured your Windows NT–based computer to allow the group Everyone to log on locally.

- Installed SQL Server on your computer. Installation procedures are covered in Chapter 2, "Installing SQL Server."

- Experience using the SQL Enterprise Manager, the SQL Enterprise Manager Query Tool, and ISQL/w.

- Knowledge of Windows NT Server user accounts, groups, Windows NT User Manager, and .CMD files. In this chapter, Windows NT User Manager is referred to, although your Windows NT–based computer might display User Manager for Domains. Both utilities function the same for purposes of this chapter.

# Lesson 1: SQL Server Security Concepts

SQL Server security is a combination of a login security mode and database security features such as usernames, groups, and aliases. Planning your security system thoroughly before you implement it will help you avoid problems during implementation.

### After this lesson you will be able to:

- Describe the different types of login security.
- Describe login IDs, usernames, aliases, and groups.
- Plan how to implement security for your SQL Server installation.

### Estimated lesson time  10 minutes

*Login security* limits access to a server to a specified list of login IDs. Login security can be implemented using one of three login security modes: *integrated* (SQL Server logins verified by Windows NT login security), *standard* (verified by SQL Server), or *mixed* (verified by either Windows NT or SQL Server).

Once login security has been set up, database access is controlled by a list of *permissions* to input data, run statements, or modify objects that have been granted to specific *usernames*. A database user is known to the database, and is correlated to a login ID.

The following figure illustrates that to work with a particular database object, a user must have a valid login ID, be registered as a database user, and have permission to work with the database object.

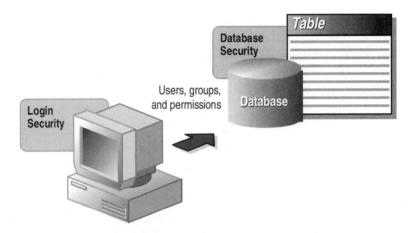

## Security Concepts

The following concepts are key to understanding how security is implemented in SQL Server.

### Login Security Mode

The login security mode determines the manner in which a SQL server validates a login request. There are three modes of login security: integrated, standard, and mixed.

*Integrated security* allows a SQL server to use Windows NT authentication mechanisms to validate logins for all connections. Only network protocols such as multiprotocol or named pipes, that support trusted or authenticated connections between clients and servers are allowed.

*Standard security* uses SQL Server's own login validation process for all connections. To log in to a SQL Server, each user must provide a valid login ID and password. Standard security is implemented when SQL Server is installed.

*Mixed security* allows login requests to be validated using either integrated or standard security. Both trusted connections (used by integrated security) and nontrusted connections (used by standard security) can be established.

### Login Security and Client-Requested Trusted Connections

Regardless of the server's login security mode, Microsoft ODBC and DB-Library client applications can be configured to always request a trusted connection from the server.

Requesting a trusted connection allows the SQL Executive service to connect to remote servers as long as the SQL Executive service is running under a Windows NT user account that has been granted system administrator (SA) access to the SQL server. Requesting a trusted connection also allows users who have been granted SA privileges to access the SQL Server when they use a client application that is configured to force trusted connections. This feature forces a trusted connection, but the appropriate user privilege levels must exist if the login is to succeed.

You can prevent logging on over client-requested trusted connections. Preventing client-requested trusted connections restricts applications and features that use trusted connections.

## Login IDs

Login security is managed with login IDs or *logins*. A login ID is a name by which a user is known to SQL Server. A login ID does not grant access to any databases. To log in to a SQL server that is running standard security, a user must provide a valid login ID and password. The following table describes the login IDs created automatically by SQL Server.

| Login ID | Description |
| --- | --- |
| system administrator (SA) | A special login ID that operates outside SQL Server's protection system. Anyone who knows the SA password can log in and act as system administrator (unless the server is running in integrated security mode). |
| probe | A special login ID that is reserved for use by some applications (for example, SQL Performance Monitor) to connect to SQL Server if it is configured for standard security. If SQL Server is configured for integrated security, the SA login ID is used instead of probe. The probe login ID is automatically created during installation. |
| | Users should not log in using this login ID. |
| repl_publisher and repl_subscriber | These special logins are reserved to allow replication processes to connect to servers configured for replication. They should not be modified, and users should not use them to log in. |

Other login IDs are created by a system administrator. Login IDs are stored are on each server. If a user needs access to multiple servers, the user must have a login ID on each of those servers.

### Remote Servers and Login IDs

A *remote server* is a SQL server on the network that a user can access through his or her local server, allowing the user to execute stored procedures on the remote server. Certain conditions must be in place to use remote servers:

- A server must allow remote access from other servers.

  Access is allowed by default. If you do not want the server to use remote stored procedures, turn off the Remote Access configuration option using **sp_configure**.

- Each server must store both its own name, as the local server, and the name of the other server in its *sysservers* table.

- The login ID that the local server uses when opening the connection must exist on the remote server.

There are three variations that are available when setting up login IDs on a remote server:

- Designate a login ID that will be used whenever the local server logs on to the remote server so that the local server is considered the client of the remote server.

- Specify that the login ID of the client-to-local server connection is the login ID to be used. Thus the client of the local server is treated as being the client of the remote server.

- Map specific login IDs on the local server to specific login IDs on the remote server using the **sp_addremotelogin** stored procedure.

---

**Note**   The type of SQL Server security chosen (integrated, mixed, or standard) does not affect the management of remote users.

---

You can also manage remote servers with the following system stored procedures:

| | |
|---|---|
| sp_addremotelogin | sp_helpremotelogin |
| sp_addserver | sp_helpserver |
| sp_dropremotelogin | sp_remoteoption |
| sp_dropserver | sp_serveroption |

## Usernames

To access a specific database, a user must have a *username* in that database. In SQL Server, a database username is a name assigned to a login ID for the purpose of allowing a user to have access to a database. The abilities a user has within a database depend on the permissions granted to the username and to any groups the username is a member of. User permissions can also be defined within SQL Server using *aliases* and *groups*.

---

**Note**  A SQL Server username is not a Windows NT username. In Windows NT, a username is the name by which the user is known to the domain, or to an individual Windows NT–based computer.

---

The following table describes the usernames created automatically by SQL Server.

| Username | Description | Databases |
|---|---|---|
| dbo | The username assigned to the database owner (DBO) or creator of a database (the SA login, by default). There is only one DBO. The DBO has full privileges inside the database that he or she owns, and determines the access and capabilities provided to other users. | *master*, *model*, *pubs* |
| guest | A special username that enables any user with a SQL Server login ID to access a database. Not created by default for most databases. | *master*, *pubs* |
| probe | A special username associated with the probe login ID. Reserved for use by applications to connect to SQL Server if it is configured for standard security. The probe username is automatically created during installation. Users should not use this username. | *master* |
| repl_subscriber | A special username reserved for the replication process. This database username should not be modified, nor should users use it to access the database. | *master* |

You may want to create a *guest* username in your databases to enable any user with a login ID for SQL Server to access the database. By default, no guest user is created in all new databases. If you want to create a guest user in all of your new databases, add a guest username to the *model* database. Any database created after that point will contain the guest user. The *master* database always contains a guest user, so users can execute system procedures.

---

**Note**  There is no SA username associated with the SA login because SQL Server does no permission checking for the system administrator login.

---

## Aliases

Aliases are usernames that are shared by several login IDs. A database alias allows you to treat more than one person as the same user inside a database, with the same permissions. Any username in a database can also serve as an alias. If a login ID is assigned an alias in a database, that login ID cannot also have a username within the database.

Aliases are often used so that several users can assume the role of database owner. Aliases can also be used to set up a collective user identity, within which the identities of individual users can be traced.

## Groups

SQL Server users can also be made members of groups. In SQL Server, a group is a collection of database users. Users in a group receive the database permissions granted to the group. Groups simplify managing large numbers of database users, because they provide a convenient way to grant and revoke permissions to more than one user at the same time.

The group Public is automatically created in every database. Each user automatically belongs to Public and can be added to only one other group. You cannot remove a user from Public.

---

**Note**  A SQL Server group is not a Windows NT group. In Windows NT, a group is a collection of Windows NT users. A Windows NT user can be a member of several Windows NT groups.

---

## User Status

SQL Server grants special status to three types of users. The SA is the person responsible for the administrative and operational functions that are independent of any particular application, and is likely to be a person with a comprehensive overview of SQL Server and all its applications and databases.

The system administrator operates outside the protection system, and does not have a username in any database. The system administrator is also treated as the owner of whatever database he or she is using. Anyone who knows the SA password can log in and act as system administrator (unless the server is running in integrated login security mode).

The database owner (DBO) is the creator of a database. There is only one DBO in a database. The DBO has full privileges inside the database that he or she owns, and determines the access and capabilities provided to other users. Although a login ID may be recognized as DBO in one database, it may be associated with a different username in another database. DBO status is automatically assigned to the SA login, but can be reassigned to a different user. The DBO username can be assigned to only one login ID, although other login IDs can be aliased to DBO.

The user who creates a database object is the *database object owner (DBOO)* and is automatically granted all permissions on it. The database object owner can grant permission to other users to use that object. Database object ownership cannot be transferred.

## Permissions

SQL Server uses permissions to enforce database security. The SQL Server permissions system specifies which users are authorized to use which Transact-SQL statements, views, and stored procedures. The ability to assign permissions is determined by each user's status (as SA, database owner, or database object owner).

There are two types of permissions: *object* and *statement*. *Statement permissions* provide the privilege to issue certain object creation statements. Statement permissions can be granted only by the SA or the database owner. *Object permissions* regulate the use of data modification statements on certain database objects. They are granted and revoked by the owner of the object.

# Planning for SQL Server Security

Before you create the user environment, it is important to plan each user's access to SQL Server and to each database. As you plan, keep in mind that each user must have:

- One login ID for each SQL server.

- A username or alias associated with the login ID in each database to which the user requires access.

## Planning Phase Guidelines

Follow these guidelines when planning for SQL Server and database security:

1. Determine which tasks users will be doing with each database. Decide if users will be updating a database and entering data, reviewing and analyzing data, or developing and implementing the database.

2. Logically group users with common tasks. This helps you determine which groups to create and, ultimately, how you administer users. Create each group based on what users do with the database. For example, you might create a group named Managers for users who have to see the data, and a group named DataEntry for users who update the database. Users who develop and implement the database can be aliased to DBO.

3. Determine which login security mode best meets your needs.

## Implementation Phase Guidelines

Follow these guidelines when implementing SQL Server and database security:

1. Implement the login security mode you decided upon, create groups for each database, and create a login ID for each user who needs access to the server. If there are multiple servers, you can create identical login IDs on each server.

   When you create groups, use meaningful names. Create groups based on organizational structure, tasks, or a combination of both. For example, groups named Managers, DataEntry, or Accounting are better choices than GroupA, GroupB, or GroupC.

2. Assign a default database. The default database is the database that the user automatically connects to after logging in to SQL Server. It should be a database that the user accesses frequently.

3. For each login ID, create a username or alias in each database that the user requires access to.

   A login ID can be aliased to a username that already exists in database. For example, the SA login is assigned the DBO username in each database by default. Alias all other users who create objects to DBO.

4. Assign each username to a group.

# Lesson Summary

SQL Server security is based on a login security mode, login IDs, usernames, aliases, groups, and permissions. Planning how to implement security before you begin saves you time and effort.

# Lesson 2: Integrated Security

Integrated security allows a SQL server to use Windows NT authentication mechanisms to validate logins for all connections. Only trusted connections are allowed. You can use integrated security in network environments where all clients support trusted connections.

### After this lesson you will be able to:

- Describe how Windows NT and SQL Server security can be integrated.
- Implement integrated security.

### Estimated lesson time  40 minutes

## Windows NT and SQL Server Integrated Security

Integrated security lets SQL Server applications take advantage of the security capabilities of Windows NT, including encrypted passwords, password aging, domain-wide user accounts, and Windows-based user administration. Windows NT users can be authorized to log in to the SQL server because Windows NT user accounts can be associated with SQL Server login IDs. With security integration, users maintain one login ID and password for both Windows NT and SQL Server.

When SQL Server login security is integrated with Windows NT login security, the security attributes of a Windows NT network user control login access to SQL Server. A user's network security attributes are established at network login time and are validated by Windows NT through a sophisticated authentication mechanism. When a network user tries to connect to SQL Server, SQL Server uses Windows NT facilities to determine with certainty the validated network username of the client. SQL Server then permits or denies login access based on that network username alone, without requiring a separate login name and password to be sent in the client connection request.

Login security integration operates over network protocols that support authenticated, or trusted, connections between clients and servers. Trusted connections support multiprotocol Net-Library and named pipes sessions from:

- Windows NT–based clients.
- Windows for Workgroups-based clients.
- Windows 95-based clients.
- Microsoft LAN Manager clients running under the Microsoft Windows or Microsoft MS-DOS operating systems.
- Windows 3.1–based clients using Novell NetWare software. The user will be prompted for a Windows NT username and password at SQL Server connect time.

Other network protocols or clients do not support authenticated connections, so other clients or clients connecting over other protocols must be handled using SQL Server standard security.

If multiple SQL Server computers participate in a domain managed by a Windows NT server, a single network login for each user is sufficient to enable access to all of the SQL servers that have added Windows NT Server accounts as SQL Server login IDs. The following figure shows the separate but interrelated security elements that verify integrated Windows NT and SQL Server security.

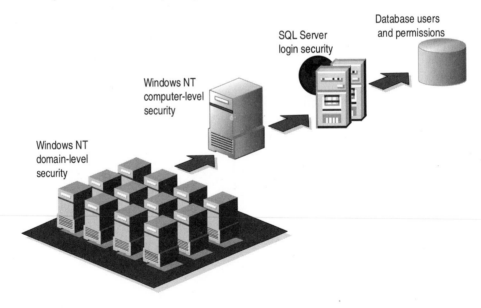

## The Integrated Security Login Validation Process

When a server's login security mode is set to integrated, a user's login is validated as follows:

1. To access SQL Server, a user first logs on to Windows NT using a Windows NT username and password.

   - If the user logs on to a domain, the username and password are validated by the domain controller's security accounts database.

   - If the user logs on to a Windows NT–based computer, the username is validated by the local security accounts database.

2. A user connects to SQL Server, and SQL Server looks in the *syslogins* table for a mapping to a SQL Server login ID, to a default SQL Server login ID (usually called *guest*), or—if the user has Windows NT administrative privileges—to SA. If there is no entry for the login ID and there is no default login, the user is denied access to SQL Server.

3. Once the login process is complete, access to individual SQL Server databases is managed through the users and permissions granted within a SQL Server database.

The following figure illustrates the integrated security login verification process.

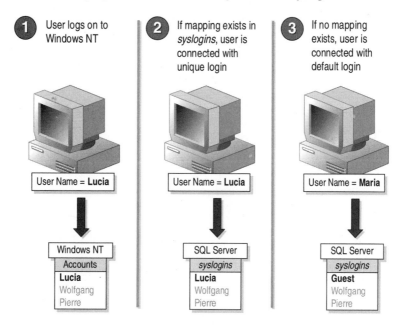

## Implementing Integrated Security

The following steps summarize the tasks performed to set up integrated security. Only a system administrator can perform the following tasks.

1. Set the SQL Server security options.

   Use SQL Enterprise Manager or **setup** to set the login security mode to integrated. Also set the other security options: Default Login, Default Domain, Set Hostname to Username, Audit Level, and Mappings.

2. Create the Windows NT users and groups authorized to access SQL Server over trusted connections.

   Use Windows NT User Manager. If you have not been granted access to User Manager to administer Windows NT users and groups, have a Windows NT Administrator perform this task for you.

3. Authorize selected Windows NT users and groups to access SQL Server.

   If a server is configured for integrated security with Windows NT, it is not necessary to create a login ID for each user. Use the SQL Security Manager utility provided with SQL Server to automatically associate the Windows NT usernames with SQL Server login IDs or with a default login ID.

---

**Note**  The **setup** program grants SA access for the local Windows NT Administrators group on the server. You can revoke this access later if you prefer.

---

The following figure depicts the tasks you perform setting up integrated security.

**SQL Enterprise Manager**
Set login security to integrated

**User Manager**
Create Windows NT users and groups

**SQL Security Manager**
Authorize Windows NT users and
groups  to access SQL Server

## Setting the SQL Server Security Options

The security options determine the server's login security mode, login auditing level, and mapping of characters in Windows NT usernames to SQL Server characters. You can set SQL Server Security options using **setup**, or from SQL Enterprise Manager.

### Login Security Mode Options

The login security mode options include:

- Login Security Mode—Standard, integrated, or mixed.

- Default Login—A SQL Server login ID (usually *guest*) to be used when a valid login ID does not appear in the *syslogins* table. The *guest* login ID does not exist by default, so you must create it if you want to include a default login ID.

- Default Domain—The name of the Windows NT domain to which the majority of your users belong. If your server computer does not participate in a domain, set the Default Domain to the server computer name.

  SQL Server uses the domain name to distinguish between more than one user with the same network username from different domains. For network usernames defined in domains other than the specified default, SQL Server adds the default domain name and a map character such as an underscore ( _ ) to the network username before attempting the lookup in the *syslogins* table.

- Set Hostname to Username—Enables you to view the network username in the output of the **sp_who** system stored procedure for those clients logged in using trusted connections.

### Audit Level

The Audit Level options enable you to determine whether to log successful logins, failed logins, or both. Where the events will be logged (in the Windows NT event log or in the SQL Server error log, or in both), depends on how you configure event and error logging for your SQL Server.

### Mappings Options

Windows NT usernames can include certain characters that are not valid in SQL Server login IDs (for example, hyphens, spaces, and periods). When you use any of the integrated security options or client-requested trusted connections, mappings let you indicate how to map these characters in SQL Server.

The following table lists the mapping characters available in SQL Server.

| Mapping option | Description |
| --- | --- |
| Map _ | Determines which Windows NT character will be mapped to the valid SQL Server character underscore ( _ ). The default is domain separator (\). Choose this mapping if you have users who are not members of your default domain that need access to the SQL Server. If chosen, the username that is not from your default domain will be mapped to *domainname_username* in SQL Server. |
| Map # | Determines which Windows NT character will be mapped to the valid SQL Server character pound sign (#). The default is hyphen (-). A user whose Windows NT username is T-USER1 will map to T#USER1 in SQL Server. |
| Map $ | Determines which Windows NT character will be mapped to the valid SQL Server character dollar sign ($). The default is space ( ). A Windows NT username of John Doe will be mapped as John$Doe. |

The following valid Windows NT characters are invalid in SQL Server and can be mapped to any of the three SQL Server map characters.

| | | |
| --- | --- | --- |
| Domain separator (\) | space ( ) | hyphen (-) |
| single quotation mark (') | "at" sign (@) | percent sign (%) |
| exclamation point (!) | ampersand (&) | period (.) |
| | caret (^) | |

**Tip** To avoid mapping problems, create Windows NT usernames using only valid SQL Server characters.

The following figure illustrates the Security Options in the Server Configuration/Options dialog box.

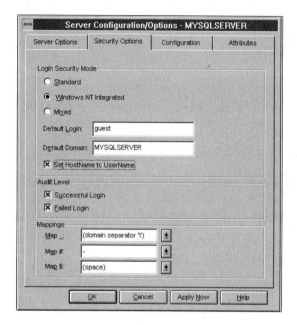

▶  **To configure the SQL Server security options for integrated security**

1.  Open SQL Enterprise Manager and, in the Server Manager window, select your server in the Server list.

2.  On the SQL Enterprise Manager Server menu, click SQL Server, and then click Configure.

    The Server Configuration/Options dialog box appears.

3.  Click the Security Options tab, and under Login Security Mode, click the Windows NT Integrated option.

4.  In the Default Login box, verify that guest appears.

5.  In the Default Domain box, if your server computer is part of a workgroup, verify that your computer name appears.

    If your server computer is part of a domain, verify that your Windows NT domain name appears as the Default Domain.

6.  Select the Set Hostname to Username check box.

7. Under Audit Level, select both Successful Login and Failed Login.

8. Accept the default mappings.

9. Click OK to accept the changes you have made.

10. Stop and restart the MSSQLServer service using either the Stop/Pause/Start Server button on the toolbar, or the SQL Service Manager.

## Creating Windows NT Users and Groups

To take advantage of integrated security for SQL Server, you must create the Windows NT users and groups that are authorized to access SQL Server.

User Manager, provided as part of the Windows NT operating system software, is the tool you use to create the Windows NT users and groups. You can start User Manager from the Administrative Tools group. For information about using this tool, see User Manager Help. If you have not been granted access to User Manager, have a Windows NT Administrator use this tool for you.

The following guidelines help you set up Windows NT accounts that can then be associated with SQL Server login IDs:

- When you create names for Windows NT users and groups, use only valid SQL Server identifiers. Limit group names to 30 characters or fewer. In addition, do not use the underscore ( _ ), dollar sign ($), or pound sign (#) in the user or group names because these characters are used by SQL Server as special mapping characters.

- Avoid placing Windows NT users in more than one Windows NT group that can access SQL Server, because SQL Server does not allow overlapping group membership within databases. Keeping your Windows NT users limited to membership in only one group that has SQL Server access privilege allows you to use SQL Security Manager to keep database groups consistent with Windows NT groups.

- Create one administrator-level group and one or more user-level groups for the accounts that will access SQL Server. The groups should correspond to the security levels that you want to grant in your SQL Server databases.

  If you want your Windows NT administrators to be the same as your SQL Server system administrators, you can leave the default permissions created by the **setup** program.

If you do not want the members of your Windows NT administrators group to be SQL Server system administrators, you can create a separate group for SQL Server administrators and grant that group administrative privilege on both Windows NT and SQL Server. After you have granted SQL Server system administrator privileges to the group, you can revoke privilege from the Windows NT Administrators group.

---

**Important**   A SQL Server login ID that maps to SA but is not part of the Windows NT Administrators group is unable to perform certain tasks that are Windows NT functions, such as starting and stopping services.

---

▶   **To create Windows NT local groups and user accounts**

In this procedure you create two Windows NT local groups, and several users. The users are made members of the local groups. You can use User Manager to create the accounts, or you can run the ADDUSERS.CMD file provided on the compact disc. In following procedures, you associate these users and groups with SQL Server Login IDs.

1. Log in to Windows NT as an administrator.

2. Start a command prompt and run the ADDUSERS.CMD file, or start User Manager and create the following Windows NT Server local groups and user accounts. Do not require users to change passwords at next logon. Add only these users to the appropriate local groups.

| Username | Full name | Description | Password | Local group |
|----------|-----------|-------------|----------|-------------|
| Dan | Dan Koch | Systems Support | dan | SQLAdmins |
| Rob | Rob Feinstein | Systems Support | rob | SQLAdmins |
| Eiko | Eiko Yim | Accounting | eiko | SQLUsers |
| Hilde | Hilde Anderson | Accounting | hilde | SQLUsers |
| Tom | Tomas Hart | Accounting | tom | SQLUsers |
| Steph | Stephen Johnson | Sales | steph | <none> |

3. Close the command prompt or exit User Manager.

## Authorizing Windows NT Users and Groups to Access SQL Server

In integrated security mode, you map Windows NT users and groups to SQL Server login IDs. Granting privileges to a Windows NT group grants access to SQL Server to each member of that group. When you use SQL Security Manager to map your Windows NT user accounts to SQL Server login IDs, a randomly generated password is created for each login ID and written to the *syslogins* table. When a user connects to a SQL server configured with integrated security, the password in *syslogins* is ignored because SQL Server is using the Windows NT username and password.

You can grant either SA privilege or user privilege to a group. When you grant SA privilege to a group, the users in that group are automatically associated with the SA login ID and to *master* as the default database. When you grant user privilege to a group, you also determine whether each user has a separate SQL Server login ID or accesses SQL Server through the default login ID. By default, login IDs are added for group members, creating SQL Server login IDs in the *syslogins* table for each user in the group.

If you do not want each user in the group to have a separate SQL Server login ID, the only way users in the group can access SQL Server is through a default login ID, which is usually *guest*.

The following figure shows the SQL Security Manager's Grant User Privilege dialog box.

▶ **To map members of a Windows NT group to SQL Server login IDs with SA privileges**

1. Open SQL Security Manager.

   The Connect Server dialog box appears.

2. In the Server box, type the name of your server, and then click Connect.

   Why did you not have to provide a Login ID or password?

   _____

   _____

   _____

   _____

3. Click the SA privilege button on the toolbar, or on the View menu, click SA Privilege.

   Which group automatically has SA privileges?

   _____

4. On the Security menu, click Grant New.

   The Grant System Administrator Privilege dialog box appears.

5. Select Local Groups to see all local groups on the Windows NT–based computer.

   What groups appear?

   _____

   _____

6. In the Grant privilege list, select SQLAdmins.

   Why are the Add login IDs for Group Members and the Add Users to Database check boxes unavailable?

   _____

   _____

   _____

7. Click Grant.

   A SQL Security Manager message appears that states "Permission granted to SQLAdmins."

8. Click OK to close the message, and then click Done to close the Grant System Administrator Privilege dialog box.

   Notice the SQLAdmins group is now listed in the Security Manager window, along with Administrators.

▶ **To map members of a Windows NT group to SQL Server login IDs with user privileges**

In this procedure, you associate each user in the Windows NT local group SQLUsers with a separate login ID, and assign *pubs* as the default database for these users. Remember that Windows NT passwords are case-sensitive.

1. In SQL Security Manager, click the User Privilege button on the toolbar.

2. On the Security menu, click Grant New.

   The Grant User Privilege dialog box appears.

3. In the Grant Privilege list, select SQLUsers.

   The Add Login IDs For Group Members check box is selected by default.

4. Select Add Users To Database, and then select the *pubs* database for the default database.

5. Click Grant.

   The Adding SQL Server Login IDs/Users message box appears, indicating the number of login IDs, users, and groups that were created, and the number of errors, if any.

6. Click Done to acknowledge the message, and then click Done again to close the Grant User Privilege dialog box.

   Notice that the SQLUsers group is now listed in the Security Manager window.

Once you have created SQL Server accounts, you can use SQL Security Manager to view information about accounts, including privileges and details.

▶   **To view account privileges**

In this procedure, you use Security Manager to view the groups, and group membership, that have SQL Server privileges.

1. On the SQL Security Manager View menu, click SA Privilege.

   What groups appear with SA privilege?

   _____

2. Double-click the SQLAdmins group to view a list its members.

   Which user accounts have SA privilege?

   _____

3. On the SQL Security Manager View menu, click User Privilege.

   What groups appear with User privilege?

   _____

4. Double-click the SQLUsers group to view a list of its members.

   Which user accounts have SA privilege?

   _____

▶   **To determine the privileges for an account**

In this procedure, you determine Dan's SQL Server privilege level.

1. On the SQL Security Manager Security menu, click Search.

   The Search for Account Information dialog box appears.

2. In the Account box, type **Dan**

3. Select Find All Permissions For Account, and then click Search.

   What privilege level does Dan have?

   _____

   What SQL Server login ID (mapped name) is Dan associated with?

   _____

   What is Dan's permissions path?

   _____

4. Click Cancel.

▶ **To review account details for a user account**

In this procedure, you view the details of Tom's user account.

1. Double-click the user account for Tom, or select Tom and then on the Security menu, click Account Detail.

   The Account Detail dialog box appears.

   What is the SQL Server login ID (mapped name) for Tom?

   _____

   What database does Tom currently have a username in?

   _____

2. Click Close.

## Removing SQL Server Login IDs and Database Usernames

With integrated security, removing login IDs and users from SQL Server is accomplished by revoking privileges from a Windows NT group using SQL Security Manager. When you revoke privileges, all users in the group are dropped from SQL Server databases, and their login IDs are removed from SQL Server.

You can also drop a particular user's login ID from SQL Server, even though the user is still part of the Windows NT local group. Then, unless you also remove the user from the Windows NT group, the user can still access SQL Server through the default login if your server has a default login.

▶ **To drop a login ID**

In this procedure, you drop Tom's SQL Server login ID, while maintaining his membership in the Windows NT local group SQLUsers.

1. In SQL Security Manager, double-click the user account for Tom in the SQLUsers group.

   The Account Detail dialog box appears.

2. Click Drop Login.

   An error message appears for each database of which Tom is not a user.

3. Click OK to close each error message.

   Tom is dropped from the *pubs* database, and then dropped as a login to SQL Server. The message "SQL login successfully dropped" appears.

4. Click OK to close the message box.

   Notice that Tom is no longer defined as a user in the *pubs* database.

5. Click Close to close the Account Detail dialog box.

   What SQL Server login ID is Tom associated with? What is Eiko associated with? What is Hilde associated with?

   _____

   _____

   _____

   What user privilege does Tom have? What user privileges do Eiko and Hilde have?

   _____

   _____

   _____

6. Without exiting SQL Security Manager, start User Manager.

   Is Tom still a member of the SQLUsers group?

   _____

7. Exit User Manager.

8. Open a query window and query the *syslogins* table.

   Does Tom have a Login ID in the *syslogins* table?

   _____

## Testing Integrated Security

In the following procedures, you test integrated security by logging on to Windows NT as members of the SQLAdmins and SQLUsers groups, and then using SQL Security Manager to verify the user's privileges.

▶ **To log on as a member of a group with SA privileges**

1. Log off, and then log on to Windows NT as Rob.

2. Start SQL Security Manager.

   The Connect Server dialog box appears.

3. Do not enter a Login ID. Verify that your server appears in the Server box, and then click Connect.

   Why is Rob able to connect to SQL Server using the SQL Security Manager without supplying a Login ID?

   _____

   _____

4. Exit SQL Security Manager.

▶ **To log on as a member of a group with user privileges**

1. Log off, and then log on to Windows NT as Eiko.

2. Start SQL Security Manager.

3. Do not enter a Login ID. Verify that your server appears in the Server box, and then click Connect.

   A SQL Security Manager message box appears, stating that you must use the system administrator's (SA) account when using SQL Security Manager.

4. Click OK.

5.  In the Login ID box, type **sa** and then click Connect.

Again, a SQL Security Manager message box appears, stating that you must use the system administrator's (sa) account when using SQL Security Manager.

Why can't Eiko connect to the SQL Server using the SQL Security Manager, even when she supplies the SA's login ID and password?

_____

_____

_____

_____

6.  Exit SQL Security Manager.

▶ **To log on as a guest**

1.  Log off, and then log on to Windows NT as Tom.

2.  Start SQL Security Manager.

3.  Do not enter a Login ID. Verify that your server appears in the Server box, and then click Connect.

A SQL Security Manager error box appears, stating that the login failed for the user guest.

Why can't Tom connect to the SQL Server using the SQL Security Manager?

_____

_____

_____

_____

4.  Exit SQL Security Manager.

5.  Log off, and then log on to Windows NT as Administrator.

You can further manage logins, usernames, and groups using SQL Enterprise Manager and system stored procedures. These tools are discussed in detail in the next lesson.

## Lesson Summary

Integrated login security simplifies granting Windows NT users and administrators access to SQL Server. Implementing integrated security requires setting SQL Server security options, creating the Windows NT users and groups you want to have access to SQL Server, and authorizing the Windows NT users and groups to access SQL Server.

| For more information on | See |
| --- | --- |
| Windows NT security | Chapter 3, "How Network Security Works," in the *Windows NT Server Concepts and Planning Guide* |
| User Manager | Chapter 13, "User Manager for Domains," in the *Windows NT Server System Guide* |
| Event and error logging | "The Windows NT Event Log" and "The SQL Server Error Log" in SQL Server Books Online |
| Integrated security | "Integrated Security" in SQL Server Books Online |

# Lesson 3: Standard Security

Standard login security uses SQL Server's own login validation process. To log in to a SQL Server configured for standard security, each user must provide a valid SQL Server login ID and password.

### After this lesson you will be able to:

- List the benefits of standard security.
- Implement standard security.

### Estimated lesson time  15 minutes

Standard security mode uses SQL Server's own login validation process for all connections, except when a client application forces a trusted connection. When a server's login security mode is set to standard, a user's login is validated as follows:

1. When a user attempts to log in to the SQL server, SQL Server looks in the *syslogins* table for the user's login ID and password.
2. If the login ID and password are valid, the user is connected to the SQL server.
3. If the login ID and password are invalid, the user cannot connect to SQL Server even though the user may have been able to log on to Windows NT Server.

The following figure illustrates the standard security login validation process.

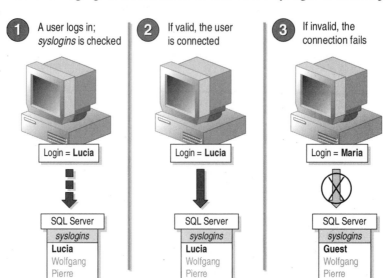

| 1 A user logs in; *syslogins* is checked | 2 If valid, the user is connected | 3 If invalid, the connection fails |
|---|---|---|
| Login = **Lucia** | Login = **Lucia** | Login = **Maria** |

| SQL Server | SQL Server | SQL Server |
|---|---|---|
| *syslogins* | *syslogins* | *syslogins* |
| **Lucia** | **Lucia** | **Guest** |
| Wolfgang | Wolfgang | Wolfgang |
| Pierre | Pierre | Pierre |

## Implementing Standard Security

Standard security is the default security mode. The following steps summarize the tasks performed to configure SQL Server for standard security. Only a system administrator can perform Steps 1 and 2. A system administrator or database owner can perform Step 3.

1. Set the SQL Server security options.

   Use SQL Enterprise Manager to verify that the login security mode of the server is Standard and to set the Audit Level options.

2. Define database groups.

   Use SQL Enterprise Manager to create groups for each database.

3. Create login IDs and assign them aliases, usernames, and groups in each database.

   Use SQL Enterprise Manager to create a login ID and password, specify a default language for each user, define the databases that can be accessed by each login ID, identify the username or alias for the login ID in each database, and identify the group to which the username or alias belongs.

The following figure depicts the tasks you perform in setting up standard security.

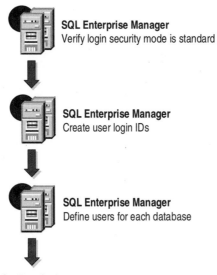

**SQL Enterprise Manager**
Verify login security mode is standard

**SQL Enterprise Manager**
Create user login IDs

**SQL Enterprise Manager**
Define users for each database

**Set Permissions**

## Setting the SQL Server Security Options

The security options for standard security determine the server's login security mode and login auditing level. You can set SQL Server Security options using **setup** or SQL Enterprise Manager.

▶ **To configure the SQL Server security options for standard security**

In this procedure, you configure your SQL Server for standard security.

1. Open SQL Enterprise Manager, and select your server from the Server list in the Server Manager window.

2. On the SQL Enterprise Manager Server menu, click SQL Server, and then click Configure.

   The Server Configuration/Options dialog box appears.

3. Click the Security Options tab.

4. Under Login Security Mode, click the Standard option.

5. Click OK to accept the changes you have made.

6. Stop and restart the MSSQLServer service using either the Stop/Pause/Start Server button on the toolbar, or the SQL Service Manager.

## Defining and Managing Database Groups

Before you create login IDs and add users to a database using standard security, you should create groups for your databases. Creating database groups before adding users simplifies adding users and, eventually, assigning them permissions. When you create groups, keep in mind that groups can be created or dropped only by the SA or DBO and must be unique to a database. A group name can have as many as 30 characters and must be unique within the database. The characters can be alphanumeric, but the first character must be a letter or the symbols # or _ , for example, DATAOPS or OPERS8.

After you have created a group, you can add new users to the group or remove users from the group at any time. In each database, a user can be a member of only one group besides Public. You cannot remove any user from the Public group.

▶ **To create a database group**

In this procedure, you add the Managers, Printing, Admin, and Sales groups to the *pubs* database.

1. In the SQL Enterprise Manager Server Manager window, select your server from the Servers list.

2. Expand the Databases folder and select the *pubs* database.

3. On the Manage menu, click Groups.

   The Manage Groups dialog box for the *pubs* database appears.

4. In the Group box, select <New Group>, type **Managers** and then click Add.

   The group is added to the database.

5. Repeat Step 4 to add the Printing, Admin, and Sales groups.

6. Click Close to close the Manage Groups dialog box.

   The new groups appear in the Groups/Users folder.

## Creating Login IDs

Before a user can gain access to SQL Server, a login ID for that user must be added to the server. When you add a login ID, you can also assign the user a password, a default language, a default database, and for each database the user will use, a username or alias, and group membership in one group in addition to Public. The following figure illustrates the SQL Enterprise Manager Manage Logins dialog box.

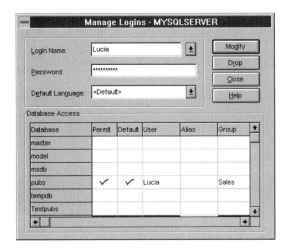

▶  **To create login IDs and usernames**

In this procedure, you create SQL Server login IDs, and assign a default database, password, username, and group membership to each ID. Use the information in the following table when creating the login IDs.

| Login ID | Password | Permit | Default database | User | Group |
|----------|----------|--------|------------------|------|-------|
| Maria | maria | pubs | pubs | Maria | Printing |
| Pierre | pierre | pubs | pubs | Pierre | Admin |
| Lucia | lucia | pubs | pubs | Lucia | Sales |
| Wolfgang | wolfgang | pubs | pubs | Wolfgang | Printing |
| Tracy | tracy | pubs | pubs | Tracy | Admin |
| Juanita | juanita | pubs | pubs | Juanita | Sales |

1. In the SQL Enterprise Manager Server Manager window, select your server from the Server list.

2. On the toolbar, click the Manage Logins button.

   The Manage Logins dialog box appears.

3. In the login name box, select <New Login>, and then type a login name from the preceding table.

4. In the password box, type the password from the preceding table.

5. In the Default Language box, accept the default language.

6. Under Database Access, click the Permit box for the *pubs* database.

   Complete the remaining columns for *pubs* as follows.

   - Under Default, verify that *pubs* is selected as the default database.
   - Under User, verify that the user's login ID appears.
   - Under Group, click the Group box, and then select the correct group name from the preceding table.

7. Click Add.

   The Confirm Password dialog box appears.

8. Type the user's password, and then click OK.

9. Repeat Steps 3 through 8 until all of the users have been added.

10. Click Close to exit.

11. In the Server Manager window, expand each group in the *pubs* database to verify that your users are members in the correct groups. You might have to update the screen to see the new information.

## Managing Users and Groups

Once you have created users and groups, the system administrator can change the password, default language, and database access (including the default database) for a login ID. Users can change their own passwords using the **sp_password** system stored procedure.

In the following procedures, you alias Pierre's login ID to DBO in the *pubs* database and change a user's group membership.

▶ **To alias a user to DBO**

In this procedure, you use the Manage Logins dialog box to change information about a Login ID. You alias Pierre to the DBO in the *pubs* database.

1. In the Server Manager window select your server, and then on the Manage menu, click Logins.

   The Manage Logins dialog box appears.

2. In the Login Name box, select Pierre.

3. Under Database Access, select the *pubs* database.

4. For the *pubs* database, click the Alias box.

   A list of available aliases is displayed.

5.  Select dbo.

Notice that when dbo appears in the Alias box, the username in the User box disappears.

6.  Click Modify, and then click Close.

► **To change a user's group membership**

In this procedure, you use the Manage Groups dialog box to move Maria from the Printing group to the Sales group.

1.  In the Server Manager window, expand the *pubs* database and double-click the Printing group.

The Manage Groups dialog box appears, displaying information for the Printing group.

2.  In the Users In Group box, select Maria, and then click Remove.

Maria's username moves to the Users box.

3.  Click Modify.

4.  In the Group box, select Sales.

5.  In the Users box, select Maria, and then click Add.

Maria's username moves to the Users In Group box.

6.  Click Modify.

7.  Click Close.

Notice that Maria now appears in the Sales group of the *pubs* database in the Server Manager window.

## Removing Users and Groups from a Database

Dropping a group deletes it from the database. When you drop a group, all users in that group are automatically removed from the group. Users who were members of the dropped group are still users in the database and remain members of the Public group.

In the following procedures, you remove the group Managers and the username Tracy from the *pubs* database. You also drop Juanita's login ID.

▶ **To remove a group from a database**

In this procedure, you remove the Managers group from the *pubs* database.

1. In the Server Manager window, select your server, and then expand the *pubs* database.

2. Expand the Groups/Users folder.

   The groups of the *pubs* database are listed.

3. Use the secondary mouse button to click the Managers group, and then click Edit on the shortcut menu.

   The Manage Groups dialog box appears with information on the Managers group. Notice there are no users in the Managers group.

4. Click Drop.

5. When prompted for confirmation, click Yes.

6. Click Close.

   The Managers group is removed from the database.

▶ **To remove a username from a database**

In this procedure, you remove Tracy's username from the *pubs* database.

1. In the Server Manager window, select your server, and expand the *pubs* database.

2. In the Groups/Users folder for the *pubs* database, expand the Admin group.

   The members of that group are listed.

3. Use the secondary mouse button to click the username Tracy, and then click Delete on the shortcut menu.

4. When prompted for confirmation, click Yes.

   The username Tracy is removed from the Admin group, and can no longer access the *pubs* database.

▶ **To drop a login ID**

In this procedure, you delete Juanita's login ID from your server.

1. From the Server Manager window, expand the Logins folder for your server.

2. Use the secondary mouse button to select Juanita, and then on the shortcut menu, click Drop.

3. When prompted for confirmation, click Yes.

   Juanita's login ID is removed.

## Managing Groups and Users Using System Stored Procedures

You can also use system stored procedures to manage groups, logins, and database users. The following table lists system stored procedures you can use to manage groups.

| To | Use this stored procedure |
|---|---|
| Add a group | **sp_addgroup** *group_name* |
| Drop a group | **sp_dropgroup** *group_name* |
| Change a user's group to the group specified | **sp_changegroup** *group_name*, *user_name* |
| See group information about a group or all groups in the current database | **sp_helpgroup** [*group_name*] |

The following table lists system stored procedures you can use to manage logins and usernames.

| To | Use this stored procedure |
|---|---|
| Get information about the logins on a server | **sp_helplogins** [*LoginNamePattern*] |
| Add a login ID to a server | **sp_addlogin** *login_id* [, *password* [, *defdb* [, *deflanguage*]]] |
| Add a username to the current database | **sp_adduser** *login_id* [, *user_name* [, *group_name*]] |
| Drop a login ID | **sp_droplogin** *login_id* |
| Drop a username from the current database | **sp_dropuser** *user_name* |
| Change a user's password | **sp_password** *old, new* [, *login_id*] |
| Change the database owner | **sp_changedbowner** *login_id* [, true] |

▶   **To view user information**

In this procedure, you use system stored procedures to view user information for the *pubs* database.

1. Open a query window, and use the *pubs* database.

2. Type and execute the following stored procedure and view the results.

   ```
   sp_helpuser
   ```

   What users exist in the database?

   _____

   To what login ID is the guest user mapped?

   _____

   _____

3. What other information does the **sp_helpuser** stored procedure provide?

   _____

   _____

4. Click the Query tab.

5. Type and execute the following stored procedure and view the results.

   ```
   sp_helpuser dbo
   ```

   What login name is aliased to DBO?

   _____

   Which login name is the DBO?

   _____

6. Close the query window.

## Lesson Summary

Standard login security provides complete login security verified by SQL Server. The steps in implementing standard security include setting SQL Server security options, defining database groups, and creating SQL Server login IDs and assigning them aliases, usernames, and groups in each database.

| For more information on | See |
| --- | --- |
| Standard security | "Standard Security" in SQL Server Books Online |

# Lesson 4: Mixed Security

The mixed security mode uses Windows NT login verification when possible, and SQL Server login verification when Windows NT login verification is unavailable.

### After this lesson you will be able to:

- Describe the process validating mixed login security.
- Configure SQL Server for mixed login security.

### Estimated lesson time  10 minutes

Mixed security mode allows SQL Server login requests to be validated using either integrated or standard security methods. Both trusted connections (used by integrated security) and nontrusted connections (used by standard security) are supported. When a server is configured for mixed login security mode, a user's login ID is validated as follows:

1. When a user attempts to log in to the server over a trusted connection, SQL Server examines the login name.

   If this login name matches the user's network username, or if the login name is blank or spaces, SQL Server uses the Windows NT integrated login rules, as it does for integrated security.

2. If the requested login name is any other value, or if the login attempt is not over a trusted connection, the user must supply the correct SQL Server password, and SQL Server uses its own login validation process as it does for standard security.

The following figure illustrates the mixed security login validation process.

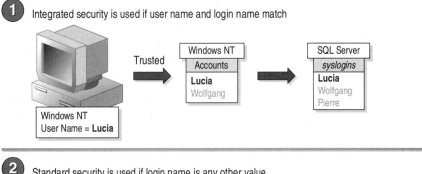

① Integrated security is used if user name and login name match

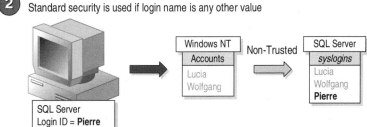

② Standard security is used if login name is any other value

## Implementing Mixed Security

The following steps summarize the tasks performed to configure your SQL server for mixed security. Only a system administrator can perform Steps 1, 3, and 4. Only a Windows NT administrator, domain administrator, or account operator can perform Step 2.

1. Set the server's security options.

   Use SQL Enterprise Manager to set the login security mode to Mixed. Also set the other security options, Default Login, Default Domain, Set HostName to Username, Audit Level, and Mappings, as shown in Lesson 2, "Integrated Security."

2. Create the Windows NT users and groups authorized to access SQL Server over trusted connections, as shown in the "Integrated Security" lesson.

   Use Windows NT User Manager. If you have not been granted access to use User Manager to administer Windows NT users and groups, have a Windows NT Administrator perform this task for you.

3. Authorize selected Windows NT users and groups to access SQL Server, as shown in the "Integrated Security" lesson.

   Use SQL Security Manager to map Windows NT users and groups to SQL Server login IDs. Decide whether each user has a separate SQL Server login ID or accesses SQL Server through the default login ID. You also choose a default database for the users.

4. Allow access to the server for those users who will not be connecting to the server over trusted connections, as shown in the "Standard Security" lesson.

   - Create groups for each database.

   - Create a login ID and password and specify a default language for each user.

   - Specify the username or alias and group within each database for each login ID.

The following figure depicts the tasks you perform in setting up mixed security.

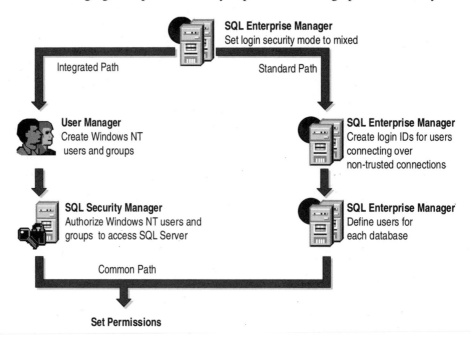

In these procedures, you configure SQL Server to use mixed security, and then test it.

▶  **To configure the SQL Server security options for mixed security**

1. Log on to Windows NT Server as Administrator.
2. Start SQL Enterprise Manager, and select your server.
3. On the toolbar, click the Configure SQL Server button.

   The Server Configuration/Options dialog box appears.
4. Click the Security Options tab.

   The Security Options dialog box displays the current setting of the options.
5. Under Login Security Mode, select Mixed.

   Do not make any other changes.
6. Click OK.
7. Stop and restart the MSSQLServer service using either the Stop/Pause/Start Server button on the toolbar, or the SQL Service Manager.
8. Exit the SQL Enterprise Manager.

▶  **To test mixed security**

In this procedure, you test connecting to SQL Server using mixed security. You first start ISQL/w and connect to your server using integrated security over trusted connections. You then connect to your server using standard security. You use usernames and login IDs created earlier in this chapter.

1. Start ISQL/w.

   The Connect Server dialog box appears.
2. In the Server box, type your server name.
3. Under Login Information, click Use Trusted Connection, and then click Connect.

   Notice the information on the title bar of the query window.

   Who are you connected as? Why?

   _____

   _____

   _____

4. On the File menu, click Connect.

   The Connect Server dialog box appears.

5. Click Use Standard Security, and then enter Maria's login ID (Maria) and password (maria).

6. Click Connect.

   Notice the information on the title bar of the query window.

   Who are you connected as? Why?

   _____

   _____

   _____

   _____

7. Exit ISQL/w.

8. Log off, and then log on to Windows NT Server as Steph with the password steph.

9. Start ISQL/w, and log in to your server using a trusted connection.

   Is Steph allowed access? Why or why not?

   _____

   _____

10. Click OK.

11. Log in to your server using standard security, with the login ID of Wolfgang and password wolfgang.

    Is Wolfgang allowed access? Why or why not?

    _____

12. Exit ISQL/w.

13. Log off, and then log on to Windows NT Server as an administrator.

## Lesson Summary

Mixed login security allows users to connect to SQL Server using Windows NT login verification over trusted connections, or SQL Server login verification over non-trusted connections. The steps in implementing mixed login security include setting SQL Server's security options; next setting up integrated security (including establishing Windows NT groups and users, and granting them access to SQL Server); and finally setting up standard security, including defining database groups, creating SQL Server login IDs, and assigning usernames and aliases.

| For more information on | See |
| --- | --- |
| Mixed security | "Mixed Security" in SQL Server Books Online |

# Review

The following questions are intended to reinforce key information presented in this chapter. If you are unable to answer a question, review the lesson and then try the question again.

1. What are the differences between standard and integrated security modes, and integrated and mixed security modes?

_____

_____

_____

_____

_____

_____

_____

2. If your environment includes clients that use both trusted and nontrusted connections, what type of login security should you implement?

_____

3. What is the difference between a trusted and nontrusted connection? In what security mode(s) is each of them used?

4. In what situation is it necessary to map characters?

# Questions and Answers

Page 573

▶ **To map members of a Windows NT group to SQL Server login IDs with SA privileges**

2. In the Server box, type the name of your server, and then click Connect.

   Why did you not have to provide a Login ID or password?

   **With integrated security, SQL Server ignores any name and password that appears, and logs you in based on your Windows NT username. You are currently logged in as a Windows NT administrator, so you automatically come into SQL Server as SA.**

3. Click the SA privilege button on the toolbar, or on the View menu, click SA Privilege.

   Which group automatically has SA privileges?

   **Administrators.**

5. Select Local Groups to see all local groups on the Windows NT–based computer.

   What groups appear?

   **All Windows NT local groups on the computer, including Administrators, SQLAdmins, SQLUsers, and others.**

6. In the Grant privilege list, select SQLAdmins.

   Why are the Add login IDs for Group Members and the Add Users to Database check boxes unavailable?

   **When you grant SA privilege to a group, the users in that group are automatically associated with the SA login ID and to master as the default database.**

Page 575

▶ **To view account privileges**

1. On the SQL Security Manager View menu, click SA Privilege.

   What groups appear with SA privilege?

   **Administrators and SQLAdmins.**

2. Double-click the SQLAdmins group to view a list its members.

   Which user accounts have SA privilege?

   **Dan and Rob.**

3. On the SQL Security Manager View menu, click User Privilege.

What groups appear with User privilege?

**SQLUsers.**

4. Double-click the SQLUsers group to view a list of its members.

Which user accounts have SA privilege?

**Eiko, Hilde, and Tom.**

Page 575

▶ **To determine the privileges for an account**

3. Select Find All Permissions For Account, and then click Search.

What privilege level does Dan have?

**Admin**

What SQL Server login ID (mapped name) is Dan associated with?

**SA**

What is Dan's permissions path?

**<your computer name>\SQLAdmins**

Page 576

▶ **To review account details for a user account**

1. Double-click the user account for Tom, or select Tom and then on the Security menu, click Account Detail.

The Account Detail dialog box appears.

What is the SQL Server login ID (mapped name) for Tom?

**Tom**

What database does Tom currently have a username in?

**The *pubs* database.**

Page 576

▸ **To drop a login ID**

5. Click Close to close the Account Detail dialog box.

   What SQL Server login ID is Tom associated with? What is Eiko associated with? What is Hilde associated with?

   **Tom is associated with guest.**

   **Eiko is mapped as Eiko.**

   **Hilde is mapped as Hilde.**

   What user privilege does Tom have? What user privileges do Eiko and Hilde have?

   **Tom has access to SQL Server with the privileges associated with guest. Eiko and Hilde have access to SQL Server with the privileges associated with their login IDs.**

6. Without exiting SQL Security Manager, start User Manager.

   Is Tom still a member of the SQLUsers group?

   **Yes.**

8. Open a query window and query the *syslogins* table.

   Does Tom have a Login ID in the *syslogins* table?

   **No.**

Page 578

▸ **To log on as a member of a group with SA privileges**

3. Do not enter a Login ID. Verify that your server appears in the Server box, and then click Connect.

   Why is Rob able to connect to SQL Server using the SQL Security Manager without supplying a Login ID?

   **SQL Server is configured for integrated security, and Rob's Windows NT username is associated with the SQL Server SA.**

Page 578

▶ **To log on as a member of a group with user privileges**

    5. In the Login ID box, type **sa** and then click Connect.

Again, a SQL Security Manager message box appears, stating that you must use the system administrator's (sa) account when using SQL Security Manager.

Why can't Eiko connect to the SQL Server using the SQL Security Manager, even when she supplies the SA's login ID and password?

**SQL Server is configured for integrated security. Eiko's Windows NT username is associated with a login ID with user privileges. When she connects to her server, SQL Security Manager does not look at the login ID she entered; instead, it uses her mapped login ID which only has user privileges.**

Page 579

▶ **To log on as a guest**

    3. Do not enter a Login ID. Verify that your server appears in the Server box, and then click Connect.

A SQL Security Manager error box appears, stating that the login failed for the user guest.

Why can't Tom connect to the SQL Server using the SQL Security Manager?

**SQL Server is configured for integrated security, and the default login ID is guest. Tom's Windows NT username is associated with the guest login ID. However, the default login ID doesn't exist because you have not created a guest login ID. Therefore, Tom's connection fails.**

Page 590

▶ **To view user information**

    2. Type and execute the following stored procedure and view the results.

```
sp_helpuser
```

What users exist in the database?

**dbo, guest, Lucia, Maria, and Wolfgang.**

To what login ID is the guest user mapped?

**The login is associated with null. This means any login ID that does not have a username in the *pubs* database will have privileges in *pubs* associated with guest.**

    3. What other information does the **sp_helpuser** stored procedure provide?

**The group that each user is a member of and each user's default database. It also shows that the LoginName Pierre is aliased to dbo.**

5. Type and execute the following stored procedure and view the results.

```
sp_helpuser dbo
```

What login name is aliased to DBO?

**Pierre**

Which login name is the DBO?

**sa**

Page 595

▶ **To test mixed security**

3. Under Login Information, click Use Trusted Connection, and then click Connect.

Notice the information on the title bar of the query window.

Who are you connected as? Why?

**SA. You are logged on to Windows NT as an administrator. When you connected to SQL Server using the trusted connection, SQL Server used integrated security to map your Windows NT username to the sa.**

6. Click Connect.

Notice the information on the title bar of the query window.

Who are you connected as? Why?

**Maria. You are logged on to Windows NT as an administrator. However, you specified Use Standard Security, and provided Maria's login ID and password. Because you provided a valid login ID, you were validated using standard security. Maria's login ID maps to user Maria in the *pubs* database.**

9. Start ISQL/w, and log in to your server using a trusted connection.

Is Steph allowed access? Why or why not?

**No. Steph has a valid Windows NT user account, but he does not have a SQL Server login ID.**

11. Log in to your server using standard security, with the login ID of Wolfgang and password wolfgang.

Is Wolfgang allowed access? Why or why not?

**Yes. You supplied a valid login ID and password for Standard Security.**

Page 598

## Review Questions

1. What are the differences between standard and integrated security modes, and integrated and mixed security modes?

   **Standard security: User logins are validated by SQL Server over nontrusted connections. Login ID and password are created by SQL Server.**

   **Integrated security: User logins are validated by Windows NT over trusted connections. Login ID and password are created by Windows NT. SQL Server login IDs are ignored.**

   **Mixed security: User logins over trusted connections are validated by Windows NT. User logins over nontrusted connections are validated by SQL Server. Login ID and password for users using trusted connections are created by Windows NT. Login ID and password for users using nontrusted connections are created by SQL Server.**

2. If your environment includes clients that use both trusted and nontrusted connections, what type of login security should you implement?

   **Mixed security.**

3. What is the difference between a trusted and nontrusted connection? In what security mode(s) is each of them used?

   **Trusted connection is a connection validated by Windows NT. SQL Server and SQL Server clients must be configured to use multiprotocol Net-Library or named pipes.**

   **Nontrusted connection is a connection validated by SQL Server.**

4. In what situation is it necessary to map characters?

   **When using integrated or mixed security, characters used in Windows NT user and group names must be valid in SQL Server. If they are not, each invalid character must be mapped to a valid character.**

CHAPTER 14

# Managing Database Permissions

## About This Chapter

SQL Server uses permissions to enforce database security. Permissions specify which users are authorized to use which database objects, and what they are allowed to do with those objects. It is important to carefully plan the permissions of each user and group, and to implement the permissions appropriately.

## Before You Begin

To complete the lessons in this chapter, you must have:

- Installed SQL Server on your computer. Installation procedures are covered in Chapter 2, "Installing SQL Server."

- Experience using the SQL Enterprise Manager, the SQL Enterprise Manager Query Tool, and ISQL/w.

- Knowledge of SQL Server login security, login IDs, usernames, groups, and aliases.

- Your SQL server configured for mixed security.

- Window NT user accounts and SQL Server Login IDs, users, and groups created in Chapter 13, "Managing SQL Server Security." If you do not have these accounts created, you can execute the \SCRIPTS\C13_SECU\ADDUSER.CMD and \SCRIPTS\C13_SECU\ADDSQLU.SQL files.

# Lesson 1: Overview of Permissions

Permissions specify which database objects (tables, indexes, views, stored procedures, triggers, defaults, and rules) users are authorized to use, and what the users can do with those objects. Without appropriate permissions, a user can connect to SQL Server but cannot use database objects. The types of permissions a user has within a database is dependent on the role the user plays within the database (system administrator, database owner, and so on). It is important to plan which permissions to grant each user or group.

## After this lesson you will be able to:

- Explain the difference between statement permissions and object permissions.
- Identify the permissions associated with the system administrator, database owner, and database object owner.

## Estimated lesson time  20 minutes

Each database has its own independent permissions system. Permissions granted in one database have no effect on other databases.

SQL Server provides two types of permissions: *statement* and *object*. Statement permissions allow an individual user or a group to execute specific CREATE and DUMP Transact-SQL statements that create database objects, or back up databases or transaction logs. Statement permissions are associated with users, not objects. Statement permissions can only be granted by an SA or DBO. The following statements require statement permissions:

| | |
|---|---|
| CREATE DATABASE / ALTER DATABASE* | CREATE DEFAULT |
| CREATE PROCEDURE | CREATE RULE |
| CREATE TABLE | CREATE VIEW |
| DUMP DATABASE | DUMP TRANSACTION |

*Permission to execute the CREATE DATABASE statement automatically confers permission to execute the ALTER DATABASE statement.

Object permissions regulate the use of object modification statements on certain database objects. They are granted and revoked by the owner of the object.

Permissions are required to execute the object modification statements listed in the following table.

| Statement | Table | Column | View | Stored procedure |
|---|---|---|---|---|
| SELECT | X | X | X | |
| INSERT | X | | X | |
| UPDATE* | X | X | X | |
| DELETE | X | | X | |
| EXECUTE | | | | X |
| REFERENCES (DRI— declarative referential integrity) | X | X | | |

*Users must have SELECT permissions in addition to UPDATE permissions to update a table column or a view.

Any user can view a database's statement and object permissions from SQL Enterprise Manager.

▶ **To view statement permissions**

In this procedure, you view the users and groups that have statement permissions in the *pubs* database.

1. Open SQL Enterprise Manager, and then select your server.
2. Expand the Databases folder, and then double-click the *pubs* database.

   The Edit Database dialog box appears.
3. Click the Permissions tab.

   By default, who can create stored procedures in the *pubs* database?

   _____

   By default, what statement permissions does a guest user have in the *pubs* database?

   _____

4. Click Cancel.

▶ **To view object permissions**

In this procedure, you view object permissions in the *pubs* database from the perspective of the object and from the perspective of the user or group.

1. Open SQL Enterprise Manager, and then select your server.

2. Expand the Databases folder, and then select the *pubs* database.

3. On the Object menu, click Permissions.

   The Object Permissions dialog box appears.

4. Click the By Object tab.

5. In the Object list, select *authors* (dbo).

   By default, what object permissions does a guest user have for the authors table in the *pubs* database?

   _____

6. Click the By User tab.

7. In the User/Group list, select Public.

   By default, what object permissions does a member of the Guest group have for the view objects in the *pubs* database?

   _____

8. Click Close.

---

**Note**   You can also view permissions by executing the **sp_helprotect** system stored procedure or by directly viewing the *sysprotects* table.

# The Permission Hierarchy

SQL Server's permissions system recognizes four types of users: the system administrator, database owners, database object owners, and other users of the database. The SA is recognized by SQL Server as a "superuser" who works outside SQL Server's permissions system. The SA is not necessarily an individual user, rather, it is a role in the SQL Server environment.

Only the SA and database owners can grant statement permissions to other users. The following figure illustrates the permissions of each type of user.

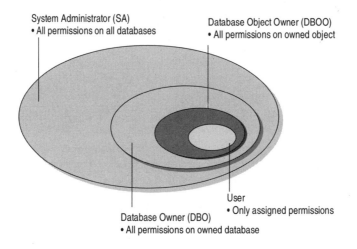

**Note**  By default, the group Public is granted SELECT permissions on the system tables.

## System Administrator (SA) Permissions

The SA login is not associated with a username. There are no restrictions on what the SA can do within SQL Server. This gives the SA the ability to repair any damage inadvertently done to the permissions system. The SA handles tasks not specific to an application or a particular database.

The following table lists the tasks (and their associated commands) that only the SA can perform. Permission to perform these tasks cannot be granted to other users.

| Tasks | Commands |
|-------|----------|
| Creating a device | device (DISK INIT, DISK REFIT, DISK REINIT) |
| Mirroring a device | DISK MIRROR, DISK REMIRROR, DISK UNMIRROR |
| Stopping a process | KILL |
| Shutting down SQL Server | SHUTDOWN |
| Reconfiguring SQL Server | RECONFIGURE |
| Performing some DBCC operations | |
| Adding or dropping extended stored procedures | |

The SA also has CREATE DATABASE statement permission. CREATE DATABASE statement permission is reserved for the SA because during database creation the amount and location of storage are allocated for each database. The SA can grant CREATE DATABASE permission to another user; however, that user is also automatically granted ALTER DATABASE statement permission.

**Important**  To maintain database permission integrity, it is recommended that you not grant CREATE DATABASE permission users other than SA.

## Database Owner (DBO) Permissions

By default, the SA is the database owner (DBO) in each database and always retains all permissions in that database. A DBO has full permission to do anything inside a database he or she owns. If necessary, you can change a database's owner using the **sp_changedbowner** system stored procedure.

The following table lists the tasks (and their associated commands) that the DBO can perform. Permission to perform these tasks cannot be granted to other users.

| Tasks | Commands |
| --- | --- |
| Restoring a database and transaction log | LOAD DATABASE, LOAD TRANSACTION |
| Deleting a database | DROP DATABASE |
| Using DBCC commands | DBCC |
| Impersonating a database user | SETUSER |
| Issuing a checkpoint | CHECKPOINT |
| Granting and revoking statement permissions | GRANT, REVOKE |
| Altering a database | ALTER DATABASE |

The following table lists the tasks (and their associated commands) that the DBO can perform that can be granted to other users.

| Tasks | Commands |
| --- | --- |
| Creating objects | CREATE TABLE, CREATE VIEW, CREATE PROCEDURE, CREATE DEFAULT, CREATE RULE |
| Backing up a database | DUMP DATABASE |
| Backing up a transaction log | DUMP TRANSACTION |
| Using objects | SELECT, UPDATE, INSERT, DELETE |

**Important**  To maintain database permission integrity, it is recommended that you not grant create object permissions to users other than the DBO.

## Database Object Owner (DBOO) Permissions

A user who creates a database object (table, view, or stored procedure) is its owner and is automatically granted all permissions on the object. Users other than the object owner, including the DBO, are denied all permissions on that object unless the owner explicitly grants them permission. (However, the DBO can impersonate the owner using SETUSER if necessary.) The only exception to users denied all permissions is the SA. The SA is unaffected by any permissions granted to or revoked from the DBO.

The following table lists the tasks—and their associated commands—that the DBOO of a table can perform. Permission to perform these tasks cannot be granted to other users.

| Tasks | Commands |
|---|---|
| Altering, truncating, or dropping a table | ALTER TABLE, TRUNCATE TABLE, DROP TABLE |
| Creating and dropping indexes | CREATE INDEX, DROP INDEX |
| Updating statistics for one or more indexes | UPDATE STATISTICS |
| Creating and dropping triggers | CREATE TRIGGER, DROP TRIGGER |
| Granting object permissions to other users | GRANT, REVOKE |

The owner of a view, stored procedure, rule, or default has statement permission to drop the object which cannot be transferred. Database object owners have the appropriate object permissions on the objects they create.

---

**Note**  The ability to grant and revoke object permissions is inherent in the create object statements. For example, if a user is granted permission to create a view, the user becomes the object owner, and can create a new view and then grant and revoke permission to access the view for other users in the database. Object ownership cannot be transferred; if you need to drop a user that owns an object, you must first drop the object.

---

## Default Group and User Permissions

The following table summarizes the SQL Server statement permissions system. The table lists the lowest user level to which the permission is automatically granted. If the permission is transferable, this user can grant or revoke the permission from other users.

| Statement | Defaults to | | | | Can be granted/revoked | | |
|---|---|---|---|---|---|---|---|
| | SA | DBO | DBOO | Public | Yes | No | N/A |
| ALTER DATABASE | — | X | — | — | (1) | — | — |
| ALTER TABLE | — | — | X | — | — | X | — |
| BEGIN TRANSACTION | — | — | — | X | — | — | X |
| CHECKPOINT | — | X | — | — | — | X | — |
| COMMIT TRANSACTION | — | — | — | X | — | — | X |
| CREATE DATABASE | X | — | — | — | X | — | — |
| CREATE DEFAULT | — | X | — | — | X | — | — |
| CREATE INDEX | — | — | X | — | — | X | — |
| CREATE PROCEDURE (2) | — | X | — | — | X | — | — |
| CREATE RULE | — | X | — | — | X | — | — |
| CREATE TABLE | — | X | — | (3) | X (2) | — | — |
| CREATE TRIGGER | — | — | X | — | — | X | — |
| CREATE VIEW | — | X | — | — | X | — | — |
| DBCC | — | X | — | — | — | X | — |
| DELETE | — | — | X (4) | — | X | — | — |
| DISK INIT | X | — | — | — | — | X | — |
| DISK MIRROR | X | — | — | — | — | X | — |
| DISK REFIT | X | — | — | — | — | X | — |
| DISK REINIT | X | — | — | — | — | X | — |
| DISK REMIRROR | X | — | — | — | — | X | — |
| DISK UNMIRROR | X | — | — | — | — | X | — |
| DROP any object (5) | — | — | — | — | — | X | — |
| DUMP DATABASE | — | X | — | — | X | — | — |
| DUMP TRANSACTION | — | X | — | — | X | — | — |
| EXECUTE (6) | — | — | — | — | X | — | — |
| GRANT | — | X | — | — | — | X | — |
| GRANT on object (5) | — | — | — | — | — | X | — |

*(continued)*

| Statement | Defaults to | | | | Can be granted/revoked | | |
|---|---|---|---|---|---|---|---|
| | SA | DBO | DBOO | Public | Yes | No | N/A |
| INSERT | — | — | X (4) | — | X | — | — |
| KILL | X | — | — | — | — | X | — |
| LOAD DATABASE | — | X | — | — | — | X | — |
| LOAD TRANSACTION | — | X | — | — | — | X | — |
| PRINT | — | — | — | X | — | — | X |
| RAISERROR | — | — | — | X | — | — | X |
| READTEXT | — | — | X | — | (7) | — | — |
| RECONFIGURE | X | — | — | — | — | X | — |
| REFERENCE | — | — | X | — | X | — | — |
| REVOKE | — | X | — | — | — | X | — |
| REVOKE on object (5) | — | — | — | — | — | X | — |
| ROLLBACK TRANSACTION | — | — | — | X | — | — | X |
| SAVE TRANSACTION | — | — | — | X | — | — | X |
| SELECT | — | — | X (4) | — | X | — | — |
| SET | — | — | — | X | — | — | X |
| SETUSER | — | X | — | — | — | X | — |
| SHUTDOWN | X | — | — | — | — | X | — |
| TRUNCATE TABLE | — | — | X | — | — | X | — |
| UPDATE | — | — | X (4) | — | X | — | — |
| UPDATE STATISTICS | — | — | X | — | — | X | — |
| UPDATETEXT | — | — | X | — | — | — | — |
| WRITETEXT | — | — | X | — | (8) | — | — |

(1)  Transferred with CREATE DATABASE permission.

(2)  Permissions to create temporary procedures are granted by default. A user can create and execute temporary procedures in a database even if not explicitly granted CREATE PROCEDURE permission.

(3)  Members of Public can create temporary tables; no permission required.

(4)  If a view, permission defaults to view owner.

(5)  Defaults to object owner.

(6)  Defaults to stored-procedure owner.

(7)  Transferred with SELECT permission.

(8)  Transferred with UPDATE permission.

## Planning a Database's Permissions

Although it is possible to have separate users acting as database owner and database object owners, it is not recommended. In most systems, the SA should be the database owner for all databases, and any other users who must act as database owners should be aliased to DBO. It is also not recommended that the DBO grant object ownership permissions to individual users. Splitting the SA and database owner responsibilities and the DBO and DBOO responsibilities can result in broken ownership chains for views and stored procedures.

The *ownership chain* of a view or stored procedure is the list of its underlying objects (such as views, tables, or stored procedures) and who owns them. Typically, the owner of a view also owns its underlying objects (other views and tables), and the owner of a stored procedure often owns all of the procedures, tables, and views that the procedure references. If all objects in the chain are not owned by the same user, the ownership chain is *broken*.

Broken ownership chains are not an issue while creating views and stored procedures, but they can be an issue when using the views and stored procedures. If the owner of a view or stored procedure owns all of its underlying objects, the owner has to grant permission only on the view or stored procedure for it to be used. However, if the owner of a view or stored procedure does not own all of the objects it depends on, the person being given permissions must also be given object permissions from the other owners; otherwise, permission to use the view or stored procedure is denied. SQL Server checks permissions on each object in the ownership chain whose next lower link is owned by a different user. This allows the owner of the original data to retain control over who is authorized to access it.

In the following figure, a complex ownership chain is broken. If a user tries to execute **Lucia.procedure1**, SQL Server checks the permissions on **Lucia.procedure1**, **Maria.procedure3**, **Maria.view2**, **Lucia.table2**, and **Maria.table3**. Permissions are checked on these objects because the next lower objects in the chain are owned by a different user.

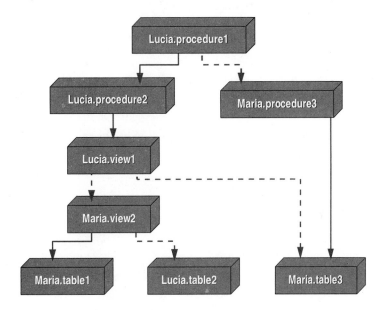

To avoid broken ownership chains, the following aliasing strategy is recommended:

1. Leave the SA (and no one else) as DBO in all databases.

2. Alias all users who need DBO permissions to DBO in each database.

3. Leave the database owner as the creator and owner of all objects in the database.

4. Grant object permissions to groups, not to individual users.

## Permissions Precedence

You can administer permissions for both groups and users. Permissions granted directly to a user take precedence over the permissions granted to a group that includes the user. The permissions granted to a group are provided to the users who are members of that group, which do not have individual user permissions that conflict with the group permissions. When granting or revoking permissions, it is recommended that you perform the steps in this order:

1. Grant permissions to the Public group. The permissions applied to the Public group are effective for users and groups with no other conflicting permissions assignments.

2. Grant or revoke permissions to other groups.

3. Grant or revoke permissions to individual users. The permissions applied to an individual user take precedence over any previously assigned permissions.

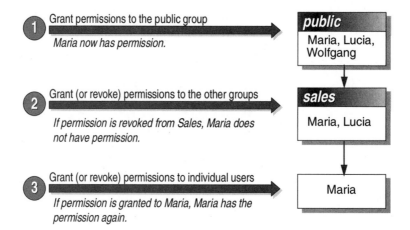

Granting and revoking permissions in this order allows you to set the more general permissions first, and requires assigning fewer additional permissions.

Permissions are sensitive to the order in which they are assigned, because of how they are written to the *sysprotects* table. The *sysprotects* table maintains information about user and group permissions. SQL Server determines what to write to the *sysprotects* table based on the current content of the table. SQL Server follows the process below in determining what to write to *sysprotects*.

1.  SQL Server evaluates whether a row exists in the *sysprotects* table for the specific permission, action, object, and user or group.

    - If a row exists, and the current GRANT or REVOKE statement duplicates the existing row, nothing is entered in *sysprotects*.

    - If a row exists, and the current GRANT or REVOKE statement is the converse (the opposite) of the previously-entered row, the previously-entered row is deleted from *sysprotects*.

2.  If no row exists in *sysprotects* relating to the specific permission, SQL Server performs one of the following steps, depending on who the permission is being granted to or revoked from, and what other permissions exist in the *sysprotects* table:

    - If a permission is granted, SQL Server enters a row in the *sysprotects* table.

    - If a permission that has been granted to the Public group is being revoked from a group, SQL Server enters a row in the *sysprotects* table revoking the permission.

    - If a permission that has been granted to any group a user is a member of is being revoked from that user, SQL Server enters a row in the *sysprotects* table revoking the permission.

The following figure illustrates how SQL Server writes to the *sysprotects* table in various circumstances. The first step in the figure demonstrates the grant rows that are written to the *sysprotects* table when SELECT permission is granted to the Sales group and to the user Maria.

The second step demonstrates that revoking SELECT permission from the Sales group removes the Sales group's GRANT SELECT row from the *sysprotects* table, but does not affect Maria's permission.

The third step demonstrates that granting SELECT permission to the Public group writes a GRANT SELECT row to *sysprotects*.

The fourth step demonstrates that revoking SELECT permission from the Sales group after granting SELECT permission to the Public group writes a REVOKE SELECT row for the Sales group in the *sysprotects* table.

**1** GRANT SELECT
ON *authors* TO Sales

GRANT SELECT
ON *authors* TO Maria

| object_id | user_id | action | protect type | ... |
|-----------|---------|--------|--------------|-----|
| authors | Sales | select | grant | |
| authors | Maria | select | grant | |

**2** REVOKE SELECT
ON *authors* FROM Sales

| object_id | user_id | action | protect type | ... |
|-----------|---------|--------|--------------|-----|
| ~~authors~~ | ~~Sales~~ | ~~select~~ | ~~grant~~ | |
| authors | Maria | select | grant | |

**3** GRANT SELECT
ON *authors* TO Public

| object_id | user_id | action | protect type | ... |
|-----------|---------|--------|--------------|-----|
| authors | Maria | select | grant | |
| authors | Public | select | grant | |

**4** REVOKE SELECT
ON *authors* FROM Sales

| object_id | user_id | action | protect type | ... |
|-----------|---------|--------|--------------|-----|
| authors | Maria | select | grant | |
| authors | Public | select | grant | |
| authors | Sales | select | revoke | |

**Note** The preceding discussion and figure demonstrate the function of the *sysprotects* table, not its actual appearance. The *sysprotects* table contains codes for each column, rather than names.

## Lesson Summary

Permissions enable you to determine what groups and users can do within a database. The permissions automatically available to a user depend on the role the user plays in a database (SA, DBO, DBOO). In most instances, it is recommended that you not grant statement (object creation) permissions to any user but the DBO. Planning your database permissions enables you to precisely map and implement your needs without having to grant and revoke many permissions.

| For more information on | See |
|-------------------------|-----|
| Permissions | "About Permissions" in SQL Server Books Online |

# Lesson 2: Implementing Permissions

You can grant both statement and object permissions to users and groups of each database. It is important that you consider carefully which groups and users should be granted each permission.

### After this lesson you will be able to:

- Grant statement permissions.
- Revoke statement permissions.
- Grant object permissions.
- Revoke object permissions.

### Estimated lesson time  20 minutes

Before you grant statement or object permissions, you must create the groups and users you want to grant permissions to. Determine which groups and users should have object creation capabilities, and assign the groups and users statement permissions. Determine which groups and users should have object manipulation permissions, and which database objects these groups and users require access to. For example, a Managers group might require permission to execute certain stored procedures to analyze data and prepare reports, or a DataEntry group might require SELECT, INSERT, UPDATE, and DELETE access on specific tables.

You can grant or revoke both statement and object permissions using either the SQL Enterprise Manager or the GRANT and REVOKE statements.

## Granting or Revoking Statement Permissions

In SQL Enterprise Manager, you set statement permissions through the Edit Database dialog box. The dialog box, illustrated in the following figure, lists the users and groups for the current database and the permissions that are granted to them. When a permission is newly selected, a green check mark appears in the check box, indicating that the permission will be granted. When an existing permission is selected, a red circle with a slash appears in the check box, indicating that the permission will be revoked. You can also grant or revoke object permissions from any query window.

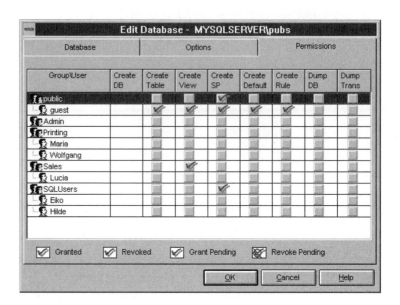

The following table lists and describes what each statement permission enables a user to do.

| Permission | Allows the user to |
|---|---|
| Create DB | Create a database. This permission can be granted only by SA, and only to users in the *master* database. |
| Create Table | Create a table. |
| Create View | Create a view. |
| Create SP | Create a stored procedure for the database. |
| Create Default | Create a default, which is a value that SQL Server inserts into a column if a user does not explicitly enter one. |
| Create Rule | Create a rule, which determines what a user can enter in a particular column or in any column that has a given user-defined datatype. |
| Dump DB | Make a backup copy of a database and its transaction log. |
| Dump Trans | Make a copy of a database's transaction log. |

**GRANT Syntax**

GRANT {ALL | *statement_list*}
    TO { PUBLIC | *name_list*}

**REVOKE Syntax**

REVOKE {ALL | *statement_list*}
    FROM {PUBLIC | *name_list*}

The *statement_list* parameter takes a list of statements a user or group is allowed to execute. The *name_list* parameter can specify group names and database usernames.

▶ **To grant and test statement permissions**

In this procedure, you grant a group statement permissions, and then test the permissions.

1. In the SQL Enterprise Manager Server Manager window, double-click the *pubs* database folder.

   The Edit Database dialog box appears.

2. Click the Permissions tab.

   The Edit Database dialog box displays all user permissions for the selected database. Existing permissions are indicated by blue check marks.

3. Click the box for the Sales group in the Create View column to grant permission to create views to the Sales group.

   Notice that Lucia and Maria are members of the Sales group.

   When a permission is newly selected, a green check mark appears in the check box.

4. Grant permission to Create SP (stored procedures) to the SQLUsers group.

   Notice that Eiko and Hilde are members of the SQLUsers group.

5. Click OK.

   The permissions are not granted until you click OK.

6. Minimize SQL Enterprise Manager.

7. Start ISQL/w, and connect to your server using as Lucia using standard security.

8. Type and execute the following statement to create a view on the *authors* table showing the author's first and last names and state.

```
CREATE VIEW view1 AS
    SELECT au_lname, au_fname, state
    FROM authors
```

Can Lucia create the view? Why or why not?

_____

_____

9. Type and execute the following statement to select from the view you created on the *authors* table.

```
SELECT * FROM view1
```

Can Lucia select from this view? Why or why not?

_____

_____

_____

10. Exit ISQL/w.

## Granting or Revoking Object Permissions

In SQL Enterprise Manager, you set object permissions through the Object Permissions dialog box. The dialog box, illustrated in the following figure, shows the users and groups for the current database and the permissions that can be granted to them.

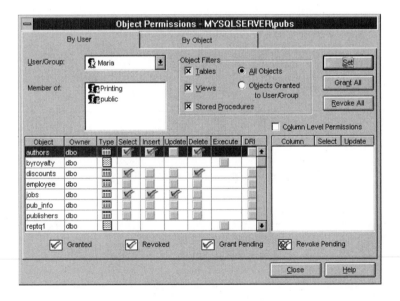

You can set object permissions either from the perspective of the user or group, or from the perspective of the object. To grant and revoke permissions by user or group, select the By User tab. To grant and revoke permissions by object, select the By Object tab. Both tabs provide the same options, but present them differently.

The permissions you can set are as follows:

| Permission | User or group can |
|---|---|
| Select | Select data from a table, view, or column. |
| Insert | Insert new data in a table or view. |
| Update | Update existing data in a table, view, or column. |
| Delete | Delete data from a table or view. |
| Execute | Execute a stored procedure. |
| DRI (References) | Reference a table without having SELECT permissions on the table. |

You can also grant or revoke statement permissions from any query window.

**Syntax**

GRANT {ALL [PRIVILEGES][*column_list*] | *permission_list* [*column_list*]}
   ON {*table_name* [(*column_list*)]
   | *view_name* [(*column_list*)]
   | *stored_procedure_name*}
   TO {PUBLIC | *name_list* }
   [WITH GRANT OPTION]

The WITH GRANT OPTION enables a user or group to whom an object permission was granted to grant the permission to other users (not groups).

**Syntax**

REVOKE [GRANT OPTION FOR]
   {ALL [PRIVILEGES] | *permission_list* } [(*column_list*)]
   ON { *table_name* [(*column_list*)]
   | *view_name* [(*column_list*)]
   | *stored_procedure_name* | *extended_stored_procedure_name*}
   FROM {PUBLIC | *name_list*}
   [CASCADE]

The CASCADE option revokes any WITH GRANT OPTION privileges that were granted by the user, including those of the user.

A GRANT or REVOKE statement can operate only on one object's permissions at a time.

## Granting Permissions on a View

Rather than granting permission to specific columns in a particular table, it is recommended that you create a view of the desired columns and grant permissions on the view. Granting permissions on a view eases administration and use. Users will have permissions to select all columns from the view, but not the table.

## Granting Permissions on a Stored Procedure

You can grant a user permissions on a stored procedure even if he or she has no permissions on objects the stored procedure references, as long as there is no break in the stored procedure's ownership chain. For example, a user might have permission to execute a stored procedure that updates a row-and-column subset of a table, even though the user does not have any permissions on that table. The same user must own the stored procedure and the referenced tables and views.

## Allowing Updates on System Tables

Permissions on the objects referenced by a stored procedure are checked when the procedure is used, not when it is created. However, for a stored procedure to update system tables, the creator of the stored procedure must be allowed to update the system tables when the stored procedure is created. The stored procedure can run successfully even if the system is reconfigured to not allow updates to the system tables.

You can use the **sp_configure** system stored procedure to enable or disable updates to system tables.

Syntax

**sp_configure** ['*config_name*'[, *config_value*]]

To enable updates to system tables from stored procedures, set *config_name* to 'allow updates', and *config_value* to 1. To disable updates to system tables, set *config_name* to 'allow updates', and *config_value* to 0.

## Implementing Object Permissions

In the following procedures you grant, test, and revoke object permissions from groups and users.

▶ **To re-register a server in SQL Enterprise Manager**

In this procedure, you register your server in SQL Enterprise Manager to use standard security and log in as Pierre, the DBO of *pubs*. Registering your server in SQL Enterprise Manager determines who you connect as when you select the server the next time you open SQL Enterprise Manager.

1. In the SQL Enterprise Manager Server Manager window, select your server.
2. On the Server menu, click Register Server.

   The Register Server dialog box appears.
3. In the Server list, select your server.
4. Select Use Standard Security, and then enter the Pierre login ID and pierre password.
5. Click Modify, and then click Close.
6. Exit and restart SQL Enterprise Manager.

▶ **To grant permissions to select from tables**

In this procedure, you grant object permissions to groups and users.

1. In the Server Manager window's Server list, select your server.

2. Expand the server's Databases folder, and then select the *pubs* database.

3. On the Object menu, click Permissions.

   The Object Permissions dialog box appears with the By Object tab selected. Notice that the dialog box shows you all object permissions for the selected database.

4. In the Object list, select the *authors* table.

5. Grant the Public group permission to select from the *authors* table.

6. Grant the Printing group permission to update the *authors* table.

7. Grant Maria permission to delete from the *authors* table.

8. Click Set.

9. In the Object box, select the **byroyalty** stored procedure.

10. Grant the SQLUsers group permission to execute the **byroyalty** stored procedure.

11. Click Set.

12. Click the By User tab.

13. In the User/Group list, select the Printing group.

    Object permissions are shown for this group. The Group Members box lists all users of the group. (To limit the amount of information displayed, select or clear Object Filters.)

14. Grant the Printing group permission to select from the *publishers* table.

15. Click Set.

16. Close the Object Permissions dialog box.

▶ **To test permissions of users connecting with standard security**

1. Start ISQL/w.

2. To verify the permissions you granted to the Public group, connect to your server as Lucia.

3. Select from Lucia's view on the *authors* table by typing and executing the following statement:

```
SELECT * FROM view1
```

4. To verify the permissions you granted to the Printing group, connect to your server as Wolfgang.

5. Update the author Ann Dull to Ann Dulle by typing and executing the following statement:

```
UPDATE authors
    SET au_lname = 'Dulle'
    WHERE au_lname = 'Dull'
```

6. To verify the permissions you granted to Maria, connect to your server as Maria.

7. Delete an author from the *authors* table by typing and executing the following statement:

```
DELETE authors
    WHERE au_id = '893-72-1158'
```

8. Exit ISQL/w.

▶ **To test permissions of users connecting with trusted connections (integrated security)**

In this procedure, you verify the permissions you granted to the SQLUsers group. Hilde is a member of SQLUsers.

1. Log off Window NT, and then log on as Hilde.

2. Start ISQL/w and connect to your server using Trusted Connections.

3. Type and execute the following statement:

```
EXEC byroyalty 100
```

4. Exit ISQL/w.

5. Log off, and then log back on to Window NT as Administrator.

▶  **To revoke object permissions**

In this procedure, the *pubs* DBO revokes permissions from users. Your server is currently registered to log in as Pierre, the *pubs* DBO, when starting SQL Enterprise Manager.

1. Start SQL Enterprise Manager, and then in the Server Manager window, select your server.

2. Expand the server's Databases folder, and then select the *pubs* database.

3. On the Object menu, click Permissions.

4. Revoke Maria's authority to delete from the *authors* table.

5. Click Set, and then click Close.

6. Log in to ISQL/w as Maria and attempt to delete from the *authors* table, where the au_id is 807-91-6654.

7. Close ISQL/w.

8. Switch to SQL Enterprise Manager and re-register your server using Standard Security with the SA login ID.

## Lesson Summary

Statement and object permissions can be granted to groups and users. Careful initial planning makes implementing permissions easier.

| For more information on | See |
|---|---|
| Implementing permissions | "Managing Object Permissions," and "Managing Statement Permissions" in SQL Server Books Online |

# Review

The following questions are intended to reinforce key information presented in this chapter. If you are unable to answer a question, review the lesson and then try the question again.

1. You want everyone in your group to be able to read the data in your database, except your interns. You want Jeannelle to be able to update the data, and Marisa to have "full control" of the database. In what order should you implement permissions?

_____

_____

_____

_____

2. You want members of the DataEntry group to have SELECT permission, but do not want members of Public to have any permissions. Which of the following will accomplish this?

   - REVOKE SELECT from Public and then GRANT SELECT to DataEntry.
   - GRANT SELECT to DataEntry and then REVOKE SELECT from Public.
   - GRANT SELECT to DataEntry.

_____

_____

_____

# Questions and Answers

Page 610

▸ **To view statement permissions**

3. Click the Permissions tab.

   By default, who can create stored procedures in the *pubs* database?

   **All members of the Public group, including the guest user.**

   By default, what statement permissions does a guest user have in the *pubs* database?

   **CREATE TABLE, CREATE VIEW, CREATE PROCEDURE, CREATE DEFAULT, and CREATE RULE.**

Page 611

▸ **To view object permissions**

5. In the Object list, select *authors* (dbo).

   By default, what object permissions does a guest user have for the authors table in the *pubs* database?

   **Select, Insert, Update, Delete and DRI (reference) permissions.**

7. In the User/Group list, select Public.

   By default, what object permissions does a member of the Guest group have for the view objects in the *pubs* database?

   **No permissions.**

Page 625

▸ **To grant and test statement permissions**

8. Type and execute the following statement to create a view on the *authors* table showing the author's first and last names and state.

   ```
   CREATE VIEW view1 AS
       SELECT au_lname, au_fname, state
       FROM authors
   ```

   Can Lucia create the view? Why or why not?

   **Yes, because she is a member of the Sales group, and the Sales group was granted permission to create views.**

9. Type and execute the following statement to select from the view you created on the *authors* table.

   ```
   SELECT * FROM view1
   ```

   Can Lucia select from this view? Why or why not?

   **No. Lucia does not have permission to select from her view because of a broken ownership chain. The authors table is owned by the DBO, not Lucia.**

Page 632

## Review Questions

1. You want everyone in your group to be able to read the data in your database, except your interns. You want Jeannelle to be able to update the data, and Marisa to have "full control" of the database. In what order should you implement permissions?

   **Grant SELECT to the Public group.**

   **Grant SELECT and UPDATE to Jeannelle.**

   **Revoke SELECT from the Interns group.**

   **Grant ALL to Marisa.**

2. You want members of the DataEntry group to have SELECT permission, but do not want members of Public to have any permissions. Which of the following will accomplish this?

   - REVOKE SELECT from Public and then GRANT SELECT to DataEntry.

   - GRANT SELECT to DataEntry and then REVOKE SELECT from Public.

   - GRANT SELECT to DataEntry.

   **All three options accomplish the task. The third option only works if no other permissions have been granted in a database.**

C H A P T E R   1 5

# Backing Up System and User Databases

## About This Chapter

This chapter provides an overview of the fault tolerance methods used to prevent data loss in Microsoft Windows NT Server and SQL Server. The main focus is on the different methods used to implement a backup strategy using SQL Enterprise Manager. In this chapter, you use SQL Enterprise Manager to schedule a backup, and then back up a database and transaction log. You also use the Maintenance Wizard to maintain the system.

## Before You Begin

To complete the lessons in this chapter, you must:

- Know how to create a database and a database device.
- Log in to Windows NT as administrator.
- Created the *testpubs* database.

  If you need to create *testpubs*, execute **sp_helpdevice**. Look under the *device_number* column and verify that device (VDEVNO) numbers 102 and 103 are not listed. If the numbers 102 and 103 are listed, make the appropriate changes in the \SCRIPTS\BLD_TPUBS\INSTTP.SQL script. This script creates the *testpubs* database for you. If you need to create these devices on a location other than C:\MSSQL\DATA, edit the location for the PHYSNAME parameter in the script. Load and execute the INSTTP.SQL script file.

  | Database name | Devices | Size |
  |---|---|---|
  | *testpubs* (8 MB) | TESTPUBSDATA | 5 MB |
  | | TESTPUBSLOG | 3 MB |

- Create the following new devices, and an empty database called *sender*, or execute the MKSENDER.SQL script file.

  | Database name | Devices | Size |
  |---|---|---|
  | sender | SENDERDATA | 5 MB |
  | | SENDERLOG | 5 MB |

# Lesson 1: Preventing Data Loss

Implementing a strategy to prevent data loss is an important part of system administration. There are several strategies for preventing data loss that can be implemented through Microsoft Windows NT Server and Microsoft SQL Server. There are also several types of backup devices you can use depending on the amount of data you want to back up and how critical it is that the data is current at all times.

### After this lesson you will be able to:

- Describe reasons for backing up data.

- Give two or more examples of backup devices.

### Estimated lesson time  10 minutes

## The Importance of Backing Up Data

Because system and product failure can occur even with the most reliable hardware and software components, you should have measures in place that get you back into production quickly and with minimal loss of data.

Data loss may happen for any number of reasons, such as:

- Accidental or malicious use of delete statements; for example, delete from *prod_table*, drop database *customers*, format drive C.

- Accidental or malicious use of updating statements; for example, accidentally updating all rows in a table by not qualifying with a WHERE clause.

- Destructive viruses.

- Natural disasters, such as fire, flood, earthquake.

- Theft.

If a physical disk device becomes damaged or unreadable, the damaged databases must be recovered by dropping and then recreating them from backups. Therefore, it is important to have a good backup strategy in place so your recovery goes smoothly.

## Types of Backup Devices

SQL Server can back up data to several types of devices.

**Tape**   Tape is the preferred media for backups. Tapes are easy to send off-site for safekeeping. Tape backups can be performed only to a tape drive that is attached to the local server.

**Hard disk**   Different physical drives are also recommended for backups. If the database and the backup are on the same physical drive, and the drive crashes, data cannot be recovered.

**Diskette**   Diskette backups are useful only with small databases.

**Named pipe**   Named pipe backups allows third-party vendors a flexible and powerful way to connect their own software and provide specialized backup and restoration capabilities.

**Null**   DISKDUMP is a special device created when SQL Server is installed. Backing up to DISKDUMP sends the data to the null device, and is the equivalent of backing up the data without saving it. You can use this null device to correct problems with the transaction log during backup.

## Lesson Summary

Data loss is prevented by backing up data to a storage device. Tape is the most common media for backups. You can also back up to hard disk or to a different physical disk drive.

# Lesson 2: Planning to Back Up Your Data

To back up a database, you make a copy of it on another device. A typical backup cycle consists of a backing up an entire database, backing up its transaction log, and then repeating backups at regular intervals.

Databases and transaction logs are backed up onto backup devices. A backup, or *dump,* device is usually a disk file, tape drive, or diskette (with earlier releases). You can back up a database to one device or multiple devices, and you can back up multiple databases or transaction logs to a common device or separate devices.

---

### After this lesson you will be able to:

- Describe a good backup strategy.

- Describe why you should back up your database.

- Describe what you need to back up.

- Describe when you would back up a database.

- Describe the function of a transaction log.

- Describe dynamic backup.

- Describe ways to check database integrity.

### Estimated lesson time  20 minutes

---

## Backing Up a Database

A regular backup schedule should be maintained on any database. The system administrator or the database owner has permission to back up the database. However, the database owner can grant that permission to other users. The person who is responsible should then set up the backup schedule.

## Frequency and Type of Backups

The frequency and type of backup you perform depends on the volume of transactions and the amount of work that might be lost due to a media failure. Systems used for high-volume, on-line transaction processing (OLTP) might have to be backed up daily and the transaction logs backed up hourly. Those used primarily for decision support could be backed up weekly and transaction logs backed up daily as shown in the following figure.

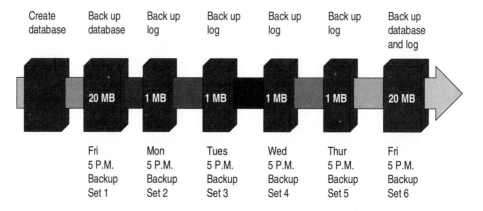

| Create database | Back up database | Back up log | Back up log | Back up log | Back up log | Back up database and log |
|---|---|---|---|---|---|---|
| | 20 MB | 1 MB | 1 MB | 1 MB | 1 MB | 20 MB |
| | Fri 5 P.M. Backup Set 1 | Mon 5 P.M. Backup Set 2 | Tues 5 P.M. Backup Set 3 | Wed 5 P.M. Backup Set 4 | Thur 5 P.M. Backup Set 5 | Fri 5 P.M. Backup Set 6 |

A common scenario is to perform a database backup after initially creating a database, and on a regular basis thereafter. You should perform transaction log backups between database backups.

## Backup Strategies

Backup strategy planning is a key component of any project. The strategy chosen should provide adequate protection for recovering data, and should also be appropriate for your environment. A solid backup plan should be in place before an application is moved from a development or test environment to a production environment. As with any application, you should always test your backup strategy prior to its going into production.

Once a backup strategy is in place, test it thoroughly. Check for vulnerable areas that could jeopardize the recovery of data by simulating as many failures as possible. For example, you could implement a redundant device and disk mirroring with multiple disks on one computer. If one of the disk drives fails, operation continues uninterrupted. After your backup strategy is in place, ask yourself whether or not it is effective in the event of computer theft.

Testing your backup strategy gives you an estimate of the amount of time required to restore the databases from backups. If the amount of time is unacceptable, you may want to re-evaluate the frequency of database and transaction log backups, or examine the feasibility of maintaining a backup server.

## What Data to Back Up

Backing up a database makes copies of its system tables, user-defined objects, and data. All of your company data is contained in user databases and should be backed up regularly. The *master*, *msdb*, and *distribution* databases should also be backed up on a regular schedule in the same way as user databases.

### The *master* database

Make backups of *master* after using any statement or system procedure that records information in it. When you create new user databases and other objects, changes occur in *master*.

*Master* cannot be separated from its transaction log; therefore, its transaction log cannot be backed up separately.

### The *msdb* database

The *msdb* database supports the SQL Executive service and provides a storage area for scheduling information. This database is modified by tasks that you schedule in the Manage Scheduled Tasks window, the automatic backups in the Database Backup/Restore dialog box, and all replication tasks. If the server is configured as a replication distributor, replication tasks are automatically created as necessary.

Because the **setup** program installs *msdb* and its transaction log on separate devices, you can perform both database and transaction log backups for it.

### The *distribution* database

When a server is configured for replication, either as a remote distribution server or as a combined publisher/distributor, it has a database dedicated to replication distribution activities. The default name for this database is *distribution*, although the user setting up replication can change that name.

The *distribution* database should have its transaction log on a separate device so that you can perform both database and transaction log backups.

## When to Back Up Data

You should back up each database immediately after creating it and then on a fixed schedule thereafter. If you create a database on Monday and wait until Friday afternoon to back it up, you risk losing an entire week of work if there is a media failure on Friday at noon.

You must load the transaction log backup after you load the database backup. You cannot use transaction log backups created between the creation of the database and the first backup of the database.

### After Performing a Non-Logged Operation

In addition to backing up each database on a fixed schedule, you must also back up a database any time you perform an operation that is not logged. Non-logged operations are not recorded in the transaction log. If an operation is not logged, the database and the log may be out of sync, in which case you cannot recover the operation if there is a media failure. Non-logged operations include bulk copying data into a database using **bcp** in fast mode and performing a SELECT INTO query.

### After Creating an Index

You should back up the database each time you create an index. If you do this, SQL Server does not have to recreate the index when you load the transaction log during the restore process. It also speeds up the restore process and reduces the amount of work performed by SQL Server during the recovery of the database.

**Example**

```
sp_dboption inventory,offline,true
```

## When to Back Up System Databases

It is strongly recommended that you back up the *master* database each time it is changed. The most common statements and system procedures—and the equivalent actions in SQL Enterprise Manager that modify *master* are listed in the following table.

| Actions | Statements and/or system-stored procedures |
|---|---|
| Creating, altering, or dropping a database | CREATE DATABASE, ALTER DATABASE DROP DATABASE |
| Creating, altering, or dropping a device | DISK INIT, DISK RESIZE, **sp_addumpdevice**, **sp_dropdevice** |
| Altering a transaction log | **sp_logdevice** |
| Mirroring or unmirroring a device | DISK MIRROR, DISK UNMIRROR, DISK REMIRROR |
| Adding or dropping servers | **sp_addserver, sp_dropserver** |
| Adding or dropping logins | **sp_dropremotelogin, sp_addlogin, sp_droplogin, sp_addremotelogin** |
| Changing configuration options | **sp_configure** |

All data is lost if a *user* database is created, expanded, or shrunk after the most recent backup of the *master* database. Therefore, always back up the *master* database after any one of these activities.

### When to Back Up Transaction Logs

Although the database and associated transaction logs can be stored on the same database devices, it is not recommended. Typically, the log portion of the database and the data portion of the database are stored on different devices, which means that you can back up the transaction log separately. Backups of the transaction log are usually coordinated with those of the database as part of an overall backup procedure.

---

**Note**  Always use the Microsoft SQL Server backup facility to back up your databases. Using Microsoft Windows NT Server to make copies of your databases does not ensure their integrity.

---

## Managing a Transaction Log

Managing the transaction log is an important system administrator function. If the transaction log is full, databases cannot be updated by users. This jeopardizes your ability to fully restore the system in the event of failure. To manage transaction logs, you can do the following:

- Place the transaction log on a separate device from its database.
- Monitor the transaction log with the **sp_spaceused** and **sp_helpdb** system procedures or the DBCC SQLPERF (LOGSPACE) statement.
- Keep the transaction log at a reasonable size (when it is on a separate device) by regularly backing up the log using either SQL Enterprise Manager or the DUMP TRANSACTION statement.

▶  **To monitor the size of a transaction log**

In this procedure, you monitor the size of a transaction log by looking at the size of logs.

1. In a query window, execute DBCC SQLPERF (LOGSPACE).

   Compare the size of each existing log and note the Log Space Used column.

2. Close the query window for the next procedure when finished.

If you do not separately back up the transaction log, the log maintains its old transactions and is not cleared out. This can cause you to run out of log space. You can clear the log by using DUMP TRANSACTION WITH TRUNCATE_ONLY before you back up the database.

It is important to back up a database anytime you perform an operation on it that is not logged. Non-logged operations cause the transaction log to become out of sync with the data in the database. After a non-logged operation, the transaction log can be truncated but not backed up. To allow the log to be backed up, first back up the associated database, creating a new point of synchronization between the database and the transaction log.

- DUMP TRANSACTION using the WITH TRUNCATE_ONLY option removes the inactive part of the log without making a backup copy of it. This frees up disk space used by the transaction log. If the log is too full to record that you have performed the TRUNCATE_ONLY option, you must use the NO_LOG option so that the truncate operation is not logged. After backing up a transaction log, you should immediately back up the database.

- When you use non-logged WRITETEXT, UPDATETEXT, or SELECT INTO on a permanent table, and then fast bulk copy, SQL Server does not log the data insertions made by these statements, and there is no way to recover them in case of media failure.

The following table lists the options used to back up the log.

| Option | Description |
|---|---|
| TRUNCATE_ONLY | Removes the inactive part of the log without making a backup copy of it, freeing disk space used by the transaction log. If your log is completely full, then you cannot use TRUNCATE_ONLY. You must backup the log with NO_LOG. |
| | After the transaction log has been backed up using TRUNCATE_ONLY, the changes that had been recorded in the log cannot be recovered. You should immediately execute DUMP DATABASE. |
| | You cannot use both TRUNCATE_ONLY and NO_LOG in the same statement. |
| NO_LOG | Removes the inactive part of the log without making a backup copy of it. NO_LOG saves space by not recording this procedure in the transaction log. |
| | Used when you have run out of space in the transaction log and cannot execute DUMP TRANSACTION WITH TRUNCATE_ONLY to retrieve some space from the log. Similar to TRUNCATE_ONLY, NO_LOG. |
| | After the transaction log has been backed up using NO_LOG, the changes that had been recorded in the log cannot be recovered. You should immediately execute DUMP DATABASE. |
| NO_TRUNCATE | Saves the complete log (everything that has happened since the last DUMP TRANSACTION) even if the database is inaccessible. Unlike the TRUNCATE_ONLY and NO_LOG options, the NO_TRUNCATE option does not purge the log of committed transactions. |
| | If the database and the log are on separate devices, and if you lose the database device, you can still back up the current contents of the log. After the failure condition is resolved (for example, after hardware is repaired), you can recover up to the exact time of the failure. |

### How Checkpoint Is Used

The checkpoint mechanism guarantees that completed transactions are automatically written from SQL Server's own disk cache to the database device. A checkpoint writes all committed transactions—cached pages (sometimes called *dirty pages*) that have been modified since the last checkpoint—to the database device. There are two types of checkpoints:

- Checkpoints that are carried out automatically by SQL Server.
- Checkpoints that are forced by database owners or the system administrator with the CHECKPOINT statement.

Forcing dirty pages onto the database device means that all completed transactions are written out. By doing so, the checkpoint shortens the time it takes for the database to recover. This is because the database pages are current, and there are no transactions that need to be rolled forward. A typical checkpoint takes only a second or two.

Checkpoints occur automatically at regular intervals as determined by the system. The automatic checkpoint interval is calculated by SQL Server on the basis of system activity and the recovery interval configuration option, which specifies the maximum acceptable recovery time. Checkpoints also occur automatically when you change a database option with the **sp_dboption** system procedure and when you stop the server with the SHUTDOWN statement or with the SQL Service Manager. The checkpoint, actually the CHECKPOINT process, also performs other tasks, including truncating the log (removing all committed transactions) if the database option has been set.

# Dynamic Backup

Dynamic backup allows a database or transaction log to be backed up while the database is active. Users can continue working with the databases during a backup, although performance might slow down. Dynamic backups are important because they encourage frequent backups, which helps you recover the database quickly in the event of a media failure.

If media failure does occur, the database must be reconstructed from database and transaction log backup media. The more recent the backup, the less recovery involved.

Backup responsibility is usually assigned to the system administrator or database owner (DBO). However, the DBO can transfer permission to back up a database and transaction log to other users.

## How Dynamic Backup Works

Dynamic backup works by writing a *snapshot* of the database to the backup device.

During a backup, SQL Server backs up a page before it handles any data modification on that page. A snapshot of the database is taken at the time the DUMP DATABASE command is executed. All unread pages are share-locked during the backup.

A dynamic backup is performed using the following steps:

1. The transaction log is checked for committed transactions.

2. All committed transactions are written to disk (the checkpoint).

3. All database pages are written to the backup device. Users attempting to write to a page during a backup must wait until that page is written to the backup device. A dynamic backup includes the steps shown in the following figure and summarized in the following list:

   a. The backup begins at the first page.

   b. If, while the page is being backed up, a request for data modification is received, SQL Server jumps ahead and backs up the affected page before allowing the modification.

c. After the affected page is backed up, SQL Server returns to the original sequence and continues to back up each page.

d. When SQL Server gets to the affected page, it skips it, and then continues with the next page.

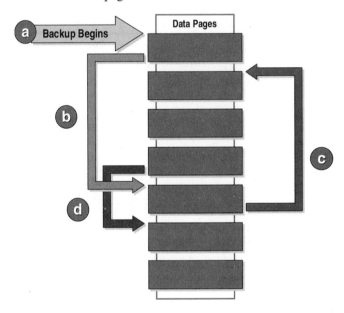

4. The transaction log (*syslogs* table) is updated to reflect the completion of the DUMP DATABASE command.

---

**Note**   Changes made by transactions that complete before the start of the backup are not reflected in the backup.

---

## Online vs. Offline Backups

Usually, a *backup operator* performs backups while the database is being used by other clients. This is called an *online* backup. You should perform online backups during off-peak hours or when the transaction volume is low. By using a fixed schedule, users will know when a backup will occur and can expect a slight delay in performance or plan to do non–SQL Server-related work during that time.

If you must take the database offline, use the query analyzer to execute the system stored procedure **sp_dboption** and set the offline parameter to True. The following example sets the offline parameter for a database called *inventory*.

**Example**

```
EXEC sp_dboption inventory, offline, true
```

## Checking the Database Integrity

If a database or transaction log contains errors, you might have a backup that cannot be loaded successfully. For this reason, it is important to perform consistency checks on your database.

The database consistency checker (DBCC) statements check the logical and physical consistency of a database. It is recommended that you execute the following DBCC statements prior to backing up a database.

| Command | Description |
|---------|-------------|
| DBCC CHECKDB | Checks all tables in a database to see that index and data pages are correctly linked, indexes are in proper sorted order, all pointers are consistent, the data information on each page is reasonable, and that page offsets are reasonable. |
| DBCC CHECKALLOC or NEWALLOC | Checks the specified database to make sure that all pages are correctly allocated and used. Unlike CHECKALLOC, NEWALLOC does not stop processing if it encounters an error. CHECKALLOC is provided for backward compatibility. |
| DBCC CHECKCATALOG | Checks for consistency in and between system tables. |

Executing these commands can be time consuming; therefore, it is recommended that no other activities take place while running them. Too many activities can lead to incorrect or misleading results.

Transactions can occur during or after running a consistency check and before a backup is performed. Check the database after a backup to ensure that it was consistent at the time it was backed up. If a database or transaction log containing errors is backed up, the errors will still exist when the data is reloaded. Under some conditions, this can prevent successful reloading.

## Lesson Summary

A good backup strategy is a critical component of any backup and recovery process. Components of a good strategy include knowing what you want to back up, when to back up, and how you are going to back up. Transaction log backups are typically coordinated with those of the database and are incorporated as part of the overall backup strategy. Prior to backing up a database, check the integrity of the database or transaction log is for errors that may interfere with a successful load.

| For more information on | See |
|--------------------------|-----|
| The CHECKPOINT statement | "Checkpoint" in SQL Server Books Online |

# Lesson 3: Implementing Backups

You should back up a database after you create it, and then maintain a regular backup schedule to ensure smooth recovery in case of database or media failure. SQL Enterprise Manager allows you to set and maintain a schedule of automatic backups. You can schedule backups when you define a backup. You can also manually back up at any time.

### After this lesson you will be able to:

- Create a backup device.
- Use Transact SQL and SQL Enterprise Manager to back up data.
- Back up to a secondary storage device.
- Back up multiple file databases.
- Perform parallel and striped backups.
- Schedule backups appropriate to your environment.

### Estimated lesson time 25 minutes

## Creating a Backup Device

You can create backup devices using SQL Enterprise Manager or by using the **sp_addumpdevice** stored procedure.

There are two ways to access the New Backup Device dialog box in SQL Enterprise Manager: You can create a backup device from the Database Backup/Restore dialog box of SQL Enterprise Manager, or you can create a backup device directly from the Server Manager dialog box by selecting the backup device folder and using a right-mouse click.

You must provide the following information to create a backup device:

- A device name—the logical name that follows the rules for identifiers and is no longer than 30 characters (longer names are truncated).
- The device location—the full path for the file location.

You also need to select the appropriate device type: disk or tape.

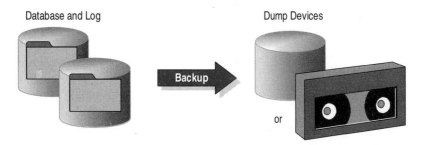

For tape devices, you have the option to skip headers. When the Skip Headers option is selected, SQL Server ignores any existing ANSI tape labels on the specified tape device. The ANSI label of a tape provides warning information about the expiration date of the tape and enforces write permissions.

### The sp_addumpdevice Stored Procedure

Another way to add a disk or tape backup device is to use the **sp_addumpdevice** system procedure. To add a disk backup device, you must use **sp_addumpdevice.** This feature is not supported in SQL Enterprise Manager.

When a backup device is added, its logical and physical names are entered in the *sysdevices* table in the *master* database.

▶ **To create a disk backup device**

In this procedure, you create backup devices for database and transaction log backups.

1. Create a directory on your local server named \SQLDUMPS on a partition with at least 30 MB of free space.
2. Using SQL Enterprise Manager, in the Server Manager window, select your server.
3. On the Tools menu, click Database Backup/Restore.

   The Backup/Restore dialog box appears.
4. Click New.

   The New Backup Device dialog box appears.

5. In the Name box, type:

**pubs_dump**

6. In the Location box, type:

**C:\SQLDUMPS\PUBS_DUMP.DAT**

7. Click Create.

8. Use File Manager to view the C:\SQLDUMPS directory.

   Does the backup device you just created appear in the directory? Why or why not?

   _____

   _____

   _____

9. Use the same steps to create the following disk backup devices in the C:\SQLDUMPS directory.

   - MASTER_DUMP
   - SENDER1_DUMP
   - SENDER2_DUMP
   - TESTPUBS_DUMP
   - TESTPUBS_TL_DUMP

10. Close the Database Backup/Restore dialog box.

11. In the Server Manager window, verify that the devices exist by opening the Backup Devices folder for your server.

## Performing a Backup

SQL Enterprise Manager makes it easy to back up your databases, transaction logs, or individual tables.

### Using SQL Enterprise Manager

You can use either SQL Enterprise Manager or the DUMP statement to back up a database transaction log or an individual table. It is usually rare to back up individual tables. If you must back them up, you should be familiar with the following issues:

- You cannot load an individual table that contains text columns indexes, or one that is published for replication.

- It is recommended that you load a table only from a backup created specifically of that particular table.

**Note**  SQL Enterprise Manager cannot be used to backup to diskettes. You must use the DUMP statement.

To back up a database or transaction log in SQL Enterprise Manager, you first select a server, and then open the Database Backup/Restore dialog box, in which you can provide or change the following information about the current backup:

- The name of the database or individual table you want to back up.

- The name of the device or devices you want to use.

- Whether SQL Server should back up the entire database, only the transaction log, or an individual table.

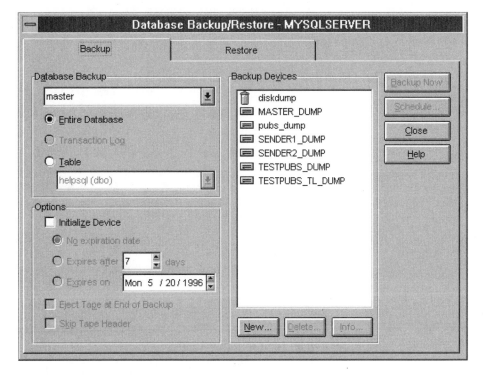

- Whether to append or overwrite the current backup to previous backups by choosing the Initialize Device option.

- Whether to set an expiration date.

- Whether SQL Server should read or skip existing ANSI tape header labels.

- Whether SQL Server should unload the tape when finished.

- Whether to run the backup immediately or schedule it for later execution.

**Note** You can back up the transaction log only when it is on a different device from its database. How a table is backed up, what its contents and datatypes are, and how many indexes it contains affect how it is restored.

The SQL Enterprise Manager Database Backup/Restore dialog box can also be used to create new backup devices.

▶ **To back up a database**

In this procedure, you back up the *master* database to the MASTER_DUMP device and view the contents of the device when the backup is complete.

1. In the Server Manager window of SQL Enterprise Manager, select your server.
2. On the Tools menu, click Database Backup/Restore to open the Database Backup/Restore dialog box.
3. Verify that the Backup tab is selected.
4. In the Database box, select *master*.
5. Under Backup Devices, select the MASTER_DUMP device.
6. Make sure the following options are selected:
   - Entire Database. The *master* database cannot be separated from its log. They are backed up as a unit.
   - Initialize Device. You must initialize a backup device the first time you use it. You can also write over the contents of an existing device by selecting the Initialize Device option.
   - No Expiration Date.
7. Click Backup Now.

   The Backup Volume Labels dialog box appears.
8. Click OK.

   When the backup is completed, the cursor returns.
9. Under Backup Devices in the Database Backup/Restore dialog box, double-click MASTER_DUMP device.

   What information is provided about the database backup?

10. Click Close.

11. To view the contents of the C:\SQLDUMPS directory, use the File Manager. Does the MASTER_DUMP device appear? Why or why not?

## Using Transact SQL

Database transaction logs and individual tables can be backed up using the Transact SQL DUMP commands. DUMP DATABASE makes a backup copy of a database and its transaction log. DUMP TRANSACTION makes a backup of only the transaction log. The maintenance options for truncating or clearing the log are available only with the DUMP TRANSACTION statement and are not available with the SQL Enterprise Manager. All of these backups can be read into SQL Server using the LOAD statement.

**Syntax**

DUMP DATABASE {*dbname* | @*dbname_var*}
   TO dump_device [, dump_device2 [..., dump_device32]]

Backing up a transaction log:

DUMP TRANSACTION {*dbname* | @*dbname_var*}
   [TO dump_device [, dump_device2 [..., dump_device32]]]
[WITH {TRUNCATE_ONLY I NO_LOG I NO_TRUNCATE}

Backing up a table:

DUMP TABLE [[*database*.]owner.]*table_name*
   TO dump_device [, dump_device2 [..., dump_device32]]

▶ **To back up using Transact-SQL**

In this procedure, you use the DUMP DATABASE command to back up directly to a file without first creating a backup device.

1. Using ISQL/w or the SQL Query Tool, execute the following command:
   ```
   DUMP DATABASE pubs to DISK='C:\SQLDUMPS\PUBS_DIR.BAK'
   ```

2. Use File Manager to go to the \SQLDUMPS directory and verify that the file exists.

**Note**  To restore from this backup, you create a backup device that points to this location or use LOAD DATABASE with the filename as follows:

LOAD DATABASE pubs FROM DISK = 'C:\SQLDUMPS\PUBS_DIR.BAK'

### Backing Up to Tape

SQL Server makes use of the Windows NT backup feature. Any tape device supported by the Windows NT operating system can be used with SQL Server. Although Windows NT is equipped with tape backup capability for file backups, you must use the SQL Server tape backup interface to back up and restore databases and transaction logs.

SQL Server allows multiple backups to a single tape, providing you with the flexibility of completely unattended tape backups. When a backup or a load is issued, the console (if active) is used. Otherwise, the server performs the tape backup in a batch operation. If any non-critical errors or specific options are overridden, the client receives the information immediately while the server continues operations. For example, if the drive does not contain a tape and the DUMP and LOAD commands are issued under batch mode, the client immediately gets a message that no tape is mounted, and the server waits until a tape is mounted to continue the operation.

During the backup operation, information about the backup is recorded on the tape label. This information includes up to 17 characters of the database name, the time and date of the backup, and whether the backup was a database or a transaction log.

If a tape contains Windows NT–based file backups, you cannot use that tape for SQL Server backups. If the tape contains data in a foreign format, that is, not SQL Server backup files, the tape is rejected and you must overwrite the existing data in order to use that tape.

## Performing a Multifile Disk Backup

It is useful to put more than one backup on a single backup device. The multifile disk backup feature automatically performs a multifile disk backup to either disk or tape as depicted in the following figure. This capability is the default and does not have to be explicitly specified as long as the backup device is initialized.

You can perform a multifile disk backup using SQL Enterprise Manager and command syntax.

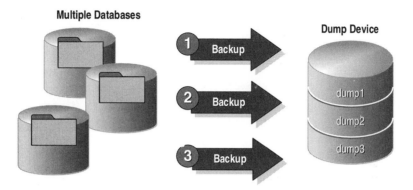

**Using SQL Enterprise Manager**

By default, SQL Enterprise Manager is configured to perform a multifile disk backup (the Initialize Device check box is cleared). If you select the Initialize Device check box in the Database Backup/Restore dialog box, the backup will be written as the first file in the backup device file.

▶ **To append multiple backups to one backup device**

In this procedure, you back up the following databases one at a time to the specified backup device. Verify that the Initialize Device check box is cleared for the second backup.

1.  Back up the *sender* database to the PUBS_DUMP device.

2.  Confirm that the Initialize Device is selected.

    This overwrites any old backups on the device or initializes a device that has never been used.

3.  Back up the *testpubs* database to the PUBS_DUMP device.

4.  Confirm that the Initialize Device option is cleared.

    This backup can now be appended to the PUBS_DUMP device.

5.  In the Dump Devices box, double-click the PUBS_DUMP device.

    What database backups appear on the PUBS_DUMP backup device? How large is backup device?

▶   **To write over an existing backup**

In this procedure, you write over an existing backup on the PUBS_DUMP device.

1. Open the Database Backup/Restore dialog box.
2. Select Initialize Device.
3. Select the *pubs* database.
4. Click Backup Now.
5. In the Dump Devices box, double-click the PUBS_DUMP Device.

   What database backups appear on the PUBS_DUMP backup device?

---

### Using Command Syntax

The following example backs up the *pubs* database to the disk backup device with a given name. The current backup is appended to the end of any existing backups on the device.

**Example**

```
DUMP DATABASE pubs TO dump1
```

The following example backs up the *pubs* database to the disk backup device as the first backup. If the device contains existing backups, the device file is truncated and reopened, and the current backup is written as the first one in the device file.

**Example**

```
DUMP DATABASE pubs TO dump1 WITH INIT
```

# Performing a Parallel Striped Backup

Performing a backup can be a time consuming operation. SQL Server gives you a way to speed up the operation significantly.

SQL Server can concurrently back up databases or transaction logs to multiple backup devices by performing a parallel striped backup. This is useful for backing up very large databases. The set of backup devices is called a stripe set. The array of backup devices can be a combination of any supported device, including tape or disk. A parallel backup does the following:

- Generates one thread per device.
- Processes an extent (eight 2K pages) at a time.
- Uses asynchronous I/O with multiple threads.

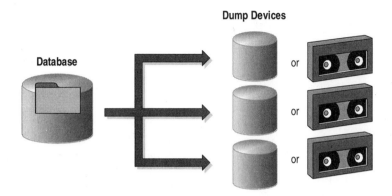

Database pages are read by multiple threads one extent at a time. Processing progresses from extent to extent, skipping unallocated extents. The *sysdevices* table is used to locate devices in a stripe set. The number of threads used is determined by the backup threads configuration option. The default setting is 5. The minimum value is 0, and the maximum value is 32.

**Note**  A database backup performed to more than one tape device can be restored from fewer devices than used for the original backup. This can be very useful if the site performing the load does not have the same equipment as the backup site.

You can perform a parallel striped backup using SQL Enterprise Manager or using command syntax.

## Using SQL Enterprise Manager

To perform a parallel striped backup, you specify multiple backup devices as the backup destination.

▶  **To back up one database to multiple devices (striped backup)**

1. Open the Database Backup/Restore dialog box, and confirm that the Backup tab is selected.

2. Select *sender* database.

3. Click Initialize Device.

4. Under Backup Devices, select the SENDER1_DUMP and SENDER2_DUMP devices. (Press CTRL while clicking the device names in the list.)

5. Click Backup Now, and then click OK.

6. Under Backup Devices in the Database Backup/Restore dialog box, double-click the SENDER1_DUMP device and the SENDER2_DUMP.

   What backups appear on the backup device? How large is each backup device?

   SENDER1_DUMP_____

   SENDER2_DUMP_____

7. View the information for the SENDER1_DUMP and SENDER2_DUMP backup devices. To view all columns, scroll to the right.

   Is this part of a stripe set?

   _____

   How many volumes are in the stripe set?

   _____

8. Click Close to close all open dialog boxes.

## Using Command Syntax

The following example performs a striped backup of the *pubs* database to three disk backup devices. The current striped backup overwrites all of the participating devices when you add the WITH INIT option to the DUMP DATABASE statement.

**Example**

```
DUMP DATABASE pubs TO dump1, dump2, dump3 WITH INIT
```

## Scheduling Automatic Backups

Use SQL Enterprise Manager to ensure regularly scheduled backups of your
database and transaction logs. Scheduled backups can be set to occur one time or on
a recurring basis. Recurring backups can occur hourly, daily, weekly, or monthly.
To schedule a backup, in the Database Backup/Restore dialog box, click Schedule.

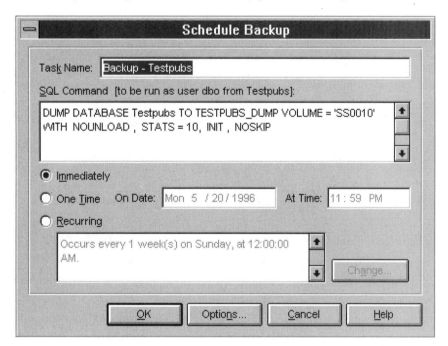

Add or change the following information in the dialog box:

- The task name for your backup.

  A backup task has a type of TSQL, which indicates that the task is a scheduled
  execution of a Transact-SQL statement. By default, the name of a backup task is
  generated by SQL Enterprise Manager using the following form: BACKUP -
  database_name.

- How often and when you want to back up.

If you choose Recurring, you can click the Change button to set various parameters
affecting scheduling, including:

- How often you want to run the recurring backup: hourly, daily, weekly, and
  so on.

- When you would like to start the recurring backup schedule and when you
  would like to stop it.

You can customize the backup command that is built by SQL Enterprise Manager by *directly editing* the text of the DUMP statement in the SQL Command box.

## Setting Backup Task Options

There are several useful options available to the system administrator when scheduling a backup task. Options are set in the TSQL Task Options dialog box. In the Database Backup/Restore dialog box, click Schedule, and then click Options.

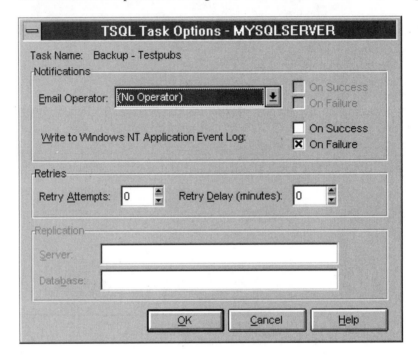

Scheduling a backup creates a backup task. When scheduling the backup, you can set task options that will:

- Send an e-mail notification to an operator when the backup fails or succeeds.
- Write an entry to the Windows NT Application Event Log when the backup fails or succeeds.
- Specify the number of retry attempts when a backup fails and the delay between each retry.

# Scheduling Backups

In the following procedures, you use the task scheduling functions of SQL Enterprise Manager and SQL Executive to schedule backups.

▶ **To schedule a database backup**

In this procedure, you back up the *testpubs* database on the TESTPUBS_DUMP device.

1. In the SQL Server Manager window in SQL Enterprise Manager, select your server.
2. On the Tools menu, click Database Backup/Restore.
3. Select the *testpubs* database as the database to back up.
4. Select the TESTPUBS_DUMP as the backup device.
5. Click Schedule.

   The Backup Volume Labels dialog box appears.
6. Click OK.

   The Schedule Backup dialog box appears. Notice the Task Name is *Backup-Testpubs*.
7. Select Recurring.
8. Click Change to change the schedule.

   The Task Schedule dialog box appears.
9. Select the following settings in the dialog box.

   | For this option | Use this setting |
   | --- | --- |
   | Occurs | Daily |
   | Daily | Every 1 day(s) |
   | Daily Frequency | Occurs once at 12:30 P.M. |
   | Duration | Start Date (today's date) No End Date |

10. Click OK to exit.
11. Click OK again to schedule the backup.

▶ **To schedule a recurring transaction log backup**

1. Using a different task name, repeat the previous procedure to add the TESTPUBS_TL_DUMP device to the Backup Destination box. Schedule a recurring backup of the transaction log of the *testpubs* database every 12 hours, starting at 9:00 A.M. and ending at 11:00 P.M.

2. Close the Database Backup/Restore dialog box.

▶ **To view the tasks in the Task Scheduler**

1. On the toolbar, click the Manage Scheduled Tasks button (the Calendar icon).

2. The Manage Scheduled Tasks dialog box appears.

   Verify that the tasks you scheduled appear in the dialog box.

3. Close the Manage Scheduled Tasks dialog box.

## Lesson Summary

SQL Enterprise Manager is the most common tool you use to back up your databases and transaction logs. Prior to backing up, you must know the device name and device path, or you can create a new device on which to back up. You also must know what you want to back up. You can use SQL Enterprise Manager to back up an entire database, the transaction logs, or a specific tables from the database. The most common medium for backing up is tape. You can schedule automatic backups to occur at intervals convenient to your working environment.

| For more information on | See |
|---|---|
| Backing up data | "Backing Up and Restoring" in SQL Server Books Online |
| **sp_addumpdevice** | "sp_addumpdevice" in SQL Server Books Online |
| Using the DBCC statements | "DBCC Statement" in SQL Server Books Online |
| The Task Scheduler | Chapter 19, "Scheduling Tasks and Setting Alerts" |

# Lesson 4: Other Methods for Preventing Data Loss

You can use a backup or standby server to prevent loss of data. In addition, you can create a mirrored copy of your data through the SQL Enterprise Manager. Deciding to use one or more of these methods depends on the type of environment in which you are working, and on your needs. It also depends on the level of security that is needed for the type of data you are backing up. The methods discussed here include using a backup or standby server, implementing Windows NT Server fault tolerance, and using SQL Server Mirroring.

### After this lesson you will be able to:

- Back up data to a standby server.
- Mirror a SQL Server device.
- Use the Database Maintenance Plan Wizard to back up your data.

### Estimated lesson time  20 minutes

## Using a Backup Standby Server

A backup server is a second server that is standing by in case something happens to the primary production server. Using a backup server shortens the time it takes to restore your databases after a failure.

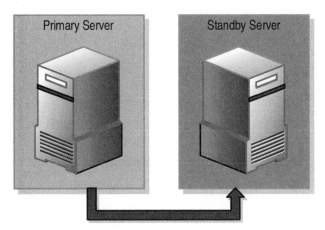

Assume that you have two servers: *Primary* is the main production SQL Server and *Standby* is another server on the network. Standby is also running SQL Server, with devices, databases, logins, and user accounts identical to those on Primary. Each time a database is copied from Primary, you manually load both it and the transaction log onto Standby. As a further precaution, it is recommended that these backups also be copied to tape (or another medium) and stored. Should a problem arise on Primary that requires significant downtime, Primary can be taken offline and Standby's server name changed to Primary.

After initially creating the databases on the Standby server, set the Read-Only and No Chkpt On Recovery options on the backup server. These options have the following effect:

**Read-Only**   Prevents users from performing any write activity in a database. When a SHUTDOWN statement is issued, it causes SQL Server to bypass writing a checkpoint record in the database.

**No Chkpt on Recovery**   Prevents SQL Server from writing a checkpoint. If the Standby server goes down and SQL Server is restarted, the databases will still show that no activity has taken place. Also, transaction logs can continue to be loaded from the Primary server.

These two options help reduce the risk of activity between log loads. If the Standby server is needed to replace the Primary server, you must turn off the No Chkpt On Recovery and Read-Only options before users can resume updating.

As an alternative to manually maintaining the Standby server with backup and restore (load), Microsoft SQL Server's replication tools can be used to establish and automatically maintain a backup server.

# Windows NT Server Fault Tolerance

*Fault tolerance* is the ability of the system to continue functioning without data loss if part of the system fails. The Windows NT operating system provides the following implementations for fault tolerance.

**Disk mirroring**   Protects against media failure by maintaining a fully redundant copy of a partition on another disk. This provides protection from the downtime and expense involved in recovering lost data and in restoring data from a backup storage facility. In a sense, mirroring is a form of continual backup. Windows NT–based disk mirroring implements RAID level 1.

**Disk duplexing**   A form of mirroring that also provides protection against controller failures by using a different disk controller on the mirror disk.

**Disk striping with parity**   Writes data in stripes across a volume that has been created from areas of free disk space. These areas are the same size and are spread over an array of disks (up to 32). It adds a parity-information stripe to each disk partition in the volume; which provides fault-tolerance protection equivalent to disk mirroring but requires less space for redundant data. Windows NT–based disk striping with parity implements RAID level 5.

When a member of a stripe set with parity fails in a severe manner—such as loss of power or a complete hardware failure—the data for that member of the stripe set is regenerated from the remaining members.

Striping with parity is recommended over mirroring for applications that require redundancy and are read-oriented. However, the use of striping with parity requires more system memory than mirroring. Also, when a member stripe is missing, it loses its performance advantage until the hardware is replaced and the member is regenerated. It is strongly recommended that when at all possible, you investigate redundant hardware-based solutions.

## Backing Up Databases

The fault tolerance methods are not a replacement for proper backup strategies. Performing frequent backups should always be part of your strategy regardless of the other fault tolerance measures you take.

# SQL Server Mirroring

Another software technique that provides a level of fault tolerance is mirroring at the SQL Server level.

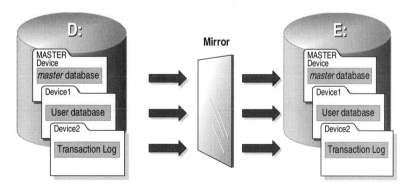

SQL Server mirroring protects against data loss in the event of media failure. Mirroring a device continuously duplicates information from one SQL Server device to another. All transactions to the device are copied to its duplicate mirror device. If one of the devices fails, the other contains an up-to-date copy of all transactions. When a read or write to a mirrored device is unsuccessful, it causes the bad device to become unmirrored, and the remaining device automatically takes over. The administrator can also choose to switch to the mirror copy of the device at any time.

You can implement SQL Server mirroring on a device-by-device basis, using a minimum, intermediate, or advanced configuration. Suggested configurations are described in the following table.

| Configuration | Description |
| --- | --- |
| Minimum | Mirror the transaction log of a *user* database on a separate disk. This configuration uses the minimum amount of disk space possible and does not provide nonstop recovery because the *master* and/or *user* databases must be recovered. |
| Intermediate | Mirror the *user* database, transaction log, and *master* database on a separate disk. This configuration uses additional disk space to provide nonstop recovery. |
| Advanced | Mirror the *user* database, transaction log, and *master* database on several disk. This configuration stores a mirror image of the transaction log and *master* database on one separate disk, and a mirror image of the *user* database on another separate disk. This option provides nonstop recovery with the highest level of redundancy. |

**Note**  SQL Server mirroring is one way you can mirror a disk for recoverability. Windows NT operating system software also allows disk mirroring and is recommended over SQL Server mirroring.

### How to Mirror a SQL Server Device

You can use SQL Enterprise Manager to set up mirroring or you can use the DISK MIRROR statement.

When you mirror a device, SQL Enterprise Manager creates a new physical device and puts an exact copy of the existing device on it. If the existing device contains a large amount of information, it may take a few minutes to create the mirror.

Place the mirror device on a separate disk. If a database or log spans more than one device, you must mirror all devices that contain the database.

# Using SQL Enterprise Manager to Mirror a Device

You can mirror a device at the time you create a new one or when you edit an existing one. After you mirror a device, you can turn mirroring off and choose to switch to the mirrored device as a replacement for the original device.

▶ **To create a mirror device**

1. On the Manage menu, click Database Devices.

2. Double-click *library_dev1*.

3. In the Edit Database Device dialog box, click Mirroring.

4. In the Mirror Device Filename box, type the physical name (the path) where you want the mirror device to be located or accept the default.

5. Click Mirror Now.

▶ **To turn off mirroring and remove the mirror device**

In this procedure, you remove the device just mirrored. Unmirror options include switching to the mirror device or turning off the mirror device.

1. Click Mirroring to open the Unmirror Device dialog box.
2. Select Turn off Mirroring - Remove Mirror Device.
3. Click Unmirror.

## Using the Database Maintenance Plan Wizard

The Database Maintenance Plan Wizard sets up and schedules core maintenance actions for a selected database. These maintenance actions include performing database and transaction log backups and other maintenance tasks such as checking data allocation, data and index linkages, and system data. You can also use it for updating optimizer information and reorganizing data and index pages. Maintenance actions can be scheduled for automatic execution at preset daily or weekly intervals.

▶ **To run the Database Maintenance Plan Wizard**

In SQL Enterprise Manager, select the database you want to run the wizard on, then on the toolbar click the Wizard icon or on the Help menu, click Database Maintenance Wizard and then follow the on-screen instructions.

## Lesson Summary

A backup standby server is used in the event something happens to the primary production server. Using one greatly shortens the time it takes to restore a database. You can also mirror your data by making a fully redundant copy of your database onto another partition on a different disk. This is a form of continual backup and is useful if you are concerned about possible downtown. The Database Maintenance Plan Wizard is used to help you schedule maintenance tasks on your database as well as help to back up and restore data.

| For more information on | See |
| --- | --- |
| How to unmirror or remirror a device | "Using SQL Server Mirroring" in SQL Server Books Online |
| How to use the DISK MIRROR command | "DISK MIRROR" in SQL Server Books Online |
| Using a backup server | "Managing a Backup Server" in SQL Server Books Online |
| The Database Maintenance Plan Wizard | Chapter 18, "Using SQL Mail, Scheduling Tasks, and Managing Alerts" |

# Review

The following questions are intended to reinforce key information presented in this chapter. If you are unable to answer a question, review the lesson and then try the question again.

1. What are some of the ways you can prevent data loss?

<br>

2. When should you back up your databases?

<br>

3. What is unique about dynamic backups?

4. What technique can you use to speed up the backup process?

_____

_____

5. Which DBCC commands should be used with backups and why?

_____

_____

_____

6. What is recorded in the transaction log and what is it used for?

_____

_____

_____

_____

7. When should you back up the *master* database to ensure good recoverability?

_____

# Questions and Answers

Page 651

▸ **To create a disk backup device**

    8. Use File Manager to view the C:\SQLDUMPS directory.

    Does the backup device you just created appear in the directory? Why or why not?

    **No, because a disk backup device is a placeholder to indicate where the database or transaction log will be backed up. A file is not created until the actual backup occurs.**

Page 654

▸ **To back up a database**

    9. Under Backup Devices in the Database Backup/Restore dialog box, double-click MASTER_DUMP device.

    What information is provided about the database backup?

    **The database name, date, size, and type of backup (database or log).**

   11. To view the contents of the C:\SQLDUMPS directory, use the File Manager.

    Does the MASTER_DUMP device appear? Why or why not?

    **Yes, because the physical file is created when the actual backup occurs.**

Page 657

▸ **To append multiple backups to one backup device**

    5. In the Dump Devices box, double-click the PUBS_DUMP device.

    What database backups appear on the PUBS_DUMP backup device? How large is backup device?

    **You should see two database backups with *testpubs* being the most recent.**

Page 658

▸ **To write over an existing backup**

    5. In the Dump Devices box, double-click the PUBS_DUMP Device.

    What database backups appear on the PUBS_DUMP backup device? How large is backup device?

    **The *pubs* database. (Results will vary.)**

Page 659

▶ **To back up one database to multiple devices (striped backup)**

6. Under Backup Devices in the Database Backup/Restore dialog box, double-click the SENDER1_DUMP device and the SENDER2_DUMP.

What backups appear on the backup device? How large is each backup device?

SENDER1_DUMP_____

SENDER2_DUMP_____

**The *sender* database. (Results will vary).**

7. View the information for the SENDER1_DUMP and SENDER2_DUMP backup devices. To view all columns, scroll to the right.

Is this part of a stripe set?

**Yes.**

How many volumes are in the stripe set?

**Two.**

Page 672

## Review Questions

1. What are some of the ways you can prevent data loss?

   **By implementing Windows NT Server disk striping with parity, disk mirroring or disk duplexing, SQL Server device mirroring, using a backup server, or backing up databases and transaction logs.**

2. When should you back up your databases?

   **On a regular basis so that your recovery time in case of failure will be an acceptable time period. Also after creating a new database, after performing a non-logged operation, after creating an index, and after performing any action which changes the *master* database.**

3. What is unique about dynamic backups?

   **Dynamic backups can be performed while users are using the database being backed up.**

4.  What technique can you use to speed up the backup process?

    **You can backup to multiple devices at the same time (parallel striped backup).**

5.  Which DBCC commands should be used with backups and why?

    **DBCC CHECKDB, DBCC CHECKALLOC OR NEWALLOC, and DBCC CHECKCATALOG. They should be used to check the logical and physical consistency of the database.**

6.  What is recorded in the transaction log and what is it used for?

    **All changes made to your databases are recorded in their respective transaction logs, along with database backups. The transaction log backups are used to recover data in the event of media failure.**

7.  When should you back up the *master* database to ensure good recoverability?

    **Back up the *master* database every time it is updated.**

CHAPTER 16

# Restoring System and User Databases

## About This Chapter

After a media failure or data corruption, a system administrator must restore the database and log. You can restore user databases, the *master* database, transaction logs, and tables. You can even restore the *master* database without a valid backup.

## Before You Begin

To complete this chapter, you must have:

- Created databases and database devices.
- Backed up a database and a transaction log.
- Completed Chapter 15, "Backing Up System and User Databases."
- Created the *testpubs* database.

   If you need to create *testpubs*, execute **sp_helpdevice**. Look under the *device_number* column and verify device (VDEVNO) numbers 102 and 103 are not listed. If the numbers 102 and 103 are listed, make the appropriate changes in the \SCRIPTS\BLD_TPUBS\INSTTP.SQL script. This script creates the *testpubs* database for you. If you need to create these devices on a location other than C:\MSSQL\DATA, edit the location for the PHYSNAME parameter in the script. Load and execute the INSTTP.SQL script file.

| Database name | Devices | Size |
|---|---|---|
| *testpubs* (8 MB) | TESTPUBSDATA | 5 MB |
|  | TESTPUBSLOG | 3 MB |

- Created the two backup devices, TESTPUBS_DUMP and TESTPUBS_TL_DUMP.

   If the two devices are not installed, execute the TESTDMP8.SQL script file. This script creates two backup devices for you.

# Lesson 1: Introduction to Restoring Databases

Every time SQL Server is started, it performs a recovery on each database. After a media failure or data corruption, the system administrator must restore the database and log from backups.

### After this lesson you will be able to:

- Describe two methods of database recovery.
- Describe some considerations about restoring a database and its transaction log.

### Estimated lesson time  10 minutes

To restore a database, you load the most recent database backup, and then load all of the transaction log backups that were made since the last database backup. The database is then restored to its state at the time of the last transaction log backup.

Depending on whether the database contains corrupt data, a device fails, or the system fails, you have different options for restoring or recovering the database. If you find that a database is corrupt, you can reload a database backup over the corrupt database. If a database device fails and the database is damaged, you can restore the database by reloading the most recent database backup and the subsequent transaction log backups. In the event of a system failure, you can recover as much of a database as possible by loading the transaction log backups.

## Recovery Methods

SQL Server uses two types of database recovery: automatic recovery and user-initiated recovery.

### Automatic Recovery

Automatic recovery is initiated every time SQL Server is started. At startup, SQL Server checks to see if any recovery is necessary. In the event of a system failure, this type of recovery can protect your database. A system crash refers to the system losing power, however, the media remains intact. Automatic recovery ensures that all transactions that were completed before a system crash are physically written to the database and all uncommitted transactions are rolled back. Automatic recovery cannot be turned off.

When SQL Server is started, an automatic recovery is performed on each database. Automatic recovery includes the following:

- Rolls back uncommitted transactions—SQL Server removes those transactions that were ongoing at the time SQL Server was shut down or when the system failed.

- Rolls forward committed transactions—SQL Server reapplies those transactions that the log has committed but have not yet been written out to the database.

Automatic recovery happens in stages. It begins with the *master* database, goes on to the *model* database, clears out the *tempdb* temporary database, recovers the *msdb* database, recovers the *pubs* database, recovers the *distribution* database (only if the server is configured as a replication distributor), and finally recovers user databases.

When using automatic recovery, you can set two configuration options by using either SQL Enterprise Manager or the **sp_configure** system stored procedure. The options are the following:

**Recovery flags**  Determines what information SQL Server displays during recovery.

**Recovery interval**  Controls the maximum time required to recover a database. An interval is set for SQL Server to determine whether to execute an automatic checkpoint.

### User-Initiated Recovery

User-initiated recovery restores the database and log from backups. This type of recovery is performed by the system administrator either in the event of media failure or when a database becomes corrupted.

## Guidelines for Restoring a Database and Transaction Log

When you restore a database and its transaction log, keep the following in mind:

- A database you are restoring from a backup cannot be in use. When you restore, all data in the target database is replaced by the loaded data.

- If you are reloading a database because of a media failure, you must first drop the damaged database by using the DROP DATABASE command, a DBCC DBREPAIR statement, or the **sp_dbremove** system-stored procedure. Then you recreate the database and restore it from a backup.

- If you load a transaction log, the changes it contains are re-executed, and any transactions that were uncommitted when the transaction log was backed up are rolled back.

- Be sure to load the backups of the transaction log in the sequence in which they were originally created. SQL Server checks the timestamps on each backed up database and transaction log and verifies that the sequence is correct. When the entire sequence of transaction log backups is loaded, the database is restored to its state at the time of the last transaction log backup, minus active transactions. In case of a system failure, this process recovers as much of a database as possible.

- If you create a database using the FOR LOAD option, and then load the database backup into the database, the DBO Use Only database option is enabled automatically. Therefore, before your users can access the database, you must disable the DBO Use Only database option.

## Examples of Restoring a Database and Transaction Log

This section contains three scenarios that show examples of restoring a database and its log. In order to restore a database and its log, you must first determine the time of the most recent database backup and the subsequent transaction logs. The following figure applies to all three scenarios.

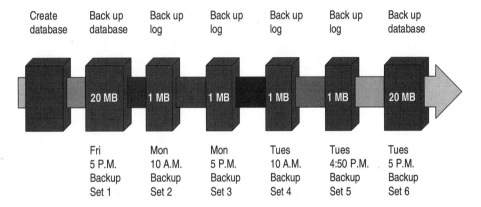

**Scenario 1**

If a problem occurs at 5:10 P.M. on Tuesday, you would have to load Backup Set 6, which is a database backup made at 5:00 P.M. The only work lost would be whatever had been done in the minutes between the last database backup and the failure.

**Scenario 2**

If a media failure occurs at 4:00 P.M. on Tuesday, you would have to load Backup Set 1 (the database backup executed at 5:00 P.M. on Friday), and then Backup Sets 2, 3, and 4 (the transaction log backups).

After all sets are loaded, the system will be in the exact state it was on Tuesday at 10:00 A.M., and all of Tuesday's work would be lost. This example shows why you should schedule frequent transaction log backups.

**Scenario 3**     If a media failure occurs on Tuesday at 4:00 P.M. on only the database device and not on the transaction log device, then the transaction log could be saved by using DUMP TRANSACTION WITH NO_TRUNCATE. In this case, all of the transactions that occurred between 10:00 A.M. and 4:00 P.M. on Tuesday would be recoverable. This scenario assumes the transaction log is on a separate physical drive from the database. With the NO_TRUNCATE option enabled, SQL Server backs up the transaction log without trying to access the database.

## Lesson Summary

Automatic recovery is initiated every time SQL Server starts. The system administrator performs a user-initiated recovery in the event of a media failure or data corruption. To ensure successful data recovery and restoration, you must schedule frequent transaction log backups.

# Lesson 2: Restoring a User Database, Transaction Logs, and Individual Tables

You can restore databases, transaction logs, and individual tables either by using SQL Enterprise Manager or by using the LOAD statement. If you restore a database from disks, you must use the LOAD statement. Before you begin restoring your database, do the following:

1.  Identify the backup device that contains the backup you need.
2.  Review the header information to determine the database name, device size, and date of the backup.

## After this lesson you will be able to:

-   Use SQL Enterprise Manager to restore a database, transaction log, or an individual table.
-   Use the LOAD statement with different options to restore a database.

## Estimated lesson time  25 minutes

## Using SQL Enterprise Manager

You can use SQL Enterprise Manager to restore a database, transaction log, or an individual table. From the Database Backup/Restore dialog box, you can specify the database or tables you want to restore, the devices or files to restore from, and a point in time up to which the database is recovered.

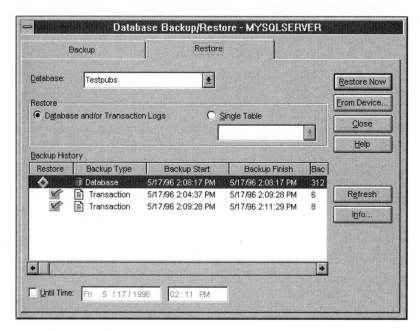

## Using the LOAD Statement

You can use the LOAD statement to restore a database by using the command syntax shown in the following examples.

To load a database:

**Syntax**

LOAD DATABASE *dbname*
    FROM dump_device [, dump_device2 [..., dump_device32]]
    [WITH options]

To load a transaction log:

**Syntax**

LOAD TRANSACTION *dbname*
    FROM dump_device [, dump_device2 [..., dump_device32]]
    [WITH options]

To load header information:

**Syntax**

LOAD HEADERONLY
    FROM dump_device

To load an individual table:

**Syntax**

LOAD TABLE [[*dbname*.]owner.]table_
    FROM dump_device [,dump_device2 [..., dump_device32]]
    [WITH options]

## Point-In-Time Recovery

Transaction logs now can be recovered up to a specified date and time. Any changes in the log after that date and time are rolled back when the log is restored. Be aware that point-in-time recovery works only when you restore a transaction log separately, and not when you restore a full database backup. You can use either SQL Enterprise Manager or Transact-SQL to accomplish a point-in-time recovery.

## Using SQL Enterprise Manager

When restoring a log in SQL Enterprise Manager from the Database Backup/Restore dialog box, on the Restore tab you can select the Until Time check box and specify a date and time up to which changes in the log should be committed.

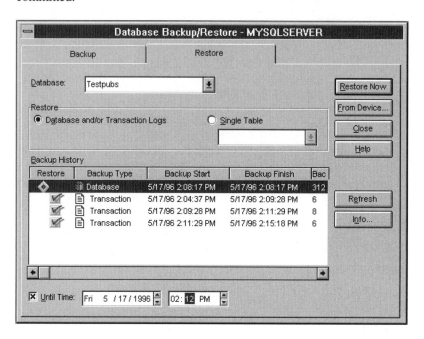

## Using Transact-SQL

You can use the Transact-SQL LOAD TRANSACTION statement with the WITH STOPAT option to do a point-in-time recovery. Suppose a user mistakenly deleted rows in a table on Sunday, August 4, 1996 at 1:00 P.M. The last transaction in the log took place on the same day at 1:30 P.M. The following example restores the log up to the time immediately before the deletions occurred (at 12:55 P.M.).

**Example**

```
LOAD TRANSACTION corporatedb from hourlydump
    WITH STOPAT = '1996 080412:55:00'
```

# Restoring Individual Tables

You can use SQL Enterprise Manager or the LOAD statement to restore an individual table in a database. This technique provides you with a more efficient way to replace an existing table with a newer version, than if you were to replace it by performing many alterations to the existing table; for example, a company may use this method to replace an outdated mailing list table. Be aware of the following issues when you are backing up and restoring an individual table:

- While it is possible to load an individual table from a complete database backup, this method is not recommended. The data in the table may become logically inconsistent with the rest of the database. Therefore, you should load a table from a complete database backup only when you need to recover from a disastrous loss of data.

- You cannot load an individual table that contains text columns, indexes, or one that is published for replication.

- The database that contains the target (receiving) table must have the Select Into/Bulk Copy option set to On before you load the table.

- During the restore process, triggers, rules, defaults, and declarative referential integrity constraints (such as PK and FK) are not enforced.

- The schema for the data source table and the target table must match. The names of the target (receiving) table and the backed up table could be different, but the underlying structure and data types must be identical. Use the SOURCE option of the LOAD TABLE statement to specify the name of the source table from which to load the data.

- The hardware platform of the source and target tables must be the same. For example, you cannot load a backup from an Alpha-based server into a table on an Intel machine.

- You can add new data into a table that already contains information by using LOAD TABLE with the Append option.

- Once you restore an individual table, you must perform a full database backup. The transaction log cannot be backed up until the database is backed up.

To load an individual table:

**Syntax**

LOAD TABLE [[*dbname.*]owner.]table_
    FROM dump_device [,dump_device2 [..., dump_device32]]
    [WITH options]

The following example restores the *customers* table from the backup device, list_dump, into the *mail_list* table and appends new records to the existing table. In this example, the source table has a different name but the same structure as the target table. This is specified by the *source* parameter.

**Example**

```
LOAD TABLE mail_list from list_dump WITH source = 'customers',APPEND
```

## Restoring a Database and Transaction Log

In the following procedures, you simulate database activity and restore a database and a transaction log from backup devices. You apply incremental transaction log backups to a database that has been restored from a backup. You then use this transaction log to recover the same number of data modifications that were recorded in the transaction log at the time of the backup.

To simulate database activity and restore a database and a transaction log from backup devices, complete the following tasks:

1. Back up the database.
2. Perform a transaction on the database.
3. Back up the transaction log.
4. Drop and recreate the device and database.
5. Load the database.
6. Load the transaction log.

▶ **To back up the *testpubs* database**

In this procedure, you clear the Truncate Log On Checkpoint option for the *testpubs* database in order to allow a backup to occur, and then backup the database.

1. Log on to Windows NT as Administrator.
2. Using SQL Enterprise Manager, from the Server Manager window, select the *testpubs* database.
3. Click the secondary mouse button, and from the shortcut menu click Edit.

   The Edit Database dialog box appears.
4. Click the Options tab.
5. Clear the Truncate Log On Checkpoint check box.

6. Click OK to close the Edit Database dialog box.

7. Back up the following database to the specified backup device:

   - Database = *testpubs*

   - Backup Devices = TESTPUBS_DUMP

   Make sure to select the Initialize Device check box.

▶ **To create changes in the database**

Simulate user activity by making a change to the database.

1. Open a query window, execute the INSPUB.SQL script, or type and execute:

```
INSERT publishers
    VALUES ('9921', 'Warehouse Publishers', 'Tulsa', 'OK', 'USA')
```

   This script inserts a row into the *publishers* table in the *testpubs* database and makes an entry into the transaction log.

2. Close the query window.

▶ **To back up a transaction log to a backup device**

After changes are made in the database, you back up the transaction log.

1. In SQL Enterprise Manager, on the Tools menu, click Database Backup/Restore.

2. In the Database Backup/Restore dialog box, back up the following transaction log to the specified backup device.

   - Transaction log = *testpubs*

   - Logical backup device name = TESTPUBS_TL_DUMP

   Make sure the following check boxes are selected:

   - Transaction Log

   - Initialize Device (if this is the first time this device is used)

   - No expiration date

3. Execute the backup.

4. In the Backup Devices box, double-click the TESTPUBS_DUMP device to open the Backup Device Information dialog box.

   What backups appear on the TESTPUBS_DUMP?

   _____

5. Close the Backup Device Information dialog box.

6. In the Backup Devices box, double-click the TESTPUBS_TL_DUMP device to open the Backup Device Information dialog box.

What backups appear on the TESTPUBS_TL_DUMP?

_____

7. Close the Backup Device Information dialog box.

8. Close the Database Backup/Restore dialog box.

▶  **To drop a database and device to simulate data loss**

1. In the Server Manager window, expand the Databases folder, and then delete the _testpubs_ database.

2. Expand the Database Devices folder, and then delete the TESTPUBSDATA device.

3. Delete the TESTPUBSDATA.DAT file in the \MSSQL\DATA directory.

▶  **To recreate a device and database**

In this procedure, you recreate the database and device in the same sequence as the original database.

1. Recreate the 5 MB TESTPUBSDATA device.

2. Recreate the 8 MB _testpubs_ database on the following devices. Make sure you select Create for Load.

| Device | Name | Size |
|--------|------|------|
| Data | TESTPUBSDATA | 5 MB |
| Log | TESTPUBSLOG | 3 MB |

3. From the Server Manager window, open the Databases folder.

What is the status of the _testpubs_ database?

_____

_____

_____

4.  From a query window, type and execute:

```
EXEC sp_helpdb testpubs
```

Scroll to the right and check the time the database was created and the database status.

What is the status?

---

▶ **To restore data to the database**

Restore the contents of the *testpubs* database from a database backup file.

1.  In SQL Enterprise Manager, on the Tools menu, click Database Backup/Restore.
2.  In the Database Backup/Restore dialog box, click the Restore tab.
3.  Click From Device.

    The Restore From Device On Server dialog box appears.
4.  In the Destination Database box, select *testpubs*.
5.  From the Devices and Files list, select TESTPUBS_DUMP. Examine the information about the device in the Backup Information box.
6.  To load the database, click Restore Now.

    What restrictions are placed on the use of the database while the load is in progress?

---

7.  To verify the results, in a query window either execute the PUBNAME.SQL script file, or type and execute:

```
USE TESTPUBS
SELECT * FROM publishers
    WHERE pub_name = 'Warehouse Publishers'
```

What are the results? Why?

---

8.  Close the query window.

▶ **To load the transaction log**

After restoring the data, you load the transaction log to recover changes that occurred since the last full database backup.

1. In the Database Backup/Restore dialog box, click the Restore tab.

2. In the Database box, select *testpubs*.

3. Click From Device.

   The Restore From Device On Server dialog box appears.

4. In the Destination Database box, select *testpubs*.

5. From the Devices and Files list, select TESTPUBS_TL_DUMP. Examine the information about the device in the Backup Information box.

6. To apply the transaction log, click Restore Now.

7. Close the Database Backup/Restore dialog box.

8. To verify the results, in the SQL Query Tool either execute the PUBNAME.SQL script file, or type and execute:

```
SELECT * FROM publishers
    WHERE pub_name = 'Warehouse Publishers'
```

What are the results? Are they what you expected? Why?

_____

_____

▶ **To disable the DBO Use Only database option**

In this procedure, you enable user access to the database.

1. Open a query window, select *master* as the current database, and then type and execute:

```
EXEC sp_dboption 'testpubs', 'dbo use only', false
```

2. In the Server Manager window, expand the Databases folder.

3. Using the secondary mouse button, click the Databases folder, and then click Refresh.

   Is the *testpubs* database in the "loading" stage? Why or why not?

_____

_____

## Lesson Summary

To restore a database and transaction log, you can use either the SQL Enterprise Manager or the LOAD statement. When you restore a database and incremental transaction log backups, you can recover as many data modifications as were recorded in the transaction log at the time of the backup.

| For more information on | See |
| --- | --- |
| Restoring transaction logs | "Recovering from Full Transaction Log in User Database" in \KB on the compact disc |

# Lesson 3: Restoring the *master* Database with a Valid Backup

SQL Server activity is controlled by the *master* database; therefore, database corruption or the loss of the *master* database can be devastating. The *master* database is important, so you should make sure you have a valid backup or are using a data redundancy technique.

## After this lesson you will be able to:

- Recover the *master* database from a backup.

## Estimated lesson time  35 minutes

If you are unable to start SQL Server, you may have one of several problems:

- Segmentation faults.
- Input/output errors.
- A physical or logical inconsistency in the database (as indicated by a DBCC statement).

Any of these problems can indicate a damaged *master* database. A media failure where the *master* database is stored can damage the database.

The procedure used to recover a damaged *master* database is different from the procedure used to recover user databases. If the *master* database becomes unusable, it must be recreated using the SQL Server **setup** program, and then restored from a previous backup. Therefore, any changes made to the *master* database since the last backup are lost. When the backup is reloaded, the changes must be reapplied.

You must rebuild the *master* database using the same character set and sort order as the *master* database backup that you reload. Also, you must use the same SQL Server installation path, location, name, and size of the existing MASTER device.

To recover a damaged *master* database, complete the following tasks:

1. Use the SQL Server **setup** program to rebuild the *master* database.
2. Add a backup device (unless the backup will be reloaded from disks).
3. Restart SQL Server in single-user mode.
4. Restore the *master* database from the most recent backup.
5. Apply to the *master* database any changes that were not included in the most recent backup.
6. Restore the *msdb* database.

# Recovering the *master* Database from a Backup

In this procedure, you assume that the MASTER device is lost, and you must rebuild the MASTER device and recover the database from a backup copy.

▶ **To check the MASTER database device size**

- Edit the MASTER database device or execute **sp_helpdevice**.

  What is the size of the MASTER database device? Record this number to use later in the procedure.

_____

▶ **To back up the *master* database**

1. Access the SQL Enterprise Manager, Database Backup/Restore dialog box.

2. To have the backup overwrite any existing backup, under Database Backup, select Entire Database, and then under Options, select Initialize Device.

3. Back up the *master* database to the MASTER_DUMP device you created previously, or create one if none exists.

▶ **To simulate activity in the *master* database**

1. Create a 2 MB database device named TEST1DEV.

2. Create a database named *test1* on the TEST1DEV device.

   This is the database that you crash and recover later in the procedure.

▶ **To simulate a crash of the MASTER device**

1. Stop SQL Server.

2. Using File Manager or Windows Explorer, rename the file MASTER.DAT to MASTER.OLD.

   Do not delete the MASTER.OLD file; you use it later.

3. Start SQL Server again.

   Were you able to connect to SQL Server?

_____

Look in the Windows NT Event Viewer Application log for startup-related error messages. Record them here.

_____

_____

▶ **To recover the MASTER device**

1. Start the SQL Server **setup** program and click Continue until you reach the Microsoft SQL Server 6.5 - Options dialog box.

2. Select Rebuild Master Database, and then click Continue.

3. Select Resume to proceed with rebuild.

4. Select all of the correct settings for your installation and proceed with the rebuild. Remember, you must use the size of the MASTER device you recorded earlier, either 30 MB or 32 MB. It takes 4 minutes to rebuild the MASTER device. Wait until **setup** finishes rebuilding MASTER.

5. In the SQL Service Manager, stop SQL Server.

6. Start SQL Server in single-user mode.

   To start SQL Server as a background service in single-user mode, complete the following tasks:

   a. In the Control Panel, click Services.

   b. In the Services list, select the MSSQLSERVER service.

      Insert the "-m" parameter in the Startup Parameters box to specify single user mode.

   c. Click Start.

7. Open SQL Enterprise Manager.

8. From the Database Backup/Restore dialog box, to recreate the backup device, select New.

   Create the MASTER_DUMP device.

9. Click the Restore tab, and then click From Device.

   The Restore From Device On Server dialog box appears.

10. Restore the *master* database from the MASTER_DUMP device. Make sure that *master* appears as the destination database and that the MASTER_DUMP device is selected in the Devices and Files list.

    When the load is finished, SQL Server stops automatically. You might receive the following error message:

    Error 10025: Possible network error: Write to SQL Server Failed. Connection broken.

    Ignore the error message.

11. In the Service Manager window, restart SQL Server.

12. Refresh the database list in Server Manager.

    You might need to close and restart SQL Enterprise Manager in order to see the changes.

All of the databases should appear in the Server Manager window, with the exception of the *test1* database. The *test1* database does not appear because it was created after you backed up *master*.

## Restoring the *msdb* Database

During a rebuild of the *master* database, the **setup** program drops and recreates the *msdb* database. All scheduling information is lost during this rebuild; therefore, after the *master* database has been restored, you then must restore the *msdb* database.

▶ **To restore the *msdb* database**

1. If necessary, expand the MSDBDATA device, and then allocate the expanded space to the *msdb* database.

   The *msdb* database must have as much or more space allocated to it as was allocated to it before the *master* database was rebuilt.

2. Restore the *msdb* database from the most recent database backup.

3. Apply all transaction log backups that were performed after that database backup.

4. Recreate any scheduled tasks that were implemented after the last transaction log backup.

If the *msdb* database becomes corrupted, you must restore it as well. The *msdb* database can be treated as a user database when it is restored.

## Lesson Summary

The procedure to recover a *master* database is different from the procedure used to recover a user database. If the *master* database becomes unusable, it must be recovered using SQL Server **setup**, and then restored from a existing backup. If you have to rebuild the *master* database, all scheduling information is lost and you must restore the *msdb* database.

| For more information on | See |
| --- | --- |
| Recovering a *master* database | "Recovering a Full Master Database" in \KB on the compact disc |

# Lesson 4: Recovering User Databases After a Media Failure

The easiest way to recreate a database is to re-run scripts that were saved when the database was created, along with scripts for any ALTER DATABASE statements that may have been executed. If you do not have this information, you can derive the size and device assignment of databases from some of the system tables.

### After this lesson you will be able to:

- Recreate lost devices.
- Recreate and reload lost databases.

### Estimated lesson time  25 minutes

When you recover a user database, the first step is to recreate the database device because the file no longer exists. After you have recreated the database devices, you then recreate and reload the database structure from backups.

## Recreating Lost Devices

If you set up a database on multiple devices, you gain speed in sending queries, updating, and in overall performance. However, databases that span multiple devices are more complex to restore.

A database called *mydb* takes 40 MB of disk space. Instead of storing it all on one device, the system administrator (SA) created the database on multiple devices. First, the SA used the CREATE DATABASE statement to create the initial 40 MB database. Then, the SA used the ALTER DATABASE statement to alter the database three times. In the following figure, the *mydb* database has allocation on four devices.

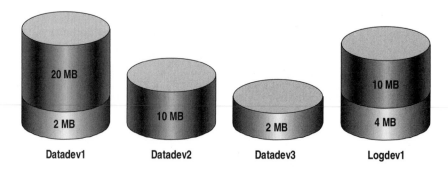

| 20 MB | | | 10 MB |
| 2 MB | 10 MB | 2 MB | 4 MB |
| Datadev1 | Datadev2 | Datadev3 | Logdev1 |

Occasionally, you might have a media failure and lose one or more devices. When you restore the database after such a failure, you must recreate the devices in the order they were created originally. To recreate lost devices, use the following steps:

1. Start SQL Server in single-user mode. At the command prompt, type and execute:

```
sqlservr /c /dmaster_device /m
```

| Where... | Does this... |
| --- | --- |
| /c | Starts SQL Server independent of Windows NT |
| /dmaster_device | Specifies a physical name for the MASTER device. For example, /dc:\mssql\data\master.dat |
| /m | Specifies single-user mode |

2. If the transaction log of the damaged or inaccessible user database is on an undamaged device, use DUMP TRANSACTION with the NO_TRUNCATE clause to back it up.

3. Drop each database that has space allocated on a lost device. You can use either the DBCC DBREPAIR statement or the **sp_dbremove** system stored procedure to drop the database.

## Using the DBCC DBREPAIR Statement

You can drop a database using the DBCC DBREPAIR statement. No user, including the person executing the statement, can be using the specified database when this DBCC statement is executed.

**Syntax**        DBCC DBREPAIR (*database_name*, DROPDB)

The *database_name* specifies which database to drop.

**Example**
```
DBCC DBREPAIR (mydb, dropdb)
```

## Using the sp_dbremove System Stored Procedure

The **sp_dbremove** system stored procedure removes a database and the associated entries in the *sysdatabases* and *sysusages* tables. Optionally, if you use the Dropdev option, any devices to which the database has exclusive use are dropped.

**Syntax**        sp_dbremove *databasename*[,dropdev]

**Example**
```
sp_dbremove testpubs, dropdev
```

▶  **To drop the database using the sp_dbremove system stored procedure**

1. Execute **sp_dbremove**.

2. If necessary, drop lost devices using the **sp_dropdevice** system stored procedure.

3. Execute CHECKPOINT.

4. Shut down SQL Server, and then start it in normal mode.

5. Recreate lost devices by executing the DISK INIT statement using the size of the original devices.

# Recreating and Reloading Lost Databases

After you have recreated your lost devices, you must then recreate and reload any lost databases. The following sections describe the process you must follow to recreate and reload a lost database.

### Query the Database

You must first examine the device allocations and uses for the damaged database. You must assign the same blocks of space for the same purposes. The following example shows the uses and sizes of the devices allocated to *mydb*:

**Example**

```
USE master
SELECT segmap, size
FROM sysusages
WHERE dbid =
    (SELECT dbid FROM sysdatabases
        WHERE name = "mydb")
```

### Examine the Output

Examine the device allocations of the damaged database. Each row that contains 3 in the *segmap* column represents a data allocation; each row that contains 4 represents a log allocation. The *size* column indicates the number of 2K blocks of data. Note the order, use, and size of this information. You must have this information in order to recreate your devices. The results of the previous example are shown in the following table.

**Results**

| segmap | size |
| --- | --- |
| 3 | 10240 |
| 3 | 5120 |
| 4 | 5120 |
| 3 | 1024 |
| 4 | 2048 |

The results set translates into the data allocation types and sizes in megabytes shown in the following table.

| Data allocation type | Size (MB) |
|---|---|
| Data | 20 |
| Data | 10 |
| Log | 10 |
| Data | 2 |
| Log | 4 |

### Recreate the Database

Recreate the database, using the CREATE DATABASE statement to duplicate all of the rows from the old *sysusages* table, up to and including the first log device.

**Example**

```
CREATE DATABASE mydb ON datadev1 = 20, datadev2 = 10
    LOG ON logdev1 = 10
```

### Use the ALTER DATABASE Command

If you need more space on the devices which you are recreating, use the ALTER DATABASE statement to recreate the rest of the entries. The following examples allocate more space on DATADEV1 and DATADEV3.

**Examples**

```
ALTER DATABASE mydb ON datadev1 = 2
```

```
ALTER DATABASE mydb ON datadev3 = 2
```

When you allocate space on existing devices, the device is assigned automatically the same type of usage: data or log. When you allocate space on a device not already in use by the database, it is always allocated as a data device.

The following example recreates the final allocation on LOGDEV1, which is already in use by the database.

**Example**

```
ALTER DATABASE mydb ON logdev1 = 4
```

LOGDEV1 is automatically entered into the *sysusages* table as a log device.

To allocate log space on a device that is not already in use by the database, follow the ALTER DATABASE command with the **sp_logdevice** stored system procedure. The following example allocates space on LOGDEV2.

**Example**

```
ALTER DATABASE mydb ON logdev2 = 4
EXEC sp_logdevice mydb, logdev2
```

## Reload the Database

Reload the database using LOAD DATABASE, and then load previously backed up logs and the newly backed up current log by using LOAD TRANSACTION.

To recover user databases after a media failure, complete the following tasks:

1. Find the necessary information about lost devices and databases.
2. Drop the lost databases and devices.
3. Recreate the lost devices in the proper order.
4. Recreate the affected databases.
5. Restore those databases from backups. All activity between the last database backup and the failure must be reapplied.

The following procedures show you how to recreate one or more lost devices. In these procedures, you assume that a media failure has occurred, and that you have lost the device on which the data for *testpubs* resides. You execute the necessary commands to drop the suspect database, then recreate the lost device and database, and finally reload the database.

▶ **To simulate normal activity prior to a crash**

1. In the Database Backup/Restore dialog box, select the Initialize Device check box, and then back up the *testpubs* database to the TESTPUBS_DUMP device.

   The initial backup of the database is the beginning of the backup cycle and will overwrite any existing backups.

2. Close the Database Backup/Restore dialog box.

3. To simulate activity prior to the crash, insert a row into the *stores* table. In the SQL Query Tool, either execute the INSSTOR1.SQL script file, or type:

   **INSERT stores**
       **VALUES ('7011', 'Flyteworks', '111 Pike Street',**
       **'Seattle', 'WA', '98002')**

4. To simulate the normal backup process, in the Database Backup/Restore dialog box, select the Initialize Device check box, and then back up the transaction log for *testpubs* to the TESTPUBS_TL_DUMP device.

5. Close the Database Backup/Restore dialog box.

6. Add another row to the *stores* table to simulate activity after the last backup. In the SQL Query Tool, either execute the INSSTOR2.SQL script file, or type and execute:

```
INSERT stores
    VALUES ('7012', 'Southridge Video Shop',
    'University Ave.', 'Seattle', 'WA', '98109')
```

▶ **To simulate the crash of a device**

1. Stop Microsoft SQL Server.

2. From either a command prompt, File Manager, or Windows Explorer, rename the device from \MSSQL\DATA\TESTPUBSDATA.DAT to TESTPUBSDATA.OLD.

3. Restart SQL Server.

   Look at the SQL Server applications error log and the Microsoft Windows NT Event Viewer Application log. What messages did you receive that indicate the database could not be recovered?

4. In a query window, attempt to execute a command using *testpubs*.

   What messages did you receive?

   _____

   _____

   _____

5. In the Server Manager window, double-click the *testpubs* database.

   What messages did you receive?

   _____

▶ **To recreate the lost device and reload the database**

1. In the SQL Query Tool, back up the transaction log with NO_TRUNCATE by typing and executing:

   ```
   DUMP TRANsaction testpubs to TESTPUBS_TL_DUMP with no_truncate,
   noinit
   ```

   This command rescues any changes in the log since the last transaction log backup, even though the database is unavailable. If you use the same device as the previous transaction log backup, make sure you use NOINIT. This ensures that this backup is appended to the backup device rather than overwriting previous log backups.

2. In the SQL Query Tool, drop the *testpubs* database by typing and executing:

   ```
   DROP database testpubs
   ```

   **Note** If the database has not been marked as suspect, but is marked as still being recovered, the DROP DATABASE command might not work. Use the **sp_dbremove** system-stored procedure to drop a database regardless of the status of the database.

3. Drop the lost device in SQL Enterprise Manager by selecting the TESTPUBSDATA device, and then choose Delete, or by typing and executing:

   ```
   EXEC sp_dropdevice testpubsdata
   ```

4. If the device still appears in the Server Manager window, use the secondary mouse button, click the Databases Devices folder, and then click Refresh. You might have to close and reopen SQL Enterprise Manager.

5. Recreate the lost device TESTPUBSDATA (5 MB) from the SQL Enterprise Manager Manage Database Devices dialog box.

6. Recreate the *testpubs* database with the data portion of the database on the TESTPUBSDATA device and the log portion of the database on the TESTPUBSLOG device. Use all of the space available on each device (8 MB total). In the New Database dialog box, select Create For Load. When first used, this option saves time by not initializing the data pages.

7. Load the *testpubs* database and transaction logs from the latest backups. Use the Restore From Device On Server dialog box to first restore the database from the TESTPUBSDUMP device, and then restore each of the log backups from the TESTPUBS_TL_DUMP device. When you load the transaction logs, you must load them in the same order in which they were backed up, finishing with the backup you did with the NO_TRUNCATE option. Make sure you choose the appropriate backups from the Backup Information list when you restore the transaction log.

8. Execute **sp_helpdb** from the *testpubs* database.

   What options are set for testpubs?

9. Turn off the DBO Use Only option by executing the following stored procedure in the SQL Query Tool.

```
EXEC sp_dboption 'testpubs', 'DBO use only', false
```

10. In the SQL Query Tool, execute the following query on the *stores* table in the *testpubs* database to see if the rows you added before the first and second transaction log backups exist.

```
SELECT * FROM stores
```

Inserts to the database completed prior to the first transaction log backup as well as inserts completed prior to the backup with NO_TRUNCATE have been recovered.

## Lesson Summary

When you recover user databases after a media failure, you first find necessary information about lost devices and databases, then recreate the lost devices in the order in which they were created originally, recreate the affected databases, and finally, restore those databases from backups. Any database activity that occurred after the backups were created is lost.

| For more information on | See |
| --- | --- |
| ALTER DATABASE | "ALTER DATABASE" in SQL Server Books Online |
| DBCC DBREPAIR | "DBCC DBREPAIR" in SQL Server Books Online |
| **sp_dbremove** | "sp_dbremove" in SQL Server Books Online |

# Lesson 5: Recovering the *master* Database Without a Valid Backup

In the unlikely event that the media where *master* resides fails, your backup of *master* is corrupt or nonexistent, and data for all other databases exists, you use the DISK REINIT and DISK REFIT statements to recover it.

### After this lesson you will be able to:

- Recreate the *master* database if the backup is corrupt.
- Use the DISK REINIT and DISK REFIT statements to recover the *master* database.

### Estimated lesson time  10 minutes

The DISK REINIT and DISK REFIT statements are used to recover the *master* database when all of the following statements are true:

- The media where *master* resides fails.
- The backup copy of *master* is corrupt or nonexistent.
- Data for all other databases exists.

If you have to recreate the *master* database and your backup is corrupt, complete the following tasks:

1. From the Microsoft SQL Server group, start the SQL Server **setup** program.
2. Rebuild the *master* database using the same character set, sort order, installation path, location name, and size of the MASTER device that were used when it was originally installed.
3. Start SQL Server in single-user mode.
4. Execute DISK REINIT to reinitialize each device in the *sysdevices* table.

   The DISK REINIT statement restores the device entries to the *system* tables when a device exists (the file is present) and the entry in the *sysdevices* table no longer exists. This situation occurs after a damaged *master* database is restored, and the *master* database is incomplete, for example, if databases and devices were added or altered since the last backup of the *master* database. Execute DISK REINIT once for each device.

**Example**

```
DISK REINIT
    NAME = 'logical_name',
    PHYSNAME = 'physical_name',
    VDEVNO = virtual_device_number,
    SIZE = number_of_2K_blocks
```

> **Important**   The DISK REINIT statement requires that you specify the virtual device number (VDEVNO) and the size of the original device or devices. If you have not maintained this information in a script file or in a printout from **sp_helpdevice**, you must obtain these numbers from the *sysdevices*, *sysdatabases*, and *sysusages* tables in the *master* database.

5. Execute DISK REFIT to rebuild the *sysusages* and *sysdatabases* tables.

   The DISK REFIT statement recreates rows in the *sysusages* and *sysdatabases* tables for all CREATE and ALTER DATABASE statements. It also drops entries in the *sysusages* table that can no longer be physically accessed, and drops the related entries in the *sysdatabases* table.

   If you do not execute DISK REFIT immediately after executing DISK REINIT, DISK REFIT will fail.

## Recovering the *master* Database Without a Valid Backup

In the following procedures, you assume that a media failure has occurred. The file MASTER.DAT is lost, and your backup of *master* is corrupted. The *test1* database you created in lesson 3 of this chapter is intact. However, without the *master* database, you have no way of getting to the data.

▶ **To simulate a crash of the *master* database**

1. Stop SQL Server.

2. From a command prompt, rename \MSSQL\DATA\MASTER.DAT to MASTER.TWO.

▶ **To recover the MASTER device without a valid backup**

1. Start the SQL Server **setup** program.

2. Rebuild the *master* database.

3. Stop SQL Server.

4. Start SQL Server in single user mode. Assuming that *master* is located at the default location, at the command prompt, type and execute:

   ```
   sqlservr /c / dc:\mssql\data\master.dat /m
   ```

   Minimize the command window, but leave it open.

5. Start ISQL/w and log in to SQL Server as SA.

6. Reinitialize the device used to store *test1* by typing and executing the following:

```
DISK REINIT
    NAME = "test1dev",
    PHYSNAME = 'C:\MSSQL\DATA\TEST1DEV.DAT',
    VDEVNO = 250,
    SIZE = 1024
```

The size to initialize to was verified in the \MSSQL\DATA directory. A virtual device number (VDEVNO) parameter of 250 was used to avoid conflicts with another device.

7. Execute DISK REFIT to rebuild the *sysusages* and *sysdatabases* tables.

What warning did you receive?

_____

_____

_____

If you do not get the warning, exit ISQL/w and reconnect to your server as SA.

8. Shut down SQL Server by executing SHUTDOWN from the SQL Query Tool or ISQL/w.

9. Restart SQL Server in normal mode. Use Control Panel, Services.

▶ **To verify the correct system information**

1. Log in to ISQL/w as SA.

2. Execute **sp_helpdevice** to see if *test1dev* is initialized.

3. Execute **sp_helpdb** to see if *test1* database exists.

4. Use the *test1* database and execute the system stored procedure **sp_help** to verify that the *system* tables exist.

▶ **To reset your server for subsequent labs**

1. Shut down SQL Server.

2. From File Manager, delete MSSQL\DATA\MASTER.DAT.

3. Rename MASTER.OLD to MASTER.DAT.

4. Restart SQL Server.

5. In SQL Enterprise Manager, select your server and click the plus sign (+) to the left of the Databases folder.

6. Verify that the following databases appear:

   ❑ *master*          ❑ *sender*

   ❑ *model*           ❑ *tempdb*

   ❑ *msdb*            ❑ *test1*

   ❑ *pubs*            ❑ *testpubs*

## Lesson Summary

The DISK REINIT and DISK REFIT statements are used to recover the *master* database when the media where *master* resides fails, the backup copy of *master* is corrupt or nonexistent, and data for all other databases exists.

| For more information on | See |
| --- | --- |
| DISK REINIT | "DISK REINIT" in SQL Server Books Online |
| DISK REFIT | "DISK REFIT" in SQL Server Books Online |

# Review

The following questions are intended to reinforce key information presented in this chapter. If you are unable to answer a question, review the lesson and then try the question again.

1. What is automatic recovery and when is it initiated?

_____

_____

_____

2. When recovering from media failure, what important information must you have about any lost databases to be able to recreate them?

_____

3. Why is it important to create a database by allocating space from devices in a certain order when recovering?

_____

_____

4. To avoid using DISK REINIT and DISK REFIT when restoring the **master** database, what steps should you take?

_____

_____

# Questions and Answers

Page 689

▶ **To back up a transaction log to a backup device**

4. In the Backup Devices box, double-click the TESTPUBS_DUMP device to open the Backup Device Information dialog box.

What backups appear on the TESTPUBS_DUMP?

**The *testpubs* database backups appear.**

6. In the Backup Devices box, double-click the TESTPUBS_TL_DUMP device to open the Backup Device Information dialog box.

What backups appear on the TESTPUBS_TL_DUMP?

**The *testpubs* transaction log backups appear.**

Page 690

▶ **To recreate a device and database**

3. From the Server Manager window, open the Databases folder.

What is the status of the *testpubs* database?

**Notice that the status of the *testpubs* database is "loading." Users cannot access the database until the administrator is finished loading the data and changes the status of the database with sp_dboption or SQL Enterprise Manager/Configure.**

4. From a query window, type and execute:

```
EXEC sp_helpdb testpubs
```

Scroll to the right and check the time the database was created and the database status.

What is the status?

**loading, dbo use only**

Page 691

▶ **To restore data to the database**

6. To load the database, click Restore Now.

What restrictions are placed on the use of the database while the load is in progress?

**DBO use only.**

7. To verify the results, in a query window either execute the PUBNAME.SQL script file, or type and execute:

```
USE TESTPUBS
SELECT * FROM publishers
    WHERE pub_name = 'Warehouse Publishers'
```

What are the results? Why?

**There were 0 rows affected, because the *testpubs* database was backed up before the new data was inserted. When the database was dropped, the new data was lost.**

Page 692

▶ **To load the transaction log**

8. To verify the results, in the SQL Query Tool either execute the PUBNAME.SQL script file, or type and execute:

```
SELECT * FROM publishers
    WHERE pub_name = 'Warehouse Publishers'
```

What are the results? Are they what you expected? Why?

**The data should now exist in the publishers table. The insert statement that was in the transaction log was restored to the database.**

Page 692

▶ **To disable the DBO Use Only database option**

3. Using the secondary mouse button, click the Databases folder, and then click Refresh.

Is the *testpubs* database in the "loading" stage? Why or why not?

**No, because disabling the DBO Use Only database option removes the loading status of the database.**

Page 695

▶ **To check the MASTER database device size**

▪ Edit the MASTER database device or execute **sp_helpdevice**.

What is the size of the MASTER database device? Record this number to use later in the procedure.

**30 MB**

Page 695

▶ **To simulate a crash of the MASTER device**

   3.  Start SQL Server again.

      Were you able to connect to SQL Server?

      **No.**

      Look in the Windows NT Event Viewer Application log for startup-related error messages. Record them here.

      **Mesg 17113: initconfig error 2 (The system cannot find the file specified.) Opening 'C:\MSSQL\DATA\MASTER.DAT for config information.**

Page 703

▶ **To simulate the crash of a device**

   3.  Restart SQL Server.

      Look at the SQL Server applications error log and the Microsoft Windows NT Event Viewer Application log. What messages did you receive that indicate the database could not be recovered?

      **Mesg 17207 : udopen: operating system error 2(The system cannot find the file specified.) during the creation/opening of physical device C:\MSSQL\DATA\TESTPUBSDATA.DAT**

      **Mesg 17218 : udread: Operating system error 6(The handle is invalid.) on device 'C:\MSSQL\DATA\TESTPUBSDATA.DAT' (virtpage 0x01000018).**

      **Error : 840, Severity: 17, State: 2 Device 'testpubsdata' (with physical name 'C:\MSSQL\DATA\TESTPUBSDATA.DAT', and virtual device number 1) is not available. Please contact System Administrator for assistance.**

      **The previous messages were in both the SQL Server Errorlog and the Windows NT Event Log. The following was found only in the SQL Server Event Log.**

      **95/06/08 10:24:42.08 spid12 Unable to proceed with the recovery of dbid <6> because of previous errors. Continuing with the next database.**

   4.  In a query window, attempt to execute a command using *testpubs*.

      What messages did you receive?

      **Mesg 921, Level 14, State 1**
      **Database 'testpubs' has not been recovered yet - please wait and try again.**

      **– Or –**

      **Mesg 926, Level 14, State 1: Database 'testpubs' cannot be opened—it has been marked SUSPECT by recovery. The SA can drop the database with DBCC.**

5. In the Server Manager window, double-click the *testpubs* database.

What messages did you receive?

**The database is marked inaccessible and cannot be edited.**

Page 704

▶ **To recreate the lost device and reload the database**

8. Execute **sp_helpdb** from the *testpubs* database.

What options are set for testpubs?

**DBO use only.**

Page 707

▶ **To recover the MASTER device without a valid backup**

7. Execute DISK REFIT to rebuild the *sysusages* and *sysdatabases* tables.

What warning did you receive?

**Warning: Disk Refit may not have the correct segment map information in *sysusages*. Please review these after the command completes to verify their accuracy.**

Page 710

## Review Questions

1. What is automatic recovery and when is it initiated?

**Automatic recovery occurs whenever SQL Server is restarted. It rolls transactions back or forward to maintain database integrity after a system failure.**

2. When recovering from media failure, what important information must you have about any lost databases to be able to recreate them?

**The devices they were created on and what size they were.**

3. Why is it important to create a database by allocating space from devices in a certain order when recovering?

**Device fragments need to be in the same order, size, and purpose as they were for the database that was backed up for the load to be successful.**

4. To avoid using DISK REINIT and DISK REFIT when restoring the *master* database, what steps should you take?

**Always have a valid up-do-date backup of *master*. That is, whenever you make any change to *master*, back it up.**

C H A P T E R   1 7

# Transferring Data

## About This Chapter

This chapter discusses methods of importing, exporting, and transferring data. Managing data can involve transferring data into a database from other sources, loading a database backup file, or upgrading a database from a previous version of SQL Server. Managing data can also involve distributing copies of data to users through removable media. In this chapter, you use tools to transfer data into or out of SQL Server.

# Before You Begin

To complete the lessons in this chapter, you must have:

- Two 3.5-inch disks.
- An understanding of managing, backing up, and restoring system and user databases.
- Completed Chapters 14, 15, and 16.
- Created the *testpubs* database.

  If you need to create *testpubs*, execute **sp_helpdevice**. Look under the *device_number* column and verify device (VDEVNO) numbers 102 and 103 are not listed. If the numbers 102 and 103 are listed, make the appropriate changes in the \SCRIPTS\BLD_TPUBS\INSTTP.SQL script. This script creates the *testpubs* database for you. If you need to create these devices on a location other than C:\MSSQL\DATA, edit the location for the *physname* parameter in the script. Load and execute the INSTTP.SQL script file.

| Database name | Devices | Size |
| --- | --- | --- |
| *testpubs* (8 MB) | TESTPUBSDATA | 5 MB |
| | TESTPUBSLOG | 3 MB |

# Lesson 1: Managing Data

As a system administrator (SA), you must know how to manage and transfer data. This chapter covers how to choose the appropriate method for data transfer based on the source of the data (from another SQL Server or from a different platform or operating system).

Managing data can involve populating a new database, transferring data into a database from other sources, loading a database backup file, or upgrading a database from a previous version of SQL Server.

Managing data can also involve distributing copies of data to users through removable media or replication. You can use removable media to distribute data to users or to place a database on a different server from the one on which it was created. As the system administrator, you are typically the person who coordinates the creation and administration of removable media.

### After this lesson you will be able to:

- Describe two or more ways to manage data.
- Describe ways to transfer data.
- Choose the best tool to use for the type of transfer you want to perform.

### Estimated lesson time  10 minutes

## Data Transfer Tools

The type of data transfer that you want to perform helps you choose the most appropriate tool for the transfer. Two SQL Server tools are used to transfer data: Transfer Manager and the Bulk Copy Program (**bcp**).

### Transfer Manager

The Transfer Manager interface (Transfer Manager) is used to transfer both database objects and data from one SQL server to another. You can also use it to transfer database objects and data from one database to another on the same server. The Transfer Manager is a graphical user interface tool; it is the tool you use most often to transfer data. Data can be exported from a Microsoft-based or non-Microsoft-based SQL server using one of the following source servers:

- Microsoft Windows NT–based Microsoft SQL Server version 4.*x* or 6.*x*.
- Non-Microsoft-based SQL Server.

The destination server must be Microsoft SQL Server version 6.5.

Using the Transfer Manager, you can:

- Import into a Windows NT–based Microsoft SQL Server.

- Transfer objects and data from one processor architecture to a different processor architecture; for example, from a SQL Server running on an Alpha AXP-based computer to a SQL Server running on an Intel-based computer.

- Transfer data from a server with one sort order to a server with a different sort order.

## The Bulk Copy Program (bcp)

The Bulk Copy Program (**bcp**) command prompt utility is used to transfer data from another database management system. It copies SQL Server data to or from an operating system file in a format specified by the user.

Use **bcp** to transfer:

- Large amounts of data to and from Microsoft SQL servers.

- Selected columns or data with customized file format definitions.

- Data in binary or ASCII format (you must be able to describe the terminators or characters used to separate columns and rows, such as comma and tab).

- Data between platforms such as a mainframe and SQL Server.

You can also use **bcp** as an intermediary step to transfer data to other applications, such as spreadsheet applications. The data is moved from SQL Server into an operating-system file that can then be easily imported into another application.

### bcp and Batch Processing

The **bcp** can be a powerful tool when combined with **isql** in batch files. Multiple operations can be performed in one batch file. For example, you could set all of the options for **bcp**, drop indexes, import data; check for integrity issues, recreate indexes, and back up the database as part of the same batch file.

## Comparison of Transfer Manager and the bcp Utility

You have a choice between using Transfer Manager and **bcp**. When transferring data from one SQL Server to another SQL Server, use Transfer Manager. When transferring data to or from a source other than SQL Server or transferring data in batch mode, use **bcp**. The following table compares the capabilities of both applications.

| Feature | Transfer Manager | bcp |
| --- | --- | --- |
| Interface. | Graphical. | Command prompt. |
| What can be transferred. | Data objects, including tables, triggers, and Declarative Referential Integrity. Security information. | Data only. |
| Types of source servers. | SQL Server to SQL Server. | SQL Server to SQL Server. |
| | Non-Microsoft-based SQL Server. | SQL Server to/from other database management systems. |
| | | SQL Server to/from other applications (for example, a spreadsheet). |
| Types of destination server. | Windows NT–based Microsoft SQL Server. | Any platform. |
| Process of moving data. | One-step process. | Two-step process. |
| | Transfer is server-to-server or if local transfer, then table-to-table. | Transfer is to a file, then from the file to a server. If local, then table to file, and file to table. |
| Transfer different sort orders. | Transfer data to server with different sort order. | Transfer data to server with different sort order (can go between non-binary compatible platforms, operating systems by using character format). |
| Transfer capabilities. | Transfer between different processor architectures. | Transfer between different processor architectures. |

(*continued*)

| Feature | Transfer Manager | bcp |
|---------|-----------------|-----|
| Batch processing. | Transfer is performed interactively; however, SQL DMO can be used to automate the process. | Scripts can be created to perform batch processing. |
| Amount of data transferred. | Entire database, or any combination of objects. | Table only. |
| Index creation. | Creates indexes as part of process. | Indexes must be created after data is transferred. |
| Logging. | Non-logged. | Logged (unless fast **bcp** is performed). |

## Lesson Summary

SQL Server provides two tools for transferring data: Transfer Manager and the Bulk Copy Program (**bcp**). Use the Transfer Manager to transfer database objects and data from one SQL Server to another or to transfer data on the same server. Use the **bcp** to transfer data from another database management system or to transfer data to other applications, such as a spreadsheet application or mainframe application.

You can use either the Transfer Manager or the **bcp** utility depending on the type of transfer you want to perform. Which method you use depends on a number of factors, including the type of destination server, the interface and types of source servers, and amount of data transferred.

| For more information on | See |
|------------------------|-----|
| Transfer Manager | "Transfer Manager" in SQL Server Books Online |
| Transferring data | "Exporting and Importing Data" in SQL Server Books Online |
| **bcp** | "**bcp**" in SQL Server Books Online |

# Lesson 2: Transferring Data and Objects

The Transfer Manager in SQL Enterprise Manager transfers objects and data from one SQL Server database to another. The Transfer Manager can transfer objects and data from one processor architecture to another; for example, from a SQL server running on an Alpha AXP-based computer to a SQL server running on an Intel-based computer.

---

### After this lesson you will be able to:

- Determine the source and destination servers you need to transfer data.
- Transfer object definitions and data.

### Estimated lesson time  40 minutes

---

You must verify the following items before you begin a data transfer using Transfer Manager:

- The SQL Server is running on both the source server and the destination server.
- The destination database exists.
- The destination database is large enough to contain all of the objects and data that you want to transfer.

## Permissions Needed to Transfer Data

You must have the following permissions to successfully transfer data using Transfer Manager:

- You must have SELECT permissions in the source database.
- You must be the database owner of the destination database.
- If the source server is a non-Microsoft-based SQL Server, you must execute the OBJECT42.SQL script on that server.

# Transfer Manager Options

Not only does Transfer Manager transfer data, it can also transfer database objects and login information. This is a convenient method for setting up multiple databases with the same structure.

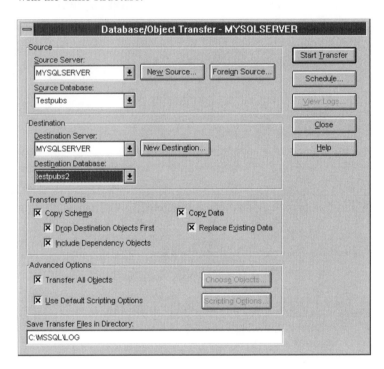

## Transfer Object Definitions and Data

In the Database/Object Transfer dialog box, you can select the source and destination servers and databases. You can also decide what objects you want to transfer and what scripting options to use. To select how to transfer data, use Transfer Options.

When you make selections, a script is generated. It is from this script that the new database takes on its characteristics based on your selections in the dialog box.

The following tables summarizes each of the options in the Database/Object Transfer dialog box:

| Dialog box option | Description |
| --- | --- |
| Source Server | Specifies the default server you are currently administering. To select another registered server, expand the box. |
| New Source | Opens the Register Server dialog box, which is used to register a server that is not listed in the Source Server box. |
| Foreign Source | Opens the Foreign Source dialog box, which is used for non-registered servers. For example, a SYBASE server is not registered. |
| Source Database | Specifies the database where data is transferred from. |
| Destination Server | Specifies a server to transfer data to. Note that the source server and the destination server can be the same server. If the required server name is not included in the list, add it to the list. Click the New Destination button and complete the Register Server dialog box that appears. |
| New Destination | Adds a server name to the Destination Server list. Click this button and complete the Register Server dialog box that appears. |
| Destination Database | Specifies the database to transfer data to. The database must already exist and have enough space for the objects and data that you are transferring. The destination database must be different from the source database. |
| Copy Schema | Copies the table schema from the source database to the destination database. |
| Drop Destination Objects First | Drops objects from the destination database before they are transferred from the source database. |
| Include Dependency Objects | Includes all objects that depend on the objects or object types selected for transfer. |
| Copy Data | Copies table data from the source database to the destination database. |
| Replace Existing Data | Replaces existing data in the destination tables with transferred data. To retain existing data and append transferred data, clear this option. |
| Transfer All Objects | Transfers all objects in the database, including tables, views, stored procedures, defaults, rules, and user-defined datatypes. |

**(continued)**

| Dialog box option | Description |
| --- | --- |
| Choose Objects | Transfers only selected objects, including tables, views, stored procedures, defaults, rules, and user-defined datatypes. You can transfer all, some, or no objects of a particular type. Click this button and make selections in the Choose Objects to be Transferred dialog box that appears. |
| Use Default Scripting Options | Specifies that default object and security scripting options will be used. The options for the default object automatically create scripts that recreate in the destination database table triggers, table DRI, table bindings, nonclustered and clustered indexes, and owner-qualified objects from the source database. The options for default security recreate users and groups, logins, and object and statement permissions. |
| Scripting Options | Specifies which scripting options to use. This is an advanced option. Click this option and complete the Transfer Scripting Options dialog box that appears. The options for the default object can automatically create scripts that recreate in the destination database table triggers, table DRI, table bindings, nonclustered and clustered indexes, and owner-qualified objects from the source database. The options for default security can recreate users and groups, logins, and object and statement permissions. |
| Save Transfer Files in Directory | Specifies where transfer scripts are stored. The default is C:\MSSQL\BINN. To change the location, type a new path in this box. If the directory does not already exist, SQL Enterprise Manager will create it. |

# Files Created by Transfer Manager

As part of the transfer process Transfer Manager creates a series of script files. When a transfer is performed, several files are created and saved on the source server in the \MSSQL\LOG directory.

The types of files created by Transfer Manager include:

| This file type | Contains |
| --- | --- |
| .DP1, .DP2 file | DROP statements for the objects |
| .IDX file | Scripts for index creation |
| .LOG file | All server messages and errors, and informative messages that will help you recover from errors |
| .TAB file | Summary information about the tables in the database, including their names, segment information, size usage, and the number of rows in each table |
| .TRG file | Scripts for trigger creation |
| .DR1, .DR2 | Scripts for declarative referential integrity and foreign keys |
| .USR, .GRP | Database users and groups |

In the following procedures, you use the Transfer Manager in SQL Enterprise Manager to create a database and login device, transfer a database, and verify the transfer.

▶ **To create database and login devices**

In this procedure, you create a database device, log device, and a database called *testpubs2*. This is the destination to which you transfer data in the next procedure.

1.  Create a 5 MB database device and a 3 MB log device.

    | Device | Name | Size |
    | --- | --- | --- |
    | Data device | TESTPUBS2DATA | 5 MB |
    | Log device | TESTPUBS2LOG | 3 MB |

2.  Create a database named *testpubs2* on the devices that you created in Step 1. Place the log on the log device. Use all of the space available on both devices. The *testpubs2* database is 8 MB total.

▶ **To transfer a database using the Transfer Manager**

In this procedure, you transfer data from the *testpubs* database to the *testpubs2* database.

1. Start SQL Enterprise Manager.

2. On the Tools menu, click Database/Object Transfer. The Database/Object Transfer dialog appears.

3. In the Source Server list, confirm that your local server is selected.

4. In the Source Database list, select the *testpubs* database.

5. In the Destination Server list, confirm that your local server is selected.

6. In the Destination Database list, select the *testpubs2* database.

7. In Transfer Options, confirm that all options are selected.

8. In Advanced Options, confirm that both Transfer all Objects and Use default scripting Options are selected.

9. Click Start Transfer.

   Notice that the Scripting in Progress dialog box shows the status of the transfer on the status bar at the bottom of the dialog box.

   When the transfer is complete, you receive a message stating that the transfer is complete and notifying you if any errors were encountered.

10. Click OK.

11. Click Close in the Database/Object Transfer dialog box.

▶ **To verify and test the transfer**

In this procedure, you verify that the transfer was completed successfully.

1. Verify that the following files were created as part of the transfer. They are located in the \MSSQL\LOG directory. The filenames are prefaced with your server name.

   TESTPUBS.ID1 and TESTPUBS.ID2

   TESTPUBS.USR

   TESTPUBS.DR1

   TESTPUBS.TAB

   TESTPUBS.TRG

2. Review the output of the files using Notepad.

   What information is contained in the files? How could this information be used?

   _____

   _____

3. Did any errors occur? Check the log file in \MSSQL\LOG\TESTPUBS.LOG. Review the output of the files using Notepad.

4. Verify that the data was transferred into the database by executing the TESTQRY.SQL script in both the *testpubs2* database on the source and the destination servers or type the following:

```
SELECT au_lname, au_fname, title
FROM authors a, titleauthor ta, titles t
WHERE a.au_id = ta.au_id
AND ta.title_id = t.title_id
ORDER BY title
```

Were the results of the query the same for both databases?

## Lesson Summary

You can use SQL Enterprise Manager to transfer data and objects from one SQL Server database to another. SQL Enterprise Manager is an easy, graphical way to transfer data quickly and to choose what data and objects you want to transfer. With the right permissions, you can transfer all data and objects using the Database/Object Transfer dialog box.

| For more information on | See |
| --- | --- |
| Transferring data | "Exporting and Importing Objects" in SQL Server Books Online |

# Lesson 3: Using the Bulk Copy Program (bcp)

You can use the Bulk Copy Program (**bcp**) to import or export data into or out of a new or existing table. For example, you can transfer large amounts of data to and from the SQL server, transfer data from another DBMS, or transfer data from one SQL server to another SQL server.

## After this lesson you will be able to:

- State permissions needed to transfer data.
- List the required parameters used in the **bcp** utility.
- List two or more ways to customize your transfer operation.
- Perform a bulk copy operation.

## Estimated lesson time  40 minutes

The **bcp** utility follows some general rules when transferring data. They include the following:

- The structure of the source table and the structure of the destination table do not need to match. This is because **bcp** is not used to copy directly from one table to another. Instead, a table is copied to a file or a file is copied to a table.
- Data copied into SQL Server is appended to any existing contents of a table.
- Data copied to a file overwrites any existing contents of the file.

The **bcp** utility uses a special set of DB-Library API calls. These calls are available to any DB-Library client application written in C.

## Permissions Needed to Execute bcp

To execute **bcp**, you must have SELECT permissions on the table you want to copy data from, and INSERT permissions on the table you want to copy data to. You also need appropriate permissions on the operating system files. You must also have SELECT permissions on the *sysobjects*, *syscolumns*, and *sysindexes* tables.

**Note**  SELECT permissions on these tables are automatically granted to the public group in the *model* database.

# Modes Used to Transfer Data

The **bcp** utility uses two modes for transferring data: fast **bcp** and slow **bcp**. Depending on the characteristics of the tables to be copied, the **bcp** utility automatically selects a copy mode. The following table compares the characteristics of the two modes.

| Fast bcp | Slow bcp |
| --- | --- |
| Occurs fastest if target table has no indexes or constraints that use indexes. | Automatically used when data is copied into a table with indexes or constraints that use indexes. |
| Is not published. | Is published. |
| The Select Into/Bulkcopy option is set to On. Set by using **sp_dboption**. | The Select Into/Bulkcopy option is set to Off. |
| When the Select Into/Bulkcopy option is set to On, dumping the transaction log is not allowed because the operations are not logged. | |
| Fast **bcp** means that only the allocation page changes are logged. | Slow **bcp** means that the data is logged. |

**Note**   Although anyone with appropriate permissions can execute **bcp**, this task is typically performed by the DBO or the table owner. To execute a fast **bcp**, you must set the database option Select Into/Bulk Copy to True. To set a database option, you must be the DBO.

## Importing Data

Because users can be using the database as data is imported, you can have locking conflicts.

## Exporting Data

To maintain data integrity and consistency, users should not be able to gain access to the database as data is exported. You can set the database option to allow only the DBO to access the database using the SQL Enterprise Manager or the stored procedure, **sp_dboption**, setting the DBO Use Only option to True.

An alternative method to restricting access when exporting data is to perform the bulk copy operation using two sessions. In the first session, begin a transaction and issue a HOLDLOCK. This assigns a sharelock to the table that allows reads, but not updates, to the database.

In the first session, you would execute the following:

```
BEGIN TRANsaction
SELECT COUNT (*) FROM tablename HOLDLOCK
```

In the second session, you would perform the bulk copy. When the bulk copy is complete, you would return to the first session and commit the transaction.

```
COMMIT TRANsaction
```

# bcp Syntax and Parameters

The **bcp** utility has many options for customizing the transfer operation. Some of the options are required and others are optional.

**Syntax**

**bcp** [[*database_name.*]*owner.*]*table_name* {**in** | **out**} **datafile**
[**/m** *maxerrors*] [**/f** *formatfile*] [**/e** *errfile*]
[**/F** *firstrow*] [**/L** *lastrow*] [**/b** *batchsize*]
[**/n**] [**/c**] [**/E**]
[**/t** *field_term*] [**/r** *row_term*]
[**/i** *inputfile*] [**/o** *outputfile*]
**/U** *login_id* [**/P** *password*] [**/S** *servername*] [**/v**] [**/a** *packet_size*]

The required options include the name of database, table name, name of operating system file or disk drive, path, transfer direction (in or out), server name, and password. The following table lists the optional parameters.

| Parameter | Description |
|---|---|
| /m maxerrors | Sets the maximum amount of errors allowed in a **bcp** operation |
| /f formatfile | Creates a format file for future use |
| /e errfile | Creates an error file in which to store rows that did not successfully transfer |
| /F firstrow /L lastrow | Specifies the first row or last row (if a subset of data is required; otherwise, the default is the first row and last row of the table) |
| /b batchsize | Sets the size of the batch file |
| /n native | Sets native formats |
| /c character | Sets character formats |
| /E | Identifies special handling of identity datatypes |
| /t field_term /r row_term | Sets field and row terminators |

(*continued*)

| Parameter | Description |
|-----------|-------------|
| /i inputfile<br>/o outputfile | Creates an input or output file |
| /v | Identifies the current DB-Library version |
| /a packet_size | Sets the packet size for data transfers |
| /U | Displays a login id |
| /P | Displays a user-specified password |
| /S | Displays the server name; which SQL server to connect to |

You must specify the direction of the copy. The **in** option copies from a file into the database table. The **out** option copies to a file from the database table or view.

The following example transfers data from the *testtable* table in the *testpubs* database to a file named TRANSFER.BCP.

**Example**

```
bcp testpubs..testtable in D:\TRANSFER.BCP /c /t"," /r \n /e
D:\TRANSFER.ERR /m100 /b500 /a4096 /Usa /Scrserver
```

The example uses the following parameters:

- In character mode.
- A comma is the field terminator.
- The error file created is D:\TRANSFER.ERR.
- New line is the row terminator.
- The maximum number of errors is set to 100.
- The batch file size is 500 rows.
- The packet size is set to 4096 bytes.
- The username is SA.
- The server name is *crserver*.

This example does not include a password. You would be prompted for the system administrator password before the transfer was completed.

# bcp Transfer Methods

There are two primary **bcp** transfer methods you can choose from when transferring data. They are interactive **bcp** and non-interactive **bcp**.

## Interactive bcp

The **bcp** utility can operate interactively, prompting you for information on a column-by-column basis unless you specify native or character modes or use a format file.

## Non-Interactive bcp

You can also transfer data non-interactively using a format file. A format file is a reusable file of frequently used default formats. You can create it by saving the format created by executing a bulk copy without using the /n or /c parameters. You can use the format file for other bulk copies by specifying the /f parameter and providing the filename.

The most common application for format files is to transfer specific columns of data. You may skip a table column on input or output by specifying 0 prefix length, 0 length, and no terminator (none).

## Naming Conventions

It is recommended that you adopt a naming convention that allows you to identify the type of file that was created. The table below provides some suggestions for naming **bcp** files.

| File extension | Description |
| --- | --- |
| .BCP | Native format |
| .TXT | Character format |
| .ERR | Error file |
| .FMT | Format file |

**Note**  Because **bcp** is an executable application, you must execute it from a command prompt. You cannot execute it from within utilities such as SQL Enterprise Manager or ISQL/w.

## Native Mode

The /n option uses native (database) datatypes. Storing data in native file format is useful when information is copied from one SQL server into another SQL server. The use of the native format saves time, preventing unnecessary conversion of datatypes into and out of character format. Native format produces a binary file.

## Character Mode

The /c option uses the character (char) format for all columns, which provides tabs between fields in a row and a new line at the end of each row. Storing information in character file format is useful when the data is used with another application such as a spreadsheet, or when the data needs to be copied into SQL Server from another database. Character format produces an ASCII file.

# Treatment of Objects in bcp

Certain objects are treated differently by **bcp** when performing transfers. For example, defaults and datatypes are always enforced. If a column with a default is left blank in the **bcp** file, the default value for that field is automatically inserted in the table.

## Defaults and Datatypes

When data is copied into a table, any defaults defined for the columns and datatypes in the table are observed. If there is a null field in the data in a file, the default value is loaded during the copy.

## Rules and Triggers

Rules and triggers are ignored for both fast and slow bulk copy operations. It is recommended that you do not bulk copy data directly into a production table. Instead, create a work table, bulk copy data into the work table, and then insert the data into the production database. The process of inserting data enforces the rules and triggers and ensures data integrity. You can then execute queries or stored procedures to test for rules and triggers in your database.

## Global Temporary Tables

The **bcp** utility can copy data into or from a temporary table. You must give the entire 30-character table name, including the number symbols (##) that precede the table name indicating that it is a global temporary table.

## Views Used As a Data Source

The **bcp** utility can copy data from a view. You can copy specific columns, add a WHERE clause, or perform special formatting such as changing data formats using the CONVERT function.

## Tables with an Identity Value Column

Use the /E parameter to use the existing identity values from the operating system file; however, do not use this step to generate identity values automatically as rows are added to the table. SQL Server assigns unique values based on the seed and increment values specified during table creation.

---

**Note**  This option is in effect only during a bulk copy into a table. It has no effect during a bulk copy from a table.

---

## Tables with or Without Indexes

The **bcp** utility performs best when bulk copying into a table that does not contain indexes. There can be severe performance problems for copying data into a table that has indexes in place.

As a rule:

- When bulk copying large amounts of data, delete all of the indexes, load the table, and then rebuild the indexes.
- When bulk copying small amounts of data, load the data without deleting indexes.

### Fast bcp: Without Indexes

A fast bulk copy does not log data inserts in the transaction log. Before you perform a fast bulk copy, set the Select Into/Bulk Copy Database option to True. You will not be able to back up the transaction log after a non-logged action has occurred. After performing a fast bulk copy, you should back up your database. You must then recreate the indexes that were deleted. Remember to allow twice the amount of space needed for the data for the construction of a clustered index.

### Slow bcp: with Indexes

A slow bulk copy writes data inserts to the transaction log. As a result, the log can become quite large. After you back up your database, you must back up the transaction log to a backup device. If you use the WITH TRUNCATE_ONLY option, you cannot restore subsequent log backups unless they are done after another full database backup.

---

**Note**  A table containing publications used for replication requires a unique index; therefore, bulk copying into such a table is executed as a slow **bcp**.

---

## Steps to Execute a Fast bcp

Follow the steps listed in the following table to execute a fast **bcp**. You should back up your database immediately after the bulk copy operation is complete.

| Step | Person responsible |
| --- | --- |
| Set Select Into/Bulk Copy option to True | SA or DBO |
| Drop indexes on table | Table owner |
| Perform the bulk copy | Any user with INSERT permission |
| Set Select Into/Bulk Copy option to False | SA or DBO |
| Issue a CHECKPOINT | SA or DBO |
| Back up the database (optional) | SA or DBO |
| Recreate indexes | Table owner |
| Check rule violations and data consistency | SA or DBO |
| Back up database | SA or DBO |

When the bulk copy out process is complete, make sure you reset the Select Into/Bulk Copy Database option to False. You can set the Select Into/Bulk Copy Database option in the Edit Database Options dialog box in SQL Enterprise Manager or by using the stored procedure **sp_dboption**.

► **To perform a bulk copy**

In the following procedures, you use the Bulk Copy Program to copy data into a SQL Server table from an operating system file. Because the destination table does not have indexes, a fast **bcp** is executed.

Several thousand records are transferred from another database table into a table in the *testpubs* database. The data from the other application is already in an ASCII file on the network. Before you can bulk copy the data, you must first create a *test* table, and then set the appropriate options in the *testpubs* database.

1. Execute the CREATABL.SQL script file. The contents of the script for the *testtable* is provided below.

```
USE testpubs
go
CREATE TABLE testtable
    (student_id int NOT NULL,
    student_name varchar(30) NULL,
    start_date char(10) NULL,
    city varchar(20) NULL,
    coursenum int NULL,
    classnum int NULL,
    course_title varchar(30) NULL,
    state char(2) NULL)
go
```

2. Execute the **sp_spaceused** stored procedure on both the *testpubs* database and *testtable* table within that database. Record your results. Compare these results with others executed later in this procedure.

| Column | *testpubs* database | *testtable* table |
|---|---|---|
| database_size | | N/A |
| unallocated space | | N/A |
| rows | N/A | |
| reserved | | |
| data | | |
| index_size | | |
| unused | | |

► **To change options for the transfer**

In this procedure, you set the Select Into/Bulk Copy database option for the *testpubs* database.

1. On the Manage menu, click Databases.

2. Double-click *testpubs*.

3. Click the Edit Database button.

4. Click the Options tab.

5. Click Select Into/Bulk Copy.

6. Click OK.

▶ **To create a directory for the bcp source file**

1. Create a directory at the root of C:\ called Transfer (C:\TRANSFER).

2. Copy the file TESTTABL.TXT from the compact disc drive to C:\TRANSFER.

▶ **To transfer data using bcp**

Next, create a batch file to execute **bcp** to transfer data from the TESTTABL.TXT file into the *testtable* table.

1. Using Notepad, create a batch/command file to execute **bcp** with the following parameters or modify the RUNBCP.BAT file to reflect your server name.

   The following information will help you determine what parameters to include.

   ___

   **Important** Do not insert hard returns. The **bcp** command syntax must include only one line of information. The **bcp** arguments are case-sensitive. Replace the server name with your server name. Use the appropriate case.

   ___

| Parameter | Setting |
| --- | --- |
| Data Direction | in |
| Transfer File | C:\TRANSFER\TESTTABL.TXT |
| Data | character only |
| Terminator | "," |
| Row Terminator | new line |
| Error File | C:\TRANSFER\TESTTABL.ERR |
| Maximum Errors | 100 |
| Number / Batch | 500 |
| Server | STUDENTx |
| User Name | sa |

2.  Name the file RUNBCP1.BAT and save it in C:\TRANSFER.

3.  From a command prompt, execute RUNBCP1.BAT.

    How many rows were copied per second?

    _____

    _____

    How many rows were copied?

    _____

4.  Review the output from the error file TESTTABL.ERR.

    Did any errors occur?

    _____

5.  Execute the **sp_spaceused** stored procedure on both the *testpubs* database and *testtable* table within that database. Record your results.

    | Column | testpubs database | testtable table |
    |---|---|---|
    | database_size | | N/A |
    | unallocated space | | N/A |
    | rows | N/A | |
    | reserved | | |
    | data | | |
    | index_size | | |
    | unused | | |

6.  Compare your results with the data from the Step 2 in the *To prepare for a bulk copy* procedure.

7.  In the Edit Database dialog box, from the Options tab, clear the Select Into/Bulk Copy check box to reset the Select Into/Bulk Copy database option for *testpubs*.

8.  Click OK.

## Lesson Summary

The bulk copy utility allows you to import or export data. Using **bcp** you can append data to existing contents of a table, overwrite existing data in a table, and copy data from one SQL Server to another.

| For more information on | See |
| --- | --- |
| The **bcp** utility | "**bcp**" in SQL Server Books Online |
| Native and character modes and creating a format file | "Using Native and Character Format **bcp**" in SQL Server Books Online |

# Lesson 4: Creating and Distributing Databases on Removable Media

In SQL Server, it is possible to create a database and then place it on removable media such as a disk, compact disc, or read/write optical disk for distribution.

### After this lesson you will be able to:

- Choose the best removable media for the database you are transferring.

- Create and reproduce data on removable media.

### Estimated lesson time  50 minutes

## Removable Media

With Microsoft SQL Server, you can create databases for distribution on removable media. You can distribute these databases on read-only removable media, such as a compact disc, or you can distribute on writable removable media, such as disks, WORM drives, or optical drives.

Removable media is an alternative for distributing large amounts of read-only data that is updated periodically, such as once a month or once a quarter. You can generate and distribute a new compact disk each time you want to distribute new data.

Some examples for the use of removable media include:

- Products that provide a subscription service to journals or periodicals, especially for scientific, medical, or legal research.

- Products based on current demographic or census data.

- Catalogs where the products offered change infrequently or seasonally.

- Any product providing monthly, quarterly, or yearly reports that do not need to be updated.

## Steps in Administering Removable Media

The removable media installation process copies a database device containing the system catalog tables and the transaction log onto the server's disk. As system administrator, you can then administer users, permissions, views, and stored procedures for the database while keeping your data on read-only removable media. The minimum database size of 1 MB enables a database to fit on a 3.5-inch disk. Note that the system tables require approximately 512K.

There are eight major steps used to administer removable media.

### Step 1: Create a Database for Removable Media on a Hard Disk

A database that will be distributed later on removable media:

- Must be created on new devices.

- Must be created on devices that are not and will not be used by any other databases to ensure contiguous space.

- Should use at least three separate devices: one for the system catalog tables, one for the transaction log, and one or more devices for the data tables.

The stored procedure, **sp_create_removable,** creates at least three separate devices (as specified earlier) and places the database on those devices. You must be the SA to use **sp_create_removable**.

**Syntax**

**sp_create_removable** *dbname, syslogical, 'sysphysical', syssize, loglogical, 'logphysical', logsize, datalogical1, 'dataphysical1', datasize1* [... , *datalogical16, 'dataphysical16', datasize16*]

**Example**

```
sp_create_removable inventory,
    invsys, 'C:\MSSQL\DATA\INVSYS.DAT', 2,
    invlog, 'C:\MSSQL\DATA\INVLOG.DAT', 4,
    invdata, 'C:\MSSQL\DATA\INVDATA.DAT', 10
```

### Step 2: Certify a Removable Media Database

The **sp_certify_removable** stored procedure prepares the database for distribution on removable media. This stored procedure checks that:

- No user-created objects are in the database.

- No permissions are granted to users.

- The SA is the DBO and the owner of all database objects.

- All device fragments are contiguous and in sequence.

The **sp_certify_removable** stored procedure also truncates the transaction log, moves it to the system device, drops the log device, and sets the database to offline, or inaccessible to users. The system administrator must be owner of the database and all database objects. The system administrator is a known user who exists on all SQL servers. The SA login can be used when the database is later distributed and installed.

> **Important** Record the information provided by this stored procedure. You must have this information to install the database.

**Syntax**

**sp_certify_removable** *dbname*[, AUTO]

### Step 3: Reproduce the Database on Removable Media (Compact Disc)

When the database is certified, create a master copy and reproduce it for distribution. The *master* database contains the system catalog tables device and the data devices. Before reproducing the *master* onto distribution disks, compare files to ensure that the *master* database is identical to the original. Distribute the information provided from executing the **sp_certify_removable** stored procedure during Step 2.

### Step 4: Install the Removable Media Database and Devices

To use a database created on removable media, you must install it on the server and then set it to online. Installing a database involves copying the device containing the system catalog tables and the transaction log to the hard disk.

The data device can remain on the distribution media (usually a compact disc), or it can be copied to the hard disk, but it remains read-only. All data must be accessible to the server. If a database spans multiple media, and there is only one compact disc drive, then some of the data devices must be copied to the server.

Use the stored procedure, **sp_dbinstall**, to install a removable media database. Perform this procedure once for each device of the database. It copies the system device to the hard disk (which places the system catalog tables and the transaction log on read/write media).

The information required by the **sp_dbinstall** parameters was provided as part of the verification process using **sp_certify_removable**. This information should accompany the distribution media.

**Syntax**

**sp_dbinstall** *database*, *logical_dev_name*, *'physical_dev_name'*, *size*, *'devtype'* [, *'location'*]

### Step 5: Place a Removable Media Database Online

Databases are initially installed as offline (unavailable). You can place the newly installed database online (ready to be used) using **sp_dboption**. To set a database online, execute **sp_dboption** using the Offline, False option. All devices belonging to the specified database are opened (if they are not already open) and marked *Nondeferred*, and the database is recovered and becomes available for use. Recovery is skipped if the database is set to read-only.

### Step 6: Use the Database

After the database is placed online, it can be administered in the normal manner to add database users, set permissions, and add views and stored procedures. Keep in mind that after the database is set to offline or uninstalled, anything written to the system tables will be lost because the system tables on the read-only drive cannot be updated.

### Step 7: Place a Removable Media Database Offline

Make sure the database has no active users. You can check to see if there are active users by viewing the Current Activity window of SQL Enterprise Manager. To set a database offline, execute **sp_dboption** using the Offline, True option. Before a removable media disk is removed from a drive, all databases on that disk must be placed offline.

### Step 8: Uninstalling a Database (Optional)

If you no longer need a removable media database, it can be uninstalled using the **sp_dbremove** stored procedure. The removable media does not need to be in the drive for you to uninstall the database. The **sp_dbremove** stored procedure does not delete the physical operating system files for the devices. You must delete the physical files manually.

**Syntax**

**sp_dbremove** *database* [, dropdev]

▶ **To create database devices and a removable media database**

In this procedure, you create a database on removable media, in this case a 3.5-inch disk. You then add data to the database.

You use the stored procedure, **sp_create_removable**, to create the database devices and the *read_floppy* database. All three devices are created on the hard disk and then copied to a 3.5-inch disk.

1. In SQL Enterprise Manager, on the Tools menu, click Query Analyzer.

2. In the *master* database, execute the **sp_create_removable** stored procedure. Use the following parameters. Remember, all paths must be in quotation marks.

| Parameter | Use this value |
|---|---|
| Database name (dbname) | read_floppy |
| System logical name (syslogical) | RF_SYS |
| System physical path ('sysphysical') | 'C:\MSSQL\DATA\RF_SYS.DAT' |
| System size (syssize) | 1 |
| Log logical name (loglogical) | RF_LOG |
| Log physical path ('logphysical') | 'C:\MSSQL\DATA\RF_LOG.DAT' |
| Log size (logsize) | 1 |
| Data logical name (datalogical1) | RF_DATA |
| Data physical path ('dataphysical1') | 'C:\MSSQL\DATA\RF_DATA.DAT' |
| Data size (datasize1) | 1 |

▶ **To certify the database as removable**

In this procedure, you certify that the database you just created is removable.

1. Verify the existence and size of the RF_SYS, RF_LOG, and RF_DATA devices. Execute the following stored procedure.

```
EXEC sp_helpdb read_floppy
```

Record the following information.

| device_fragments | Size | Usage |
|---|---|---|
| RF_DATA | | |
| RF_LOG | | |
| RF_SYS | | |

2. In the query window, execute the stored procedure:

```
EXEC sp_certify_removable read_floppy
```

3. Save the results set as **RF.RPT**.

4. Note the messages you received about device status. Always record this information and provide it with the database when it is distributed on removable media. This information is required to install a removable media database.

| Device name | Device type | Sequence | Device frag. used by database | Physical filename |
|---|---|---|---|---|
| RF_SYS | _____ | _____ | _____ | _____ |
| RF_DATA | _____ | _____ | _____ | _____ |

5. Check the existence and compare the size of the RF_SYS, RF_LOG, and RF_DATA devices. Execute the following stored procedure.

```
EXEC sp_helpdb read_floppy
```

What is the size of the database?

_____

Record the following information.

| device_fragments | Size | Usage |
|---|---|---|
| RF_DATA | _____ | _____ |
| RF_LOG | _____ | _____ |
| RF_SYS | _____ | _____ |

What changed? Why?

_____

_____

6. Insert a blank disk into your drive.

7. Copy the RF_SYS.DAT to the disk. The file is located in the C:\MSSQL\DATA directory. Label this disk RF_SYS_DAT.

8. Insert another blank disk into your drive.

9. Copy the RF_DATA.DAT file to the disk. The file is located in the C:\MSSQL\DATA directory. Label the disk RF_DATA.DAT.

▶ **To remove the database and devices**

This procedure removes all references to the database from the system tables.

1. Remove the database that you just created by executing the following stored procedure.

```
EXEC sp_dbremove read_floppy, dropdev
```

2. Verify the removal of the database from the system tables. Execute the following query.

```
EXEC sp_helpdb read_floppy
```

What message did you receive?

_____

3. Verify the removal of the devices from the system tables. Execute the following query.

```
EXEC sp_helpdevice
```

Are the RF_SYS.DAT, RF_DATA.DAT and RF_LOG.DAT devices listed?

_____

4. Manually delete the files RF_SYS.DAT, RF_DATA.DAT and RF_LOG.DAT from the C:\MSSQL\DATA directory.

▶ **To install the database**

In this procedure, you install the *read_floppy* removable media database from disk on your server.

The installation procedure needs to be executed for each device.

1. Insert the disk with the RF_SYS.DAT device into your drive.

   (This assumes that your disk drive is drive A—if it is not, make the appropriate substitutions.)

2. Install the system device which copies the system tables and transaction log to the hard disk. From the Query Analyzer, execute the following:

```
EXEC sp_dbinstall read_floppy, RF_SYS, 'A:\RF_SYS.DAT', 1, 'SYSTEM',
'C:\MSSQLDATA\RF_SYS.DAT'
```

3. Insert the disk with the RF_DATA.DAT device into your drive.

4. Execute the following statement from a query window to mount the data device for the *read_floppy* database. Because the data remains on disk, a path does not need to be specified to copy the files to the C drive.

```
EXEC sp_dbinstall read_floppy, RF_DATA, 'A:\RF_DATA.DAT', 1, 'DATA'
```

5. Verify the existence of the *read_floppy* database.

```
EXEC sp_helpdb read_floppy
```

What is the status of the database?

---

▶ **To place the removable media database online**

- Execute the following procedure:

```
EXEC sp_dboption 'read_floppy', 'offline', false
```

---

**Note**  The system stored procedure **sp_dboption** is used to set database options. Setting options can also be done in the Edit Database dialog box in SQL Enterprise Manager. However, if a database is offline, you must use the stored procedure to place the database online.

---

What messages were returned?

---

▶ **To use the database**

- Execute a query in one of the system tables in the *read_floppyy* database.

```
SELECT * FROM sysobjects
```

This query did not gather data from drive A. Why not?

---

► **To take the database offline**

1. Use *master*.

2. Execute the **sp_dboption** stored procedure as in the previous procedure, except this time set the *offline* parameter to True.

   What messages were returned? Is the disk ready to be removed from the drive?

   _____

   _____

   _____

   _____

► **To remove the database**

1. Remove the database that you just created by executing the following stored procedure.

   ```
   EXEC sp_dbremove read_floppy, dropdev
   ```

2. To verify the that the database has been removed, execute:

   ```
   EXEC sp_helpdb read_floppy
   ```

3. Delete the RF_SYS.DAT file manually from the C:\MSSQL\DATA directory.

## Lesson Summary

You can create a database and place it on removable media such as a 3.5-inch disk, compact disc, or writable optical disk. You can make the media read-only or writable depending on your distribution. The SA can create, certify, and reproduce the database on removable media. The database is then installed and placed online for use.

| For more information on | See |
|---|---|
| Using removable media | "Using Databases on Removable Media" in SQL Server Books Online |

# Review

The following questions are intended to reinforce key information presented in this chapter. If you are unable to answer a question, review the lesson and then try the question again.

1. What are three methods for transferring data into SQL Server?

 

2. You are transferring both data and a table structure from one SQL server to another. Which tool should you use?

 

3. You are transferring data from a mainframe computer to SQL Server. Which tool should you use?

 

4. When installing a removable media database, why are the system tables copied to the hard disk?

# Questions and Answers

Page 726

▶  **To verify and test the transfer**

2.  Review the output of the files using Notepad.

    What information is contained in the files? How could this information be used?

    **The files contain the Transact-SQL scripts used to created various database objects. These files could be used to build objects in other databases.**

4.  Verify that the data was transferred into the database by executing the TESTQRY.SQL script in both the *testpubs2* database on the source and the destination servers or type the following:

```
SELECT au_lname, au_fname, title
FROM authors a, titleauthor ta, titles t
WHERE a.au_id = ta.au_id
AND ta.title_id = t.title_id
ORDER BY title
```

    Were the results of the query the same for both databases?

    **Yes. 25 rows were returned in both cases.**

Page 736

▶  **To perform a bulk copy**

2.  Execute the **sp_spaceused** stored procedure on both the *testpubs* database and *testtable* table within that database. Record your results. Compare these results with others executed later in this procedure.

| Column | *testpubs* database | *testtable* table |
| --- | --- | --- |
| database_size | **8 MB** | N/A |
| unallocated space | **6.86 MB** | N/A |
| rows | N/A | **0 rows** |
| reserved | **1166K** | **16K** |
| data | **188K (may vary)** | **2K** |
| index_size | **108K** | **0 K** |
| unused | **870K (may vary)** | **14K** |

Page 737   ▶   **To transfer data using bcp**

1. Using Notepad, create a batch/command file to execute **bcp** with the following parameters or modify the RUNBCP.BAT file to reflect your server name.

   **bcp testpubs..testtable in**
   **C:\TRANSFER\TESTTABL.TXT /c /t"," /r\n**
   **/eC:\TRANSFER\TESTTABL.ERR /b500 /m100 /S<studentx> /Usa /P**

3. From a command prompt, execute RUNBCP1.BAT.

   How many rows were copied per second?

   **1450 rows per second. This number will vary depending upon the amount of memory in the server, as well as activity on the server at the time of the bulkcopy.**

   How many rows were copied?

   **6149.**

4. Review the output from the error file TESTTABL.ERR.

   Did any errors occur?

   **No. The error file is empty. If errors occurred, they are placed in the error file where the rows can be changed and then resubmitted.**

5. Execute the **sp_spaceused** stored procedure on both the *testpubs* database and *testtable* table within that database. Record your results.

| Column | testpubs database | testtable table |
|---|---|---|
| database_size | **8 MB** | N/A |
| unallocated space | **6.36 MB** | N/A |
| rows | N/A | **6149 rows** |
| reserved | **1678K (may vary)** | **528K** |
| data | **708K (may vary)** | **528K** |
| index_size | **108K (may vary)** | **0 K** |
| unused | **862K (may vary)** | **0 K** |

Page 744 ▶ **To certify the database as removable**

1. Verify the existence and size of the RF_SYS, RF_LOG and RF_DATA devices. Execute the following stored procedure.

```
EXEC sp_helpdb read_floppy
```

Record the following information.

| device_fragments | Size | Usage |
|---|---|---|
| RF_DATA | 1 MB | Data only |
| RF_LOG | 1 MB | Log only |
| RF_SYS | 1 MB | Data only |

4. Note the messages you received about device status. Always record this information and provide it with the database when it is distributed on removable media. This information is required to install a removable media database.

| Device name | Device type | Sequence | Device frag. used by database | Physical filename |
|---|---|---|---|---|
| RF_SYS | System and log | 1 | 1 MB | C:\MSSQL\ DATA\ RF_SYS.DAT |
| RF_DATA | Data | 2 | 1 MB | C:\MSSQL\ DATA\RF_ DATA.DAT |

5. Check the existence and compare the size of the RF_SYS, RF_LOG, and RF_DATA devices. Execute the following stored procedure.

```
EXEC sp_helpdb read_floppy
```

What is the size of the database?

**2 MB**

Record the following information.

| device_fragments | Size | Usage |
|---|---|---|
| RF_DATA | 1 MB | Data only |
| RF_LOG | N/A | N/A |
| RF_SYS | 1 MB | Data only |

What changed? Why?

**There are two devices instead of three. The RF_LOG was dropped and the log was placed on the RF_SYS device. The total database size is 2 MB instead of 3 MB. This is because the RF_LOG device, which was 1 MB, was dropped.**

Page 746

▶ **To remove the database and devices**

2. Verify the removal of the database from the system tables. Execute the following query.

```
EXEC sp_helpdb read_floppy
```

What message did you receive?

**The database does not exist.**

3. Verify the removal of the devices from the system tables. Execute the following query.

```
EXEC sp_helpdevice
```

Are the RF_SYS.DAT, RF_DATA.DAT and RF_LOG.DAT devices listed?

**No.**

Page 746

▶ **To install the database**

5. Verify the existence of the *read_floppy* database.

```
EXEC sp_helpdb read_floppy
```

What is the status of the database?

**Offline.**

Page 747

▶ **To place the removable media database online**

- Execute the following procedure:

```
EXEC sp_dboption 'read_floppy', 'offline', false
```

What messages were returned?

**Opening device 'RF_DATA' and marking it as non-deferred.**
**Device option set.**
**Opening device 'RF_SYS' and marking it as non-deferred.**
**Device option set.**
**Recovering database 'read_floppy.'**
**Database is now online.**

Page 747

▶ **To use the database**

- Execute a query in one of the system tables in the *read_floppy* database.

```
SELECT * FROM sysobjects
```

This query did not gather data from drive A. Why not?

**The system tables are located on the hard disk. Drive A did not have to be accessed to process this query.**

Page 748

▶ **To take the database offline**

2. Execute the **sp_dboption** stored procedure as in the previous procedure, except this time set the *offline* parameter to True.

What messages were returned? Is the disk ready to be removed from the drive?

**Database is now offline.**
**Closing device RF_DATA and marking it deferred.**
**Device option set.**
**Closing device RF_SYS and marking it deferred.**
**Device option set.**

**Yes, the database is ready to be removed.**

Page 749

## Review Questions

1. What are three methods for transferring data into SQL Server?

   **Transfer Manager, bcp, and loading a database.**

2. You are transferring both data and a table structure from one SQL server 6.5 to another. Which tool should you use?

   **Transfer Manager.**

3. You are transferring data from a mainframe computer to SQL Server. Which tool should you use?

   **bcp.**

4. When installing a removable media database, why are the system tables copied to the hard disk?

   **So that the system tables can be updated. For example, users can be added to the database, permissions can be set, and views and stored procedures can be added.**

CHAPTER 18

# Using SQL Mail, Scheduling Tasks, and Managing Alerts

## About This Chapter

As the administrator or implementor, you often perform administrative tasks such as raising errors, sending alerts through e-mail, and scheduling tasks when specified conditions are encountered. This chapter covers how to automate and streamline these administrative tasks using the SQL Mail, task scheduling, and alert management features of SQL Server.

## Before You Begin

To complete the lessons in this chapter, you must have:

- Installed SQL Server on your computer. Installation procedures are covered in Chapter 2, "Installing SQL Server."
- The *pubs* database installed. To update the *pubs* database, see \SCRIPTS\BLD_PUBS\INSTPUBS.SQL on the compact disc.

# Lesson 1: Overview of SQL Mail, Scheduling Tasks, and Managing Alerts

As the system administrator, you are responsible for daily system maintenance, such as backing up data. SQL Enterprise Manager enables you to automate and streamline administrative tasks using SQL Mail, task scheduling, and the alert management features. The SQL Executive service coordinates and controls these features. This lesson provides an overview of the SQL Mail, task scheduling, and alert management features.

---

### After this lesson you will be able to:

- List two ways in which SQL Server can be configured to send e-mail.
- Describe the types of tasks that can be scheduled.
- Describe the types of alerts available.

### Estimated lesson time  10 minutes

---

## Using SQL Mail

The SQL Server mail capability is called SQL Mail. To fully use the features of task scheduling and alert management, you must have SQL Mail configured. This allows you to send notices of events and alerts to specified operators.

You can use SQL Mail to send messages through the built-in Messaging Application Programming Interface (MAPI) in Microsoft Windows NT.

SQL Mail messages can consist of short text strings, the output from a query, or an attached file. Using the SQL Mail extended stored procedures, messages can be sent from within a trigger or a stored procedure. For example, you could set up a trigger to send an e-mail message when changes occur in the database.

You can easily configure SQL Server to send e-mail messages to operators when:

- A SQL Server alert occurs.
- A SQL Performance Monitor threshold is exceeded.
- A scheduled task—such as a database backup—succeeds or fails.

## Scheduling Tasks

You can create server tasks and schedule them for execution at specified times. The tasks can be operating system command executions, Transact-SQL statements, or replication tasks. You can schedule tasks to occur at a single specified time, on a recurring schedule, when initiated by an alert, or to be executed immediately. The SQL Server processes also automatically create and schedule tasks, such as database and transaction log backups.

You can also use the Database Maintenance Plan Wizard to create and schedule tasks. The Database Maintenance Plan Wizard sets up and schedules core maintenance actions for a selected database. These maintenance actions include: checking data allocation, data and index linkages, and system data; updating optimizer information and reorganizing data and index pages; and performing database and transaction log backups. You can schedule maintenance actions so that they are automatically performed at preset daily or weekly intervals.

## Managing Alerts

SQL Enterprise Manager can be used to automatically respond to SQL Server events by executing a predefined task, triggering an alert, or sending an e-mail or pager notice to selected operators. For example, you can generate an alert when a database is about to become full, or when a database backup is unsuccessful.

If the proper SQL Server options are set, SQL Server events are written to the Windows NT application event log. The SQL Executive service continually monitors the Windows NT application event log, waiting for events from SQL Server. When an event occurs, the SQL Executive service compares the event details with the alerts previously defined by the SQL Server administrator. If it finds a match, the SQL Executive service carries out the defined response. For each alert, SQL Server can perform the following:

- Execute a task.

  This task can be Transact-SQL statements or a Windows NT–based application (.CMD or .EXE file).

- Send e-mail or pager notices, or both, to one or more operators.

Microsoft SQL Server can send messages to designated operators through the built-in MAPI in Windows NT. An e-mail message can consist of short text strings, the output from a query, or an attached file.

## Lesson Summary

SQL Server offers several features—SQL Mail, task scheduling, and alert management—that enable you to automate and streamline administrative tasks.

# Lesson 2: The SQL Executive Service

The SQL Executive service manages the functions that control SQL Server events, tasks, alerts, and replication. This lesson describes how the SQL Executive service manages the functions controlling events, tasks, and alerts, and describes the relationships among these functions.

### After this lesson you will be able to:

- Describe the SQL Executive service.
- Describe how the SQL Executive service manages the functions that control events, tasks, and alerts.
- Describe the relationship between the functions that control events, tasks, and alerts.

### Estimated lesson time  10 minutes

SQL Executive is a service that runs on the Microsoft Windows NT Server-based computer where SQL Server is installed. It provides scheduling capabilities that enable replication, and allows you to schedule other SQL Server tasks including backups, DBCC operations, and other administrative maintenance tasks.

The SQL Executive service:

- Schedules and automates administrative functions.
- Alerts operators so they can respond to server problems in a timely manner.
- Provides event auditing with the Windows NT application event log.

SQL Executive administration is integrated within SQL Enterprise Manager. Scheduling information is maintained in the *msdb* database, which is created automatically by the SQL Server **setup** program. The *msdb* database supports SQL Executive and provides a storage area for scheduling information.

# Management of SQL Executive Functions

You can use the SQL Enterprise Manager and the SQL Executive service to manage server events, tasks, alerts, and replication.

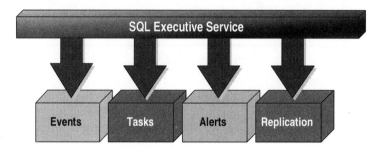

## Event Management

The SQL Executive service is registered as a callback application with the Windows NT EventLog service. When a SQL Server event is posted to the Windows NT application event log, which is the central location for application event logging, the Windows NT EventLog service notifies the SQL Executive service. Then the SQL Executive service responds to and processes the SQL Server event.

Under the following circumstances, errors and messages generated by SQL Server and SQL Server applications are entered in the Windows NT application event log and can therefore cause SQL Executive to fire alerts:

- Severity 19 or higher *sysmessages* errors.
- Non-*sysmessages* warnings/errors from SQL Server (severities 110, 120, and 130).
- Any RAISERROR statement invoked by using the WITH LOG option.
- Any event logged by using **xp_logevent.**
- Any *sysmessages* error modified by using **sp_altermessage with_log**, which forces an error to be written to the Windows NT application event log when the error occurs.

---

**Note**  RAISERROR WITH LOG is the recommended way to write to the Windows NT application event log from SQL Server.

---

Error messages with a severity lower than 19 can be logged by using RAISERROR WITH LOG, or by designating specific *sysmessages* errors as *always logged*.

When an event occurs, SQL Executive compares the event details against the alerts previously defined by the SQL Server administrator. If it finds a match, SQL Executive carries out the defined response. For each alert, the response can be either or both of the following:

- Send e-mail and pager notices, or both, to one or more operators.
- Execute a task. This can be a Transact-SQL command batch or a Windows NT–based application (.CMD or .EXE file).

## Task Management

The SQL Enterprise Manager and the SQL Executive service allow you to define, build, and automate administrative tasks that can be scheduled for execution at a specified time and date, or that can be executed on demand. Common administrative functions, such as database/log backups, index rebuilds, and data loads, can be automated as either Transact-SQL commands or Windows NT command executions that do not have a visual component.

The SQL Enterprise Manager is used to create and schedule the tasks, controlling the occurrence (daily, weekly, monthly, and so on), the frequency (once only, once every day, once every hour, and so on), and the duration of the task. When processing tasks, SQL Executive does the following:

- Runs the task as scheduled.
- If configured to do so, it:
  - Retries the task if it initially failed to run it.
  - Sends an e-mail notification.
  - Writes a success or failure of task message to Windows NT application event log.
- Writes information regarding task execution to the *syshistory* table in *msdb*.

## Alert Management

Alerts provide an early warning mechanism for administrators. Alerts can be defined on any SQL Server event and can be associated with operators or groups of operators who receive alert notifications through e-mail or pager, or both. SQL Executive service can combine the management of alerts, events, and tasks to provide a proactive management environment in which tasks can be automatically invoked in response to the alert. When processing alerts, SQL Executive does the following:

- Automatically notifies operators when events occur, by e-mail or pager as configured.
- Executes a task, if it is configured to do so.

### Replication Management

Replication, which is provided as an integral element of SQL Server, allows you to automatically distribute read-only copies of transactional data from a single source server to one or more destination servers.

SQL Executive controls three types of tasks associated with SQL Server replication: distribution, log reader, and sync.

# Relationships Among Events, Tasks, and Alerts

The management functions of the SQL Executive work together to provide an environment for distributed operations. The following figure illustrates the relationship among the management functions. An operator can receive constant updates on the operational status by defining and monitoring alerts. For example, if the server is stopped or a database is approaching capacity, you can be notified of the problem. Server tasks can be assigned and associated with server alerts, creating a fully automated administrative environment.

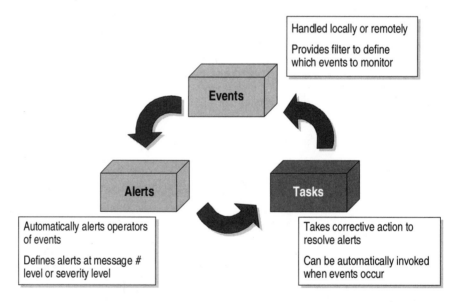

The following examples describe the relationship among the event, task, and alert functions.

### Example 1: An Event Invoking an Alert

You can set up an alert to take place if the database transaction log fills up unexpectedly. When the event occurs, the defined alert is invoked and you are notified by e-mail or pager.

### Example 2: An Alert Invoking a Task

In addition to defining an alert, you can also assign a task to an alert. For example, when an alert occurs because the database transaction log fills up, you can invoke an *on-demand* task to backup the transaction log.

### Example 3: A Task Invoking an Event (Alert)

You can schedule a task, such as backing up the database. If the backup is successful, the task is complete. However, if the backup operation fails, an event can be written to the log. If you have an alert predefined on that event, an alert occurs and the on-duty operator is notified by e-mail or pager.

## Lesson Summary

SQL Executive is a service that runs on the Microsoft Windows NT Server-based computer where SQL Server is installed. The SQL Executive service and the SQL Enterprise Manager enable you to manage the functions that control events, alerts, tasks, and replication. The management functions of the SQL Executive service—which control events, alerts, and tasks—work together to provide an enviromentment for distributed operations.

| For more information on | See |
| --- | --- |
| SQL Executive | "Running SQL Executive" in SQL Server Books Online |

# Lesson 3: Implementing SQL Mail

SQL Server includes extended stored procedures that allow SQL Server to send and receive e-mail messages through a built-in MAPI in Windows NT. This capability is called SQL Mail.

The procedures in this lesson are written for Windows NT Server 3.51. If you are running SQL Server 6.5 on Windows NT Server 4.0, replace the procedures in this lesson with the procedures found in the NT4MAIL.TXT file located in \SCRIPTS\C18_TASK\ on the compact disc.

### After this lesson you will be able to:

- Install a simple post office using Windows NT Server.
- Set up the server computer as a Microsoft Windows NT Mail client.
- Configure SQL Mail to send and receive messages.

### Estimated lesson time  30 minutes

## Sending and Receiving SQL Mail Messages

You can use SQL Mail to send messages when the following applies:

- A SQL Server alert occurs.
- A SQL Performance Monitor threshold is exceeded.
- A scheduled task, such as a database backup or a replication event, succeeds or fails.
- Transact-SQL uses extended stored procedures for mail.

Before SQL Mail can send and receive these messages, a Mail post office must be available, and your server computer must be configured as a Mail client.

SQL Mail can use Microsoft Windows NT Mail, Microsoft Exchange, or any other MAPI provider, to send e-mail messages to operators and to recieve messages sent to a SQL Server Mail account.

SQL Mail messages can consist of short text strings, the output from a query, or an attached file. With the SQL Mail extended stored procedures, operators can send messages from within a trigger or a stored procedure. For example, you could set up a trigger to send a message when changes occur in the database.

Using MAPI and your mail system in a multiserver environment, SQL Server can use system stored procedures, such as **sp_processmail**, with task scheduling to automatically receive queries through e-mail, process the query, and send the results back in an e-mail message.

The **sp_processmail** system stored procedure uses extended stored procedures (**xp_findnextmsg**, **xp_readmail**, **xp_sendmail**, and **xp_deletemail**) to process incoming e-mail messages, which can be only a single query, from the inbox for SQL Server. This system stored procedure also executes the query and returns the results set (as an attached file) to the message sender.

# Setting Up Mail

You can use the MSSQLServer service to set up SQL Mail. You use the LocalSystem Account for MSSQLServer service to:

- Set up a mail post office.
- Enable SQL Mail.
- Set up SQL Server as a SQL Mail client.

## Setting Up a Mail Post Office

Before you can set up a SQL Mail client, a mail post office must already be available. The mail post office can be set up using any e-mail application that supports MAPI, such as Windows NT Server workgroup mail or Microsoft Exchange.

The Windows NT Mail application provided with Windows NT Server 3.51 has a client side and a mail-server side. The client side includes the Mail application with its graphical user interface. The server side contains a directory structure known as the post office. All post office file manipulation is handled by the Mail client. The post office is a temporary message store, holding a message only until the Mail client retrieves it.

▶ **To install a Workgroup Postoffice on Windows NT Server 3.51**

In this procedure, you set up a basic Microsoft Mail post office on a Windows NT Server 3.51 computer. You define a mail login account based on your own name that you use to administer this post office. You use the post office and your login account to send alerts in procedures later in this chapter:

---

**Note**  If you are running SQL Server 6.5 on Windows NT Server 4.0, replace the procedures in this lesson with the procedures found in the NT4MAIL.TXT file located in \SCRIPTS\C18_TASK\ on the compact disc.

---

1. In the Main group in Program Manager, double-click the Mail icon.

    The Welcome to Mail dialog box appears.

2. Under Postoffice selection, click Create a New Workgroup Postoffice.

3. Click OK.

    A message appears asking if you want to create a post office.

4. Click Yes.

   The Create Workgroup Postoffice dialog box appears. You create the workgroup post office on the root of drive C.

5. Under Create WGPO In, double-click C:\

6. Click OK.

   The WGPO directory is created on the root of drive C.

   The Enter Your Administrator Account Details dialog box appears.

7. In Name, type your name.

   For example, if your name is Mike Greene, type Mike Greene.

8. Under Mailbox, type your first name followed by the first letter of your last name (do *not* use spaces).

   For example, if your name is Mike Greene, your mailbox would be *mikeg*.

9. Under Password, leave the default entry PASSWORD.

10. Write down the information that you provided. You will refer to this information later.

    Name _____

    Mailbox _____

    Password _____

11. Click OK.

    A message box appears stating that the Workgroup Postoffice was created in C:\WGPO.

12. Click OK.

13. On the File menu, click Exit and Sign Out.

▶ **To test your Workgroup Postoffice in Windows NT 3.51**

In this procedure, you test the Microsoft Mail Postoffice. You sign in to mail using the Mail account you just created, send an e-mail message to yourself, and then retrieve it.

---

**Note**  If you are running SQL Server 6.5 on Windows NT Server 4.0, replace the procedures in this lesson with the procedures found in the NT4MAIL.TXT file located in \SCRIPTS\C18_TASK\ on the compact disc.

---

1. In the Main group in Program Manager, double-click the Mail icon.

   The Mail Sign In dialog box appears.

2. In the Name box, enter the name of your Mailbox.

3. In the Password box, enter your password.

4. Click OK.

5. Click Compose.

   The Send Note dialog box appears.

6. In the To box, enter your Name.

7. In the Subject box, type **First Test**

8. In the body of the note, enter a message of your choice.

9. Click Send.

10. On the View menu, click New Messages to retrieve your message.

    Your new message appears in the Inbox dialog box.

11. Double-click your message to read it.

12. Press ESC to close your message when you are finished.

13. On the File menu, click Exit and Sign Out.

---

**Note**  In a multicomputer, production environment, you would share your post office on the network and ensure that the SQL Server service (MSSQLSERVER) and all Mail clients have permissions to read and write files in the shared postoffice directory.

---

## Enabling SQL Mail

To enable SQL Mail, set up:

▪ The Windows NT Server-based computer as a mail client for your mail system.

▪ SQL Server as a SQL Mail client.

### Setting Up the Server Computer As a Mail Client

Before SQL Server can send and receive messages through the MAPI client interface in Windows NT, the server computer must be configured as a Mail client for whatever mail system you are using.

When you installed the Windows NT Server 3.51 Workgroup Postoffice earlier in this lesson, your computer was automatically configured as a Windows NT Mail client.

If your Windows NT Server Workgroup Postoffice was configured on a different computer, you need to configure your SQL Server computer as a Windows NT Mail client as follows:

1.  Start Mail and click Connect to An Existing Postoffice.
2.  Specify the network path to the shared post office.
3.  Specify the account on the post office that will serve as the SQL Server Mail account.

## Setting Up a SQL Mail Client

Once the server is set up as a Windows NT Mail client, you can set up a SQL Mail client by using SQL Setup. You can also start and stop SQL Mail, and change the Auto Start Option in the Registry.

The Mail Login dialog box is used to specify a Windows NT mail client login name and password for SQL Server's SQL Mail use. The Copy SQL Mail configuration from current user account check box ensures that the current mail client configuration is used by SQL Mail.

Selecting this check box copies the post office location and mail options of the user for whom you previously set up the Windows NT Mail client to the default user. Even if you do not use the Mail Login dialog box to store a Mail username and password, you must select this option when setting up SQL Mail for the first time. Thereafter, the check box does not need to be selected unless you have changed your Mail client configuration information.

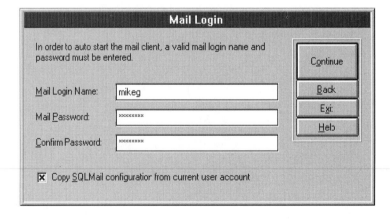

▶ **To set up a SQL Mail client**

In this procedure, you set up your computer as a SQL Mail client. You configure this client to use the Mail login account created earlier in this chapter (when you installed the Workgroup Postoffice) and to start automatically whenever SQL Executive starts.

---

**Note**  If you are running SQL Server 6.5 on Windows NT Server 4.0, replace the procedures in this lesson with the procedures found in the NT4MAIL.TXT file located in \SCRIPTS\C18_TASK\ on the compact disc.

---

1. Start the Mail client, and log in using the e-mail mailbox name you created earlier in this lesson.

2. Start SQL Setup.

3. Click Continue twice to access the Microsoft SQL Server 6.5 - Options dialog box.

4. Select Set Server Options.

5. Click Continue.

   The Set Server Options dialog box appears.

6. Select Auto Start Mail Client. This option starts a SQL Mail session each time SQL Executive starts.

7. Click Mail Login.

   When you configure SQL Server to automatically start SQL Mail sessions, you must supply an e-mail login name and password. You created this mail account earlier in this lesson when you configured your workgroup post office, and you are currently running mail using this mail name.

8. In the Mail Login Name box, type your e-mail (mailbox) name.

9. In the Mail Password box, type:

   **PASSWORD**

10. In the Confirm Password box, type:

    **PASSWORD**

11. Select Copy SQL Mail Configuration From Current User Account.

12. Click Continue.

13. Click Change Options to accept your configuration.

14. Click Continue to accept the Mail Login information.

15. Click Exit to Windows NT.

16. Stop and restart the SQL Executive service.

17. Check the application event log in Windows NT Event Viewer to verify that the Microsoft Mail session was started successfully.

▶ **To test SQL Mail using xp_sendmail**

In this procedure, you use **xp_sendmail** from inside a query window to test your installation of SQL Mail.

---

**Note** If you are running SQL Server 6.5 on Windows NT Server 4.0, replace the procedures in this lesson with the procedures found in the NT4MAIL.TXT file located in \SCRIPTS\C18_TASK\ on the compact disc.

---

1. Open a query window, and use the *master* database.

2. Type and execute the following extended stored procedure, substituting your name, to send yourself a test message.

```
xp_sendmail @recipients = '<your name>',
    @subject = 'test message',
    @message = 'This is a test.'
```

The message *Mail sent* appears when it is successful.

3. Check Mail to see your message.

4. Close the query window.

## Starting and Stopping SQL Mail

Once you have configured your SQL Server as a SQL Mail client, you might want to start or stop the mail client. If you stop the mail client, you cannot send messages using the extended stored procedures of SQL Mail.

To start or stop the SQL Mail client, use SQL Enterprise Manager and expand the tree for your server. On the SQL Mail icon, click the secondary mouse button to get the shortcut menu, and then click Start or Stop.

### Changing the Auto Start Option Using SQL Executive

After SQL Mail is installed, each time the SQL Executive service starts it automatically attempts to start the SQL Mail session if configured to do so. You can control this through the SQL Executive. To change the Auto Start option using SQL Executive, follow these steps:

1. On the SQL Executive icon, click the secondary mouse button.
2. Click Configure.

   The Configure SQL Executive dialog box appears.
3. Select or clear the Auto Start SQLMail When SQL Executive Starts option.

### Using xp_startmail

You can use **xp_startmail** to start mail sessions. If you supplied a login name and password in the Mail Login dialog box, you do not need to provide it at the **xp_startmail** command prompt. If there is an existing mail session, **xp_startmail** will not start a new one. If mail is being used on the same computer on which SQL Server is also running, the mail client must be started before **xp_startmail** is used.

---

**Note**  If you change the Windows NT Mail password for this mail login account, you need to change the password here as well.

---

# Troubleshooting SQL Mail Problems

There might be times when SQL Mail does not respond as you think it should. Most problems result from incorrect permissions or Registry settings. This section describes some steps you can take to diagnose and solve SQL Mail problems.

You can use the following troubleshooting techniques to diagnose and resolve most SQL Mail problems. Typically, errors in starting a mail session or sending e-mail fall into two categories: permission problems when accessing Shared File System (SFS) shares being used as post offices, and Registry setup problems.

If you are having problems with SQL Mail, check the following:

1. Ensure that the SQL Server service (MSSQLServer) is assigned the LocalSystem account and that the Allow Service To Interact With Desktop option is selected. Use the Services application in Control Panel to check these.
2. Ensure that the user who set up SQL Mail can successfully start a mail session and send e-mail by using the Windows NT Mail client application, MSMAIL32.EXE.

3. When starting a mail session, Mail makes use of information in the Windows NT Registry to determine startup information, such as the share name serving as a post office for the user logging in. The Registry information is configured for the current user when the SQL Server **setup** program or SQL Enterprise Manager application is run, and is copied to the default user key when the Copy SQL Mail Configuration From Current User Account in the Mail Login dialog box is selected.

The following is the Registry key used by SQL Mail:

```
HKEY_USERS\.DEFAULT\Software\Microsoft\Mail
```

If this Registry key is not set up properly, ensure that you are able to start a mail session using the account you are currently logged in under, and then rerun SQL Setup or SQL Enterprise Manager, ensuring that Copy SQL Mail Configuration From Current User Account is selected.

4. Make sure that the MSSQLServer service has at least RW access to the post office share.

If SQL Server is running under the LocalSystem account and is on the same domain as the post office server, the post office grants rights to the Windows NT *EVERYONE* group, or if it is not, grants rights to the Windows NT *GUEST* account.

Access to the file share can be tested by using the **xp_cmdshell** extended stored procedure. For instance, the following commands can be used to test read/write access to the server when you substitute the appropriate computer and share names:

```
xp_cmdshell "dir \\mailserver\poshare"
```

and

```
xp_cmdshell "echo 'hello' > \\mailserver\poshare\test.txt"
```

---

**Note**  If the post office share is on an NTFS drive, permissions must be set for both the network share and the file system.

---

5. If the post office resides on a computer running Windows NT Server version 3.5*x*, and if the MSSQLServer service on a separate Mail client computer runs under the LocalSystem account (as it should to support SQL Mail), ensure that the post office share has been added to the list of shares that can be accessed by services running under LocalSystem. This can be done by adding the share name to the Registry key on the Windows NT–based computer sharing the post office:

```
\HKEY_LOCAL_MACHINE\System\CurrentControlSet\Services
\LanmanServer\Parameters
```

Name: NullSessionShares
Type: REG_MULTI_SZ
Data: COMCFG WGPO

You can also set the SQL Server service (MSSQLServer) to run under a Windows NT user account, which does not require the NullSessionShares Registry entry. A Registry key can be checked by using the Registry Editor (REGEDT32.EXE).

**Caution**  Only experienced users should use REGEDT32 to edit the Windows NT Registry. Editing of the Registry is not generally recommended, and inappropriate or incorrect changes can cause serious configuration problems for your system.

## Lesson Summary

You use SQL Mail to send messages to operators. You must have SQL Mail set up to be able to fully use all of the task scheduling and alerts management features. Before you can use SQL Mail, you must set up a Mail post office, set up a SQL mail client, and set up SQL Server as a mail client. If SQL Server does not respond as you believe it should, you need to use troubleshootng techniqes to diagnose and resolve the problems.

| For more information on | See |
| --- | --- |
| SQL Mail | "Setting Up Mail," "SQL Mail and Microsoft Exchange Server Configuration Requirements," and "Troubleshooting SQLMail Problems" in SQL Server Books Online |
| Registry Editor | Books Online for Microsoft Windows NT |
| SQL Mail on Windows NT Server 4.0 | The file located in \SCRIPTS\C18_TASK\NT4MAIL.TXT on the compact disc |

# Lesson 4: Managing Task Scheduling

Using SQL Enterprise Manager and the SQL Executive service, you can create server tasks and schedule them for execution. The tasks can be command executions, Transact-SQL statements, or replication tasks. A task can be scheduled to occur at a single specified time, on a recurring schedule, or when initiated by an alert. A task can also be executed immediately.

SQL Server processes also automatically create and schedule tasks. Users with system administrator (SA) privileges can use SQL Enterprise Manager to modify, disable, delete, and immediately run both user-created tasks and SQL Server–created tasks. Users without SA privileges can manage only the tasks they own.

### After this lesson you will be able to:

- Demonstrate how to create a task.
- Demonstrate how to modify and remove a task.
- Demonstrate how to set task scheduling options, including task engine options.
- Demonstrate how to schedule a task to execute.

### Estimated lesson time  45 minutes

Users with SA privileges can use the Manage Scheduled Tasks window to define, build, and automate administrative tasks that can be scheduled, such as the following:

- Backing up data
- Backing up transaction logs
- Updating statistics
- Dropping and recreating indexes
- Checking data integrity

Administrators control the occurrence (daily, weekly, monthly, and so on), the frequency (once only, once every day, once every hour, and so on), and the duration of the task schedule. Task scheduling involves three activities: creating tasks, setting task options, and scheduling task execution.

## Creating a Task

You create a task when you determine that a new task needs to be performed, such as backing up data. When you create a task, you define and schedule the task.

## Defining the Task

Use the New Task dialog box to create a new task. To go to the New Task dialog box, click Manage Scheduled Tasks on the toolbar, and then click New Task.

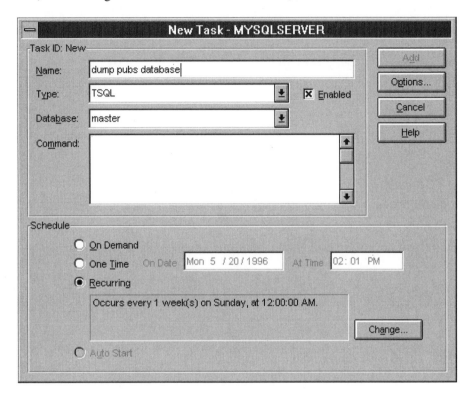

When creating a task, you must provide the following information.

| Option | Description |
| --- | --- |
| Name | Used to enter a unique name for the task. |
| Type | Used to select or enter the type of task to be scheduled. Most often you select CmdExec or TSQL. The other types are used for replication scheduling. There are five task types: |
| | CmdExec—An operating system command that does not have a visual component, or a .CMD or .EXE file as specified in the Command box. |
| | Distribution—A replication distribution process command. |
| | LogReader—A replication logreader process command. |
| | Sync—A replication synchronization process command. |
| | TSQL—A Transact-SQL statement to be run against the selected database. The statement is limited to 255 characters. |

(*continued*)

| Option | Description |
| --- | --- |
| Enabled | Used to create and schedule a task when this box is selected. When the box is cleared, the task is created, but not scheduled. |
| Process Exit Code of a Successful Task<br><br>–or–<br><br>Database | If type CmdExec is selected, the Process Exit Code of a Successful Task option appears. This field can be used to enter the Process Exit Code of a Successful Task. If the other types are selected, the Database option appears. This field can be used to select or enter the database the task is executed against. |
| Command | Used to enter text of the task to be scheduled. This can be a valid operating system command, the filename (including path) of an .EXE or .CMD file, or a Transact-SQL statement. This can also be a command to one of the replication processes. |
| Schedule | Used to schedule the task. The tasks can be scheduled to be On Demand, One-Time, Recurring, or Auto Start.<br><br>On Demand—The task is created but not scheduled. On-demand tasks are the only types of tasks that can be used by alerts. When the alert occurs, the task is run. On-demand tasks can also be run from the Task Scheduling window by clicking Run Task.<br><br>One Time—The task occurs once, at the specified date and time. After running, it will be disabled but not deleted. If One-Time is selected On Date and At Time can be set:<br><br>On Date—The date for the one-time execution of the task.<br><br>At Time—The time for the one-time execution of the task.<br><br>Recurring—Specifies a recurring schedule for the task. The schedule is displayed in the box below Recurring. The default for a recurring task is once a week on Sunday. To change the schedule, click Change.<br><br>Auto Start—Used by replication processes. SQL Server automatically starts the task when SQL Executive starts. |
| Add | Used to add the task you have specified. |
| Options | Used to specify options about e-mail and Windows NT application event log notification and retry attempts for a particular task. |

## Scheduling Task Execution

When you create a task and choose to have it executed on a recurring basis, the default is to have the task executed once a week on Sunday. However, you can specify that the task be executed repeatedly at specified intervals.

Use the Task Schedule dialog box to schedule task execution. To go to the Task Schedule dialog box, click Change in the New Task dialog box (you can also click Change in the Edit Task dialog box).

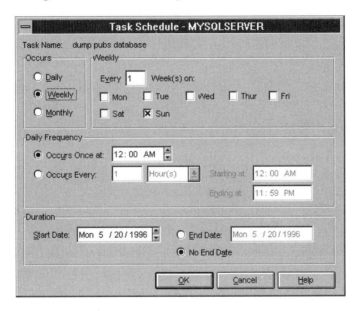

To schedule a task, you must provide the following information.

| Option | Description |
|---|---|
| Occurs | The frequency with which the task should occur: Daily, Weekly, or Monthly. |
| | Daily—If you choose Daily occurrence, then the Daily frame appears in the dialog box. Enter the number of days in the recurrence cycle. The default is Every 1 Day(s), indicating that the recurring task will be executed each day. |
| | Weekly—If you choose Weekly occurrence, then the Weekly frame appears in the dialog box. Enter the number of weeks in the recurrence cycle, and select the day. The default is Every 1 Week(s), on Sunday. |
| | Monthly—If you choose Monthly occurrence, then the Monthly frame appears in the dialog box. Complete the choices in this frame. For example, if you enter Day 4 of Every 2 Month(s), the recurring task will be executed on the fourth day of every other month. |
| Daily Frequency | The frequency with which the task should occur. This can be either once a day at a specified time or repeated at a specified interval within a specified range of hours. |
| Duration | The period during which the task is executed. You can establish the start date and whether there is an end date. |
| | Start Date—The first day on which the recurring task will be executed. |
| | End Date—The last day on which the recurring task will be executed. Not valid if No End Date is selected. |
| | No End Date—The recurring task has unlimited duration. |

▶ **To create a task**

In this procedure, you create a Transact-SQL task, *dump pubs database*, that backs up the *pubs* database to a disk file in the directory C:\MSSQL\BACKUP. You schedule the task to run daily.

1. Start SQL Enterprise Manager, and then select your server.

2. On the Server menu, click Scheduled Tasks, or click Manage Scheduled Tasks on the toolbar.

   The Manage Scheduled Tasks window appears.

3. Click New Task.

   The New Task dialog box appears.

4. In the Name box, type:

   **dump pubs database**

5. In the Type box, select TSQL.

6. Select the Enabled check box.

7. In the Database box, select *pubs*.

8. In the Command box, type:

   **dump database pubs to disk = 'c:\mssql\backup \pubs_dir.bak'**

9. Under Schedule, click Recurring, and then click Change.

   The Task Schedule dialog box appears.

10. Under Occurs, click Daily.

    Notice that the Daily Frequency occurs once at 12:00 am, starting with today's date and no end date.

11. Click OK.

    The New Task dialog box reappears.

12. Click Add.

    The Manage Scheduled Tasks window reappears. Notice the *dump pubs database* task appears in the task list.

## Modifying a Task

Once you have created a task, you can use the Edit Task dialog box to change any of the information that defines the task, or use the Task Schedule dialog box to change a recurring task execution.

## Modifying the Task Definition

Use the Edit Task dialog box to change any of the information configured for that task, including scheduling and option information. To go to the Edit Task dialog box, double-click the task name in the Manage Scheduled Tasks window, or click Edit Task on the toolbar.

If you do not want a task to run, but you do not want to delete it, you can clear the Enabled check box to temporarily disable it.

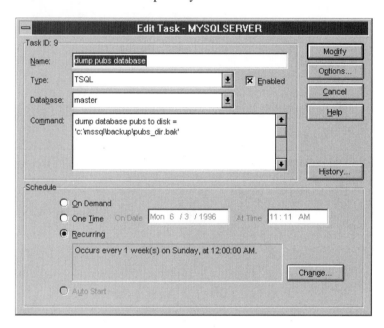

## Modifying the Task Execution

Use the Task Schedule dialog box to modify the schedule for task execution. To go to the Task Schedule dialog box, click Change in the Edit Task dialog box.

## Setting Task Options

When you create or modify a task, you can set options so that an operator receives an e-mail or pager notification upon task success or failure, so that Windows NT application event log entries are made upon task success or failure, and so that task retry parameters are set. Task options are set by clicking Options in the New Task or Edit Task box, and then completing the Task Options dialog box.

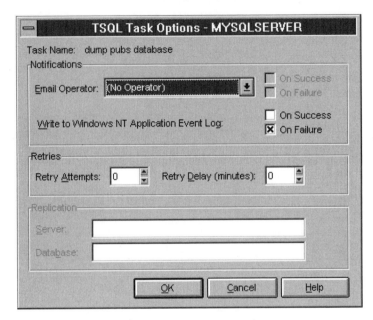

To set the task options, you must provide the following information.

| Option | Description |
| --- | --- |
| Email Operator | Specifies the operator to be notified by e-mail of the status of the task execution. Also, the e-mail check boxes for On Success or On Failure, or both, must be selected. |
| | If necessary, you can remove an assigned operator by choosing (No Operator) in the Operator box. Or, you can add a new operator by selecting (New Operator) and completing the New Operator dialog box that appears. |
| Write to Windows NT Application Event Log | Records information about the task execution in the Windows NT application event log. The check boxes On Success or On Failure, or both, must be selected. |
| | Note that regardless of this setting, information about task execution is always logged in the Task History table, *syshistory* in *msdb*. |
| Retry Attempts | Specifies the number of retry attempts for a failed task. |
| Retry Delay | Specifies the number of minutes to wait before retrying a failed task. |
| Server | Specifies a remote destination server for replication tasks. |
| Database | Specifies a remote destination database for replication tasks. |

▶ **To set options for a task**

In this procedure, you set the option to write to the Windows NT event log for the *dump pubs database* task you created earlier in this lesson.

1. Use SQL Enterprise Manager to access the Manage Scheduled Tasks window.

2. Click the *dump pubs database* task, and then click Edit Task.

   The Edit Task dialog box appears.

3. Click Options.

   The TSQL Task Options dialog box appears.

4. Select both the On Success and On Failure check boxes beside Write to Windows NT application event log.

5. Click OK.

   The Edit Task dialog box reappears.

6. Click Modify.

   The Manage Scheduled Tasks window reappears. You are now able to write success and failure notifications to the event log for this task.

# Viewing the Task List and the Running Tasks

You can use the Manage Scheduled Tasks window to view the list of tasks that are defined for a particular SQL server, to view the list of running tasks, and to run tasks immediately. To view the lists, from the Server Manager you select a server and then on the toolbar, click Manage Scheduled Tasks.

## Viewing the Task List

To view a list of existing tasks (both scheduled and disabled) for this server, click the Task List tab. You can update the information by clicking Refresh. The information in the following table is displayed.

| Option | Description |
| --- | --- |
| Task | Task name |
| Enabled | Whether the task is enabled or disabled |
| Owner | The task owner (usually the task creator) |
| Type | The type of task: |
| | CmdExec is an operating system command or executable file |
| | TSQL is a Transact-SQL statement |
| | Distribution is a replication task |
| | LogReader is a replication task |
| | Sync is a replication task |
| Frequency | The task's schedule type: |
| | Recurring |
| | One Time |
| | On Demand (an on-demand task is run by an alert when the alert occurs) |
| Last Run | The day and time the task last ran |
| Status | The status of the task last ran |

▶   **To view the scheduled tasks**

1. Use SQL Enterprise Manager to the Manage Scheduled Tasks window.

2. What tasks are currently scheduled to run?

## Viewing the Running Tasks Lists

You can also view the running tasks in the Manage Scheduled Tasks window. To view a list of the tasks that are currently running, click the Running Tasks tab. You can update the information by clicking Refresh. The information in the following table is displayed.

| Title | Description |
|-------|-------------|
| Name | Task name |
| Owner | The task owner (usually the task creator) |
| Type | The type of task: |
| | CmdExec is an operating system command or executable file |
| | TSQL is a Transact-SQL statement |
| | Distribution is a replication task |
| | LogReader is a replication task |
| | Sync is a replication task |
| Start Date | The date/time when the task began execution |
| Status | The status information about the task |

## Running a Task Immediately

A task can be scheduled to automatically run at a single specified time, on a recurring schedule, or when initiated by an alert. Any task in the task list can be run immediately by the task owner and the system administrator. For the task to run, the SQL Executive service must be running on the target server. To run a task immediately, select it and click Run Task on the toolbar, or use the **sp_runtask** system stored procedure.

▶  **To run a task immediately**

In this procedure, you run the *dump pubs database* task you created earlier in this lesson.

1. Use SQL Enterprise Manager to access the Manage Scheduled Tasks window.
2. From the Task List, select the *dump pubs database* task.
3. Click Run Task.
4. Click Yes to run the task.
5. Click OK to acknowledge the task started successfully.
6. In the Manage Schedule Tasks window, click the Running Tasks tab. If the task is still running, notice the information about the *dump pubs database* task.
7. Click the Task List tab.
8. When the task has completed, update the Manage Scheduled Tasks window.

9. When was the *dump pubs database* task last run? Was it successful?

10. If the task did not run successfully, use the Windows NT Event Viewer to determine what the problem was, correct it, and run the task again.

11. Open the Windows NT application event log and view the detailed information for the task you just ran.

# Task History

SQL Server keeps a history of each task. Users with system administrator privileges can view all of the tasks and task histories. However, users without system administrator privileges can view the tasks and tasks histories for only those tasks that they created and own.

### Viewing Task History

You can view information about the last run date of a task, the time and duration of the last run, the status of that run, and whether any e-mail was sent by SQL Executive. You can also view any messages encountered while running the task. To view the task history, you select the task in the Task Scheduling window and then click Task History.

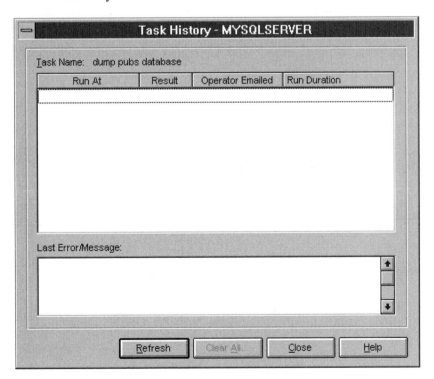

▶ **To view a task history**

In this procedure, you view the task history of the *dump pubs database* task you created earlier in this lesson.

1. Use SQL Enterprise Manager to the Manage Scheduled Tasks window.

2. From the Task List, select the *dump pubs database* task.

3. Click Task History.

4. What information does the Task History window provide?

---

5. Close the Task History window.

6. Close the Manage Scheduled Tasks window.

## Maintaining the Task History Log

To control how long task history information is retained, you need to manage the size of this log. The system maintains the task history log as information in the *syshistory* table of the *msdb* database. Only users with system administrator privileges can set the task engine options.

Use the Task Engine Options dialog box to control the size of the task history log. To go to the Task Engine Options dialog box, click Task Engine Options in the Manage Scheduled Tasks window.

You must provide the following information.

| Option | Description |
|---|---|
| Limit Size of Task History Log | If you clear this option, there is no limit on the size of the history log, and the number in the Maximum Task History Log Size has no effect. By default, this option is selected. |
| Maximum Task History Log Size (rows) | Specifies a maximum number of rows in the task history. The task history log will retain the most recent rows entered, up to the number specified. When this number is exceeded, the oldest entry (row) in the task history log is purged to make room for the newest entry. The default is 1000. |
| Maximum Task History Rows Per Task | Specifies the maximum number of rows kept per task. When the number is exceeded, the oldest row in the log for the task is purged to make room for the newest row. |
| Current Task History Log Size (rows) | Displays the actual size, in rows, of the history log. |
| Clear Task History Log | Empties the history log. |

**Important**  Depending on the activity level of the server, clearing the Limit Size of Task History Log check box can cause the size of the *msdb..syshistory* table to grow rapidly. In some cases, it can grow until it completely fills the *msdb* database. This can cause subsequent alert and history tasks to fail. If you need to keep large amounts of task history information, expand the *msdb* database to a size sufficient to accommodate the growth of *syshistory*.

# Database Maintenance Plan Wizard

The Database Maintenance Plan Wizard sets up and schedules core maintenance actions for a selected database. These maintenance actions include checking data allocation, data and index linkages, and system data; updating optimizer information and reorganizing data and index pages; and performing database and transaction log backups. Maintenance actions can be scheduled for automatic execution at preset daily or weekly intervals.

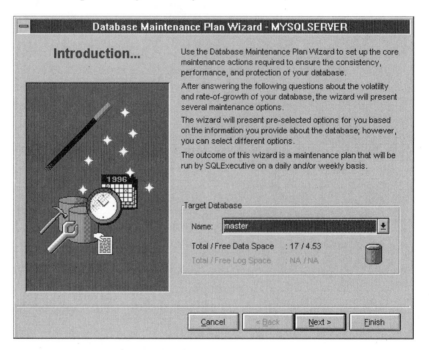

▶ **To create a weekly maintenance task using the Database Maintenance Plan Wizard**

In this procedure, you use the Database Maintenance Plan Wizard to create a task that performs core maintenance actions required to ensure the consistency, performance, and protection of the *master* database.

1. Use SQL Enterprise Manager and select your server.

2. On the Help menu, click Database Maintenance Plan Wizard, or click the Database Maintenance Plan Wizard on the toolbar.

   The Database Maintenance Plan Wizard appears.

3. In the Target Database Name box, select *master*, and then click Next.

4. Under Data Volatility, click Less than 5%.

5. Under Data Growth, click Less than 2%, and then click Next.

6. Under Data Verification Tests, select all check boxes (the default).

7. In Add the Data Verification Tests to, click The Weekly Maintenance Plan, and then click Next.

8. Under Data Optimizations, accept the defaults.

9. Under Add the Data Optimizations to, select The Weekly Maintenance Plan, and then click Next.

10. Under Backup Options, click Back Up the Database Weekly, and then click Next.

11. Under Backup Destination, accept the default location C:\MSSQL\BACKUP, and then click Next.

12. Under When to Run the Weekly Plan, select On Day Saturday, and then click Next.

13. Review the Weekly Plan Summary, and click Done.

14. If you have a printer configured, click Yes to print the wizard summary information; otherwise, click No.

15. Click Done.

16. Access the Manage Scheduled Tasks window.

   Notice a new task has been created, Master Weekly Automated Maintenance.

   What type of task did the Database Maintenance Plan Wizard create?

   _____

17. Click the Master Weekly Automated Maintenance task, and then click Edit Task.

   What application runs when this task runs?

   _____

18. Click Cancel to close the Edit Task dialog box.

19. Run the Master Weekly Automated Maintenance task now.

   Was the task successful? How do you know?

   _____

# Deleting or Disabling a Task

If a task is no longer applicable, you can delete or disable the task. You can delete or disable the task in the Manage Scheduled Tasks window.

## Deleting a Task

If a task is no longer needed, you might want to delete it. To delete a task, select the task that is no longer needed from the Manage Scheduled Tasks window, and then click Delete Task or press the DEL key.

▶ **To delete a task**

In this procedure, you delete the Master Weekly Automated Maintenance task that you created earlier in this lesson using the Database Maintenance Plan Wizard.

1. Use SQL Enterprise Manager to the Manage Scheduled Tasks window.

2. Click the Master Weekly Automated Maintenance task.

3. Click Delete Task.

4. Click Yes.

   The Manage Scheduled Tasks window reappears. Notice the Master Weekly Automated Maintenance task no longer appears in the Task List.

## Disabling a Task

If you do not want a task to run but you do not want to delete it, you can temporarily disable it. To disable a task, edit the task and clear the Enable option.

# Lesson Summary

You can use the Manage Scheduled Tasks window to create and modify tasks, such as backing up databases and transaction logs, and schedule when you want them to be performed. Once you have created and scheduled tasks, you can view them and run scheduled tasks immediately. You can also view and maintain the task history. The Database Maintenance Plan Wizard enables you to set up and schedule core mainenteance actions for a selected database, such as checking data allocation. If you decide that a task is not longer applicable, you can delete or disable it.

| For more information on | See |
| --- | --- |
| Scheduling tasks | "Scheduling Tasks" in SQL Server Books Online |
| Database Maintenance Plan Wizard | "Using the Database Maintenance Plan Wizard" in SQL Server Books Online |
| Task scheduling interface | "Task Scheduling Interface" in SQL Server Books Online |

# Lesson 5: Managing Alerts

SQL Enterprise Manager and the SQL Executive service provide an easy way to set alerts on SQL Server events. By creating alerts, you can set up SQL Server to respond automatically to events, either by executing a task that you have defined or by sending an e-mail or pager message, or both, to an operator that you have specified. When you create alerts, you must define two things:

- The conditions that cause an alert.

- The action the system takes when the defined alert occurs.

## After this lesson you will be able to:

- Demonstrate how to create an operator.

- Demonstrate how to edit and remove an operator.

- Demonstrate how to create an alert.

- Demonstrate how to set an alert.

- Demonstrate how to edit and remove an alert.

- Configure an alerts management server for event forwarding.

## Estimated lesson time  45 minutes

To manage alerts, you perform the following tasks:

- Make sure the SQL Executive service is running.

- Enable Windows NT logging.

- Create an operator for each alert. This is the person who is notified when the alert has occurred.

- Create an alert. This defines the conditions that cause an alert, and the actions the system takes when the alert occurs.

- Set alert options. Alert options include things such as designating an operator who will be notified when all pager notifications for an alert fail, or defining the events to be forwarded to another SQL server.

# Using Operators

An operator is the person (or group) who is notified, through either e-mail or a pager notification, when an alert has occurred. When you create an operator, you add information for the operator that can include an e-mail name, a pager e-mail name, and the schedule that the operator is available to be paged. You can create, edit, view, delete, or disable operators.

## Creating an Operator

You use the New Operator dialog box to create an operator. To go to the New Operator dialog box, click Manage Alerts and Operators, click the Operators tab, and then click New Operator.

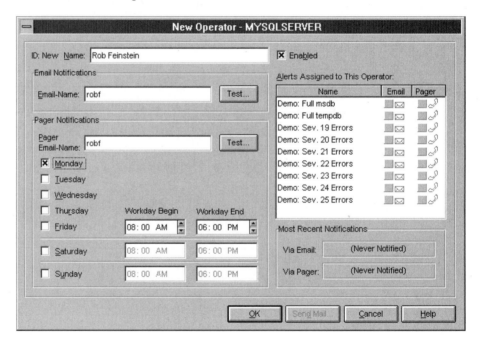

To create an operator, you must provide the following information.

| Option | Description |
| --- | --- |
| New Name | A unique name assigned to the person who is designated to receive alerts. |
| | It is useful to clear the Enabled check box if you want to create the operator now but do not want to allow the operator to receive alerts until later. Another reason to clear this box is to temporarily disable the sending of alerts to this operator (for example, if the operator will be absent on vacation). |
| Email-Name | The operator's e-mail name. Alert notification is sent to this name. |
| | The Test button sends a test e-mail message to the specified e-mail name (32-bit clients only). |
| Pager Email Name | The e-mail name designated for the pager operator. Using pager scheduling options, you can specify the days and times to use pager notification. |
| | The Test button sends a test message to the specified e-mail name (32-bit clients only). |
| Alerts Assigned to This Operator | Assign alerts to this operator. |
| | A solid envelope or solid telephone icon indicates that the alert already has a notification of that type defined on it. An outline envelope or outline telephone icon indicates that the alert does not have a notification of that type defined on it. |

If SQL Enterprise Manager is running on a 32-bit client computer (a computer where the SQL Server client utilities have been installed, but not the server software), and if the Microsoft Mail client has been started, you can use the mail integration features of SQL Enterprise Manager by clicking the Test button, and SQL Enterprise Manager attempts to resolve the entered e-mail name or (as appropriate) pager e-mail name to the closest matching *friendly* e-mail name. If there is not a close match or if the name cannot be resolved, a dialog box displays a list of possible choices.

Paging is implemented by e-mail. To support this, mail must be configured so that it is possible to send an e-mail message that results in a page being sent. E-mail interfaces to pager services are provided by many telecommunications companies, and all that is generally required is the ability to route e-mail messages (for example, using the Microsoft Mail External Mail application) to a post office at the pager provider's site. For more information, contact your telecommunications provider.

Whether you are using e-mail or pager notifications, you must be running mail on the same computer as SQL Server.

▶ **To create an alert notification operator**

In this procedure, you create an alert notification operator. You use your name for the operator, and use the e-mail name you configured when setting up SQL Mail in an earlier lesson.

1. Start SQL Enterprise Manager, and select your server.
2. On the Server menu, click Alerts/Operators, or on the toolbar, click the Manage Alerts and Operators button.
3. In the Manage Alerts and Operators window, click the Operators tab.
4. On the toolbar, click New Operator.

   The New Operator dialog box appears.

5. In the New Name box, enter your name.
6. In the Email-Name box, enter your full e-mail name.
7. Click Test to send a test e-mail message.
8. Click Yes to send the test notification.

   A Test Email-Name message appears, indicating the message was sent successfully.

9. Click OK to acknowledge the message.
10. To exit the New Operator dialog box, click OK.

    You are returned to the Manage Alerts and Operators dialog box. Notice that you are now configured as an operator.

## Editing an Operator

Once you have created an operator, you can change any of the information that defines the operator. Use the Edit Operator dialog box to edit an operator. To go to the Edit Operator dialog box, in the Manage Alerts and Operators window, click the Operators tab, and then double-click the operator name. In the Edit Operator dialog box, change any of the options configured for that operator.

## Viewing an Operator

You can determine when an operator was last notified by e-mail or pager. You can find this information in the Manage Alerts and Operators window and in the Edit Operator dialog box.

# Using Alerts

If you are going to have your alerts notify an operator, first create your operators. Then, you can create alerts. You can also view, edit, delete, or disable an alert. You can also delete or disable an operator.

## Creating an Alert

Use the New Alert dialog box to create an alert. To go to the New Alert dialog box, select a server in the Server Manager Window, click Manage Alerts and Operators on the toolbar, click the Alerts tab, and then click New Alert.

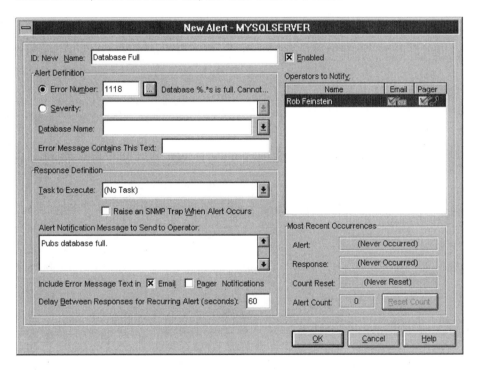

When you create an alert, you must define the conditions and the actions for the alert by providing the following information.

| Option | Description |
| --- | --- |
| New Name | The name assigned to this alert. By clearing the Enabled box, you can create the alert, but it is inactivate. |
| Enabled | Used to create an alert when this box is selected. When the box is cleared, the alert is created, but it is inactive. |
| Error Number | Specifies that an alert will occur whenever a specific error message is entered in the Windows NT application event log. |
| Severity | Specifies that an alert will occur whenever an error of a specific severity level is entered in the Windows NT application event log. |

(*continued*)

| Option | Description |
|---|---|
| Database Name | Used to narrow the alert notification criteria to a specific database. |
| Error Message Contains This Text | Alert will occur only when the error message contains a particular character string. Type the character string in the Error Message Contains String box. |
| Task to Execute | Specifies a task to execute when a qualifying alert occurs. A task can invoke an application or a Transact-SQL statement (task types CmdExec or TSQL) and can only have an "On Demand" schedule. |
| Alert Notification Message to Send to Operator | Provides additional information to the alert recipients. You can enter up to 255 characters. |
| Include Error Message Text | Includes the actual text of the error message as part of the notification message. |
| Delay Between Responses for Recurring Alerts | Sets a delay between responses for recurring alerts. For example, suppose you type 8 in this box. Later, five alerts that meet the alert definition occur within a period of eight seconds or less. Only one alert is sent to the designated operators. |
| Operators to Notify | Specifies the operators who will be notified when the defined alert occurs. For each operator, specify whether the operator will be notified by e-mail and pager. |
| | A solid envelope or solid telephone icon indicates that the operator has address information of that type defined. An outline envelope or outline telephone icon indicates that the operator does not have address information of that type defined. |
| Most Recent Occurrences | Shows the most recent occurrences of alerts. |

**Note**  An alert occurs only if the specified event is written to the Windows NT application event log. If an event occurs that matches both an alert set on an error number and an alert set on a severity, only the more specific alert (the error number alert) runs.

It is possible to create an alert that has no task or e-mail or page associated with it. In this case, an alert would be fired, an event written to the Windows NT application event log, and the occurrence of the alert would be recorded. You would do this if you only wanted to count and record occurrences of the alert, but take no immediate action.

▶ **To create an alert**

In this procedure, you create an alert named Object Not Found. This alert is based on SQL Server error number 208, and is generated for the *pubs* database.

1. In the Manage Alerts and Operators window, click the Alerts tab.
2. Click New Alert.

   The New Alert dialog box appears.
3. In the New Name box, type:

   **Object Not Found**
4. Select Error Number.
5. Click the ellipsis [...] button next to the Error Number box.

   The Manage SQL Server Messages dialog box appears.
6. In the Error Number box, type **208**
7. Click Find.
8. Click Select.

   The New Alert dialog box reappears.
9. In the Database Name box, select *pubs*.
10. In the Alert Notification Message to Send to Operator box, type:

    **test message**
11. Select the Include Error Message Text in Email check box.
12. In the Operators to Notify list, select the email check box beside your name.
13. To save the alert, click OK.

    The Alert Invocation dialog box appears.
14. When prompted to enable the error to invoke the alert, click Yes.

    The Manage Alerts and Operators window appears.

▶ **To test the alert**

In this procedure, you run a query that triggers the alert you just created. You then check the Windows NT application event log and your e-mail to verify that the alert was processed.

1. Open a SQL Query window, and use the *pubs* database.
2. Type and execute the following query:

```
select * from testobject
```

3. Open the Windows NT Event Viewer and select the application event log. Refresh the window if necessary. Does the alert appear in the event log?

4. Close the Windows NT Event Viewer.
5. Check your e-mail. Did the alert event occur?

## Viewing an Alert

You can view a list of all existing alerts, or information about a specific alert.

Use the Manage Alerts and Operators window to view an alert. This window provides the date and time the alert last occurred, along with the count of the number of times the alert has occurred. You can also find this information in the Edit Alert dialog box, which allows you to reset the alert count.

▶ **To view an alert**

In this procedure, you use the Edit Alert dialog box to determine the most recent occurrence of an alert.

1. Using SQL Enterprise Manager, access the Managing Alerts and Operators dialog box.
2. Update the window.
3. Double-click the alert Object Not Found.
4. What was the Most Recent Occurrence of this alert?

## Editing an Alert

Once you have created an alert, you can change any of the information that defines the alert. You use the Edit Alert dialog box to edit an alert. To get to the Edit Alert dialog box, in the Manage Alerts and Operators window, click the Alert tab, and then double-click the alert name, or you can click Edit Alert. You can then change any of the options configured for that alert.

## Deleting or Disabling an Alert

If an alert is no longer applicable, you delete or disable the alert, which inactivates the alert but preserves the alert information. You use the Manage Alerts and Operators window to delete or disable an alert. To delete or disable an alert, click the Alerts tab, and then do one of the following:

- To delete the alert, select the alert name and click Delete Alert.
- To disable an alert, double-click the alert name to open the Edit Alert dialog box and clear the Enable option.

### Deleting or Disabling an Operator

If an operator is no longer applicable, you can delete it. Or you can disable an operator, which inactivates the operator but preserves the operator information. Use the Manage Alerts and Operators window to delete or disable an operator. To delete or disable an operator, click the Operators tab and perform one of the following:

- To delete an operator, select the operator name, and then click Delete Operator.
- To disable an operator, double-click the operator name to open the Edit Operator dialog box, and then clear the Enable option.

## Setting Alert Engine Options

The Alert Engine Options feature enables you to do the following:

- Designate an operator to be notified when all pager notifications for an alert fail.
- Specify a server to whose Event (application) log any unhandled SQL Server events will be sent.
- Restrict the events forwarded to those of a specified severity or above.
- Format the To Line, CC Line, and Subject of pager e-mail messages.

Before the Alert Engine can function, you must set the options you require. To set options, use the Alert Engine Options dialog box. To go to the Alert Engine Options dialog box, in the Manage Alerts and Operators window click the Alerts tab, and then click Alert Engine Options.

On the Fail-Safe tab, designate the operator to notify and whether to notify that person by e-mail or pager notification. You also designate the server to forward events to, and the level of severity to forward events to.

| Field | Description |
|---|---|
| Operator to Notify | The operator who is notified when all pager notifications for an alert fail. Reasons for such a failure can include, but are not limited to, incorrect pager addresses, a problem with the mail system, or a *hole* in the pager schedules of the intended page recipients. |
| Server to Forward Events to | The remote server whose event log will receive any unhandled SQL Server events on the local server (events for which there are no locally defined alerts). |
| Forward Events for Errors with Severity of or Above | Restrict the events that are forwarded to the unhandled SQL Server event forwarding server to those of or above a the selected severity level. |

On the Pager Email tab, you create the template that is used for the To Line, CC Line, and Subject of a pager e-mail message.

Enter prefixes and suffixes as required. For the To and CC lines, select the Pager-Address option if an operator's actual pager address should be inserted after the prefix and before the suffix. When a message is constructed, the prefix is added to the beginning of the Pager Address, and the suffix is appended. If a Pager Address option is not selected, the prefix and suffix (if one is provided) are simply combined.

These entries allow you accomplish special addressing by creating a template that is used for the To, CC, and Subject lines of a pager email message. Special addressing of the pager email message might be required in order to integrate with a pager service provider's e-mail system.

A notification (for both pages and e-mail messages) consists of lines of text. To prevent the notification for a single alert from being split over multiple pages, select the option Include Body of Email in Notification Page. For pager notifications (that is, a notification page) where hardware character buffers are at a premium, it is preferrable to limit the amount of text sent. When this option in cleared, only the subject line is sent (and therefore there is much less text in the notification page).

## Managing Messages

You can manage messages that you establish when you create or edit an alert. While managing alerts, you can:

- View a list of available messages, and select one to set an alert on.
- Search for messages by message text, severity, and error number, and by only those that are always written to the Windows NT application event log.
- Select an option to always write the message to the Windows NT application event log.
- Create and edit user-defined messages.

Use the Manage SQL Server Messages dialog box to manage messages. To go to the Manage SQL Server Messages dialog box, click Messages on the Server menu. You can also get this dialog box while creating or editing an alert by selecting an Error Number option and then clicking the ellipse (...) button.

In order to view all available messages, clear all of the boxes, and then click Find. To view a subset of all available messages, complete the appropriate boxes, and then click Find.

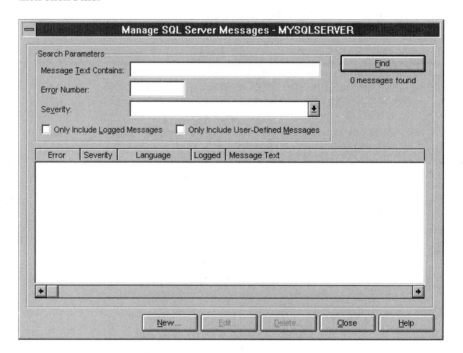

To control the messages that will be searched for, you can select from the following options:

| Field | Description |
| --- | --- |
| Message Text Contains | Searches for all messages that contain the text that is entered in this box. |
| Error Number | Searches for a message having the error number entered in this box. |
| Severity | Searches for messages of the selected severity level. |

(*continued*)

| Field | Description |
|-------|-------------|
| Only Include Logged Messages | Restricts the list to only those SQL Server messages that are always written to the Windows NT application event log. |
| | If the Only Include User-Defined Messages option is cleared, this list includes all system messages with severity levels 19 through 25, plus all user-defined messages that are configured to be written to the log. |
| | If the Only Include User-Defined Messages option is also selected, this list includes only user-defined messages that are configured to always be written to the log. |
| Only Include User-Defined Messages | Restricts the list to user-defined messages. If this option is cleared, the list includes system and user-defined messages. |

If you want to sort the list by a column attribute, click that column (Error, Severity, Language, Logged, or Message Text). This sorting option is not available if the list contains more than 750 rows. The default sort is by error number.

## How SQL Server Processes Alerts

The SQL Executive service starts up and registers itself as a callback application for the Windows NT EventLog service. The SQL Executive service connects to the SQL Server (by DB-Library) and reads the *sysalerts* table in the *msdb* database.

The following figure and text describe the steps involved in managing events, alerts, and tasks.

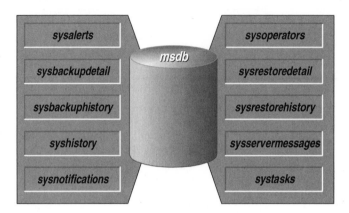

1. When an event occurs, the SQL Server records the error information in the Windows NT event log using **xp_logevent** or RAISERROR.

2. When an error is recorded in the Windows NT event log, the SQL Executive is notified that an error originating from the SQL Server has occurred. The SQL Executive retrieves the error information from the Windows NT event log.

3. To determine if any alerts and tasks are defined for this event, the SQL Executive scans the *sysalerts* table, matching the Windows NT event log to the *sysalerts* table. This match is based upon the following:

| Windows NT event log | MSDB..sysalerts |
| --- | --- |
| Event Source | sysalerts.Event_Source |
| Event Description | sysalerts.Message_ID |
| Event Description | sysalerts.Severity |

**Note**  The Event Source and the Event Description information in the Windows NT event log must match *sysalerts.event_source* and either *message_id* or *severity* information. If *sysalerts.message_id* or *sysalerts.severity* are defined, then compare them as follows: If *sysalerts.message_id* is defined, compare it with Event Description; if they match, invoke alert. If *sysalerts.severity* is defined, compare it with Event Description; if they match, invoke alert.

4. If a matching alert is found, a defined action takes place—either an e-mail message or a pager notification is sent.

   Alert handling can be invoked by either of the following methods:

   - E-mail sent to all specified operators (**xp_sendmail**).
   - Pager notification to all specified operators on duty; if all pager notifications for an alert fail, such as when no operators are on duty, send a pager notification to the pager-fail-safe-operator.

   On duty is determined in the *sysoperators* table by the various pager start and end times and page days.

   If there are no locally defined alerts enabled for this event, the event can be forwarded to the specified event forwarding server for processing.

5. Action handling is completed by the associated task if defined in *sysalerst.task_id*. The SQL Executive calls the appropriate subsystem (Transact-SQL or Windows NT command) with the task information. Then normal SQL Executive processing occurs and the *syshistory* table is updated with the status of the task.

   Record the date when the alert occurred in the sysalerts table.

**Note**  For a demonstration of how SQL Server processes alerts are processed, see SQLMOD4.EXE in \DEMO on the compact disc.

## Troubleshooting Alerts

Under conditions of rapidly occurring alerts, the delay between the event appearing in the Windows NT application event log and the response by SQL Executive may increase (ordinarily, it is only a few seconds). This can occur because the alerts engine has a top response speed governed by its architecture—SQL Executive competes with SQL Server for process bandwidth, and is designed to be economical with threads.

The rate at which SQL Executive can process alerts also depends on the complexity of the alert response—that is, the number of notifications. It is a good idea to send notifications to as few operators as possible. One technique is to send notifications to one group of e-mail address rather than notifying several individual operators.

If the rate of alert occurrence exceeds the rate at which SQL Executive can process alerts, a backlog of alerts will develop. If backlogs develop, you should increase the value for the Delay Between Responses for Recurring Alerts option for each alert.

If an alert is not firing, answer these questions:

- Is the SQL Executive service running?
- Does the event appear in the Windows NT application event log?
- Is the alert enabled?
- Are the alert's Last Occurred and Count values changing?

    If the alert's Last Occurred and Count values are changing, then that alert is occurring but there may be a problem with the response firing. If you have defined e-mail or pager notifications to occur, test the e-mail or pager addresses of the assigned operators by using the Test button (next to the address boxes in the Edit Operators dialog box). If a pager notification is not being received, check that the operator's pager notification schedule is set for the necessary days and hours.

## Lesson Summary

In this lesson you learned how to use the Manage Alerts and Operators window to create, modify, and view operators and alerts. Once you have created operators and alerts, you can use the Alert Engine Options dialog box to designate a fail-safe operator who will be notified when all pager notifications for an alert fail, specify a server to whose event log any undhandled SQL Server events will be sent, restrict the events forwarded to those of a specified severity or above, and format pager e-mail messages. You can use the Manage SQL Server Messages dialog box to manage messages that you establish when you create or edit an alert. You also learned how SQL Server processes alerts and how to troubleshoot problems.

| For more information on | See |
|---|---|
| Managing alerts | "Managing Alerts" in SQL Server Books Online |
| Alerts management interface | "Alerts Management" in SQL Server Books Online |
| Alert system troubleshooting | "Tips and Troubleshooting" and "Alert System Troubleshooting" in SQL Server Books Online |
| Setting alerts | The C18_PRI.TXT file located in \SCRIPTS\C18_TASK\ on the compact disc |

# Lesson 6: Using an Alerts Management Server

An alerts management server allows SQL Server events to be forwarded to a central location for processing and administration.

## After this lesson you will be able to:

- Describe the advantages and disadvantages of configuring event forwarding.
- Demonstrate how to configure event forwarding.

## Estimated lesson time  10 minutes

## Forwarding Events

Event forwarding allows SQL Server events to be forwarded to another SQL server—called the alerts management server—for processing instead of being processed locally. Event forwarding enables central management of alerts and allows the development of alerts neighborhoods, which are groups of servers that share a common alerts management server.

Some advantages of setting up an alerts management server are the following:

- Offers centralized control—Centralized control and a consolidated view of the events of several SQL Servers is possible from a single server.
- Scaleable—Allows a variable number of physical servers to be administered as one logical server.
- Efficient—/Configuration time is reduced because you only need to define alerts and operators once, at one server.

Some disadvantages of setting up an alerts management server are the following:

- Increases traffic—Forwarding events to an alerts management server can increase network traffic, although this can be moderated by restricting event forwarding to only higher severity events.
- Can lead to a single point of failure—The alerts management server is a potential single point of failure.
- Increases server load—Handling alerts for the forwarded events causes an increased processing load at the alerts management server.

## Considerations for Configuring Event Forwarding

When you configure event forwarding, follow these guidelines:

- Avoid running critical or heavily used applications on the alerts management server.

- Avoid configuring large numbers of servers to share the same alerts management server. If congestion results, reduce the number of servers using a particular alerts management server.

- Define server-specific alerts on the local server, instead of forwarding them.

- Failure conditions encountered by the alerts engine—for example, an inability to send an e-mail notification—are written to the local Windows NT application event log with a source name of SQL Executive. Therefore, after configuring your alert system, periodically check the Windows NT application event log for SQL Executive events.

## Configuring Event Forwarding

If you want to use event forwarding, you must first configure all servers:

- On each server that is to forward events, you need to do the following:
  - Set up unhandled event forwarding
  - Check that alerts are not defined on the events to be forwarded
- On the Alerts Management Server, you need to set alerts on events that you expect to be forwarded.

To configure event forwarding, provide the following information:

- On each server that is to forward events, set up unhandled event forwarding.
  - In the Alerts Engine Option dialog box, click the Fail-Safe tab, and then in the Server To Forward Events To box, select a server. This becomes the alerts management server.
  - In the same dialog box, select a severity level from the list in the Forward Events For Errors With Severity Of Or Above box. Unhandled alerts of a level equal to or greater than this severity will be forwarded to the alerts management server.

- On each server that is to forward events, check that alerts are not defined on the events to be forwarded or, if alerts are set, they are disabled.

If a locally defined alert is disabled and an event occurs that would have caused the alert to fire, the event will be forwarded to the alerts management server. This allows local overrides—that is, alerts defined locally that are also defined at the alerts management server—to be turned off and on as needed.

---

**Important**  Only unhandled events are forwarded, and only those of a severity equal to or greater than the setting in the Fail-Safe tab of the Alerts Engine Option dialog box. An unhandled event is one for which there is no enabled, locally defined alert.

---

- On the alerts management server, set alerts on the events that are expected to be forwarded.

## Lesson Summary

You can forward SQL Server events to another SQL server—the alerts management server—for processing instead of having them processed locally. In this lesson you learned about guidelines for configuring event forwarding, and how to configure event forwarding.

| For more information on | See |
| --- | --- |
| Setting alerts on forwarded events | "Setting Alerts on Forwarded Events" in SQL Server Books Online |

# Review

The following questions are intended to reinforce key information presented in this chapter. If you are unable to answer a question, review the lesson and then try the question again.

1. To use SQL Mail for alerting an operator of an event, under what account must the MSSQLServer service run?

2. If a Windows NT Mail post office share is on an NTFS drive, what requires permissions?

3. If the post office is on a computer running Windows NT Server 3.5*x*, and if the MSSQLServer service on a separate Mail client computer runs under the LocalSystem account, what must you do to ensure the post office share can be accessed?

4. If the Windows NT Mail password is changed, what other Mail password must be changed?

5. Where must an event be written before an alert will fire?

6. In what situation is it beneficial to use an alerts management server?

# Questions and Answers

Page 785

▶ **To view the scheduled tasks**

2. What tasks are currently scheduled to run?

**Dump Pubs Database.**

Page 788

▶ **To view a task history**

4. What information does the Task History window provide?

**Date and time when the task was run, the result, the operator that was sent e-mail, the run duration, and the last error/message resulting.**

Page 790

▶ **To create a weekly maintenance task using the Database Maintenance Plan Wizard**

16. Access the Manage Scheduled Tasks window.

Notice a new task has been created, Master Weekly Automated Maintenance.

What type of task did the Database Maintenance Plan Wizard create?

**CmdExec**

17. Click the Master Weekly Automated Maintenance task, and then click Edit Task.

What application runs when this task runs?

**SQLMAINT.EXE**

19. Run the Master Weekly Automated Maintenance task now.

Was the task successful? How do you know?

**Yes. The Task History shows a successful result, and the Event Viewer shows the master database was successfully dumped.**

Page 799

▶ **To test the alert**

3. Open the Windows NT Event Viewer and select the application event log. Refresh the window if necessary. Does the alert appear in the event log?

**Yes.**

5. Check your e-mail. Did the alert event occur?

**Yes.**

Page 813

## Review Questions

1. To use SQL Mail for alerting an operator of an event, under what account must the MSSQLServer service run?

   **The LocalSystem account. This account must be configured with the Allow Service To Interact With Desktop option selected in the Control Panel Services application.**

2. If a Windows NT Mail post office share is on an NTFS drive, what requires permissions?

   **Permissions must be set for both the network share and the file system.**

3. If the post office is on a computer running Windows NT Server 3.5x, and if the MSSQLServer service on a separate Mail client computer runs under the LocalSystem account, what must you do to ensure the post office share can be accessed?

   **Add the post office share to the list of shares in the Registry.**

4. If the Windows NT Mail password is changed, what other Mail password must be changed?

   **The SQL Mail login password.**

5. Where must an event be written before an alert will fire?

   **The Windows NT application event log.**

6. In what situation is it beneficial to use an alerts management server?

   **When there are multiple physical servers that you want to manage from a central location.**

C H A P T E R   1 9

# Tools for Monitoring and Tuning SQL Server Performance

## About This Chapter

For your server to perform well, it must be able to provide acceptable response times for each query, and to be able to maximize throughput for all users. If the response times or the throughput are not acceptable, you must monitor SQL Server and Microsoft Windows NT to see if there are any bottlenecks affecting the performance. If you find a bottleneck, you must tune your system to resolve it. Then you must run your system to verify that you did not uncover another unacceptable bottleneck.

This chapter introduces you to measuring, troubleshooting, and tuning your server's performance: why you should measure and tune SQL Server's performance, how to establish a baseline, the tools you will use to monitor and tune your server's performance, and how to use those tools to monitor and tune your server's performance. This chapter is not intended to provide you with the extensive detail necessary to optimize all aspects of SQL Server.

## Before You Begin

To complete the lessons in this chapter you must have:

- Experience using the SQL Enterprise Manager, the SQL Enterprise Manager Query Tool, and ISQL/w.

- Knowledge of basic SQL Server and programming concepts.

- Experience using Windows NT Server Performance Monitor.

- Completed Chapter 18, "Using SQL Mail, Scheduling Tasks, and Managing Alerts."

- Set up SQL Mail.

- Confirmed that the *library* database exists. If you must create the *library* database, execute the \SCRIPTS\BLD_LIB\BLDLIB.CMD file located on the compact disc.

# Lesson 1: Measuring Performance

Before you can tune SQL Server, you must understand the primary performance goals of the server and the factors that affect SQL Server performance. You must be able to measure SQL Server performance to identify any bottlenecks contributing to unacceptable performance. To effectively measure performance, you must establish a baseline for SQL Server. This lesson describes SQL Server performance goals, factors that affect performance, methods for establishing a baseline, and tools that you can use to establish a baseline.

---

### After this lesson you will be able to:

- Describe performance goals for SQL Server.

- Identify factors that affect SQL Server performance.

- Describe how to establish a baseline.

- Describe the tools used to establish a baseline.

### Estimated lesson time  10 minutes

---

## Performance Goals

When you define SQL Server performance goals, you consider two factors: throughput and response time for queries.

### Throughput

Throughput is the number of queries that can be handled by the server during a given time frame, along with the number and size of the rows that are returned to the client. SQL Server must maximize throughput by balancing resources among users.

### Response Time for Queries

Response time is the length of time required for the first row of the results set to be returned. Response time is often referred to as the *perceived time* for the user to receive visual affirmation that a query is being processed.

SQL Server must provide acceptable response time per query by doing the following:

- Minimizing network traffic

- Reducing disk I/O

- Minimizing processor time

As the number of users increases, contention for server resources increases, which can cause overall throughput to decrease and response time to increase.

# Factors That Affect Performance

Performance can be measured by the amount of I/O required to process a transaction, the amount of processor effort, and the response time. Performance varies relative to each specific environment and is dependent on the client application, the architecture and resources, the server, and the concurrent activities. You can assess each of these areas to determine where the greatest impact to performance occurs, and then tune SQL Server accordingly.

## Client Application

The client application is typically where most of the performance issues are created and resolved. These problems often appear to exist in SQL Server, but they are more often generated by the client application. SQL Server is controlled by the client application. Below is a list of general items to be considered when looking at an application:

- User requirements
- Logical and physical design
- Efficiency of user code
  - Transaction management
  - Cursor management
  - Lock usage
- Mixing decision support and on-line transaction processing (OLTP) in the server environment

## Architecture/Resources

SQL Server must work within the confines of the hardware on which it is installed. The following resources should be considered potential bottlenecks:

- Processor efficiency
- Memory, disk, and I/O throughput
- Network efficiency
- Logging
- Multiprocessing

### SQL Server (Database Management System)

Bottlenecks are not always caused by hardware—the following SQL Server components can also create problems:

- Configuration
- Query optimizer
- Lock management
- Logging
- Data distribution (devices)

### Concurrent Activities

Even if your SQL Server is optimally tuned, response time and throughput may suffer if the server computer is also performing other functions. The following activities, if performed concurrently with SQL Server production applications, can adversely impact performance.

- Maintenance/administrative activities
- Backing up/loading data
- Index creation
- Other activities on the SQL Server computer, such as screen savers, file and print sharing, and gateway services

## Establishing a Baseline for Measuring Performance

To be able to effectively manage the performance of SQL Server, you need to establish a baseline to enable you to compare the way the system is currently running to the way it runs after any changes are made.

To establish a baseline, you must determine the overall size of your database and tables, and determine the row size and number of rows per page for your database tables. You can use the **sp_spaceused** system stored procedure to determine the overall size of your database and tables, and you can use the formulas in this lesson to determine row size and number of rows per page for your database tables.

### The sp_spaceused System Stored Procedure

The **sp_spaceused** system stored procedure displays the disk space reserved, the index size, and the unused portion of the database. If a table name is specified, **sp_spaceused** also displays how many rows are in the table. If no table name (*objname*) is given, **sp_spaceused** reports on the space used by the entire current database.

**Syntax**

**sp_spaceused** [*objname*] [[**,**] @updateusage = {**true** | **false**}]

A limitation of **sp_spaceused** is that after you drop an index, it reports inaccurate information. However, **sp_spaceused** provides a quick, rough estimate of space used. If you notice incorrect values when you execute **sp_spaceused**, use the **@updateusage** option to report and correct inaccuracies in the *sysindexes* table. The **@updateusage** option executes the DBCC UPDATEUSAGE statement.

---

**Note** sp_spaceused is always performed in the current database. If you specify an (*objname*), only that object and its associated indexes will be updated.

---

Because **sp_spaceused** with the **@updateusage** option takes some time to execute on large tables or databases, use it only when you suspect incorrect values are being returned or when other users are not active.

Using the **@updateusage** option corrects the *used*, *reserved*, and *dpages* columns of the *sysindexes* table for any clustered indexes on objects of the type U (user-defined table) or S (system table). Size information is not maintained for nonclustered indexes. You can use this statement to synchronize space usage counters in *sysindexes*, which will result in accurate usage information being returned.

**sp_spaceused** was designed to compute a relatively accurate estimate of space. It requires a shared table lock on the table being processed so that it can access every row in the table.

## Estimating Rows per Page

The row is the smallest unit of measurement used when determining the I/O overhead for a query. Rows are stored on data pages. The larger the row, the fewer rows that are stored on a data page; the smaller the row, the more that are stored on a data page. It is important to know the size of a row for each table in your database.

For example, if *Table_1* has a row size of 400 bytes; based on this size, 5 rows fit on a 2K data page (2,016 bytes per page/400 bytes per row). If *Table_2* has a row size of only 80 bytes, 25 rows fit on a 2K data page (2,016 bytes per page/80 bytes per row).

If a query is executed against *Table_1*, and it returns 100 rows, you will access 20 pages (100 rows/5 rows per page). Each page accessed equals an I/O hit. In this example, this query costs 20 I/O to process.

If a query is executed against *Table_2*, and it returns 100 rows, you will access 4 pages (100 rows/25 rows per page). The cost of this query is only 5 I/O to process.

As the following example shows, the I/O overhead of a query varies significantly depending on the number of rows processed, which is directly impacted by row size and how many rows fit per page.

To estimate the row size, use the following formula:

Fixed row overhead (4 bytes)

+ Sum of bytes in all columns

+ Number of variable-length columns

= Row size

In the preceding formula, every row is estimated to have 4 bytes of fixed overhead. There is additional overhead for columns that are of variable-length. A column is considered to be variable-length if it allows NULLs, or when defined with a *varbinary* or *varchar* datatype.

The preceding formula is reasonably accurate, but cannot be completely accurate given the presence of variable-length columns in a table. The defined length of variable-length columns and the amount of data contained in the columns varies widely in every database. For example, the storage requirements of a column defined as *varchar*(255) are determined by the amount of data stored in that field. If the field contains 20 characters, then the size of the column is 20 bytes, not 255. Because of variable-length columns, it is almost impossible to determine exact row size in a database.

**Example**

Assume you are working with a 10,000 row table, and a query that returns a results set of 200 rows. This is your table definition:

```
CREATE TABLE TABLE_1
    (
    column_1 int          NOT NULL,    -- integer is 4 bytes
    column_2 char(255)    NULL,
    column_3 varchar(85)  NOT NULL,
    column_4 char(40)     NOT NULL,
    column_5 char(10)     NOT NULL
    )
```

The table's row size is 400 bytes.

| | |
|---|---|
| Fixed row overhead | 4 bytes |
| + Sum of bytes in all columns | 4 + 255 + 85 + 40 + 10 = 394 |
| + Number of variable-length columns | 2 (*column_2* and *column_3*) |
| = Row size | 400 |

Therefore:

- The table has 5 rows per page (2,016 bytes per page/400 bytes per row).
- The total number of pages in the table is 2,000
  (10,000 rows/5 rows per page).
- The I/O needed to retrieve these rows is 40 pages
  (200 rows per results set/5 rows per page).

▶  **To calculate row size and I/O requirements**

In this procedure, you calculate row size and I/O requirements for a table. Note that the assumptions for the table have been changed.

1. Assume your table has 10,000 rows and that your query returns a results set of 150 rows. This is your table definition:

```
CREATE TABLE TABLE_2
    (
    column_1 int          NOT NULL,
    column_2 char(25)      NOT NULL,
    column_3 varchar(46)   NOT NULL
    )
```

2. Calculate the row size and I/O.

   What is the sum of bytes for all columns?

   _____

   What is the number of columns that allow NULL or are variable-length?

   _____

   What is the row size?

   _____

   $4 + (\rule{1cm}{0.15mm}) + (\rule{1cm}{0.15mm}) = \rule{1.5cm}{0.15mm}$

3. Calculate the missing information.

Number of rows per page in the database.

Total number of pages in the table.

I/O to retrieve expected 150 rows?

## Lesson Summary

To be able to tune SQL Server, you must understand SQL Server and know what your performance goals are. You must also understand the four factors that affect performance: the client application, architecture/resources, SQL Server (database management system), and concurrent activities. Once you understand SQL Server, your performance goals, and factors that affect SQL Server performance, you need to gather information about SQL Server so that you can establish a baseline that you can use to measure SQL Server performance. To establish a baseline, you use **sp_spaceused** to determine the overall size of your database and tables, and you use the formulas presented in this lesson to determine the row size and the number of rows per page for your database tables.

| For more information on | See |
| --- | --- |
| The **sp_spaceused** system stored procedure | "sp_spaceused" in SQL Server Books Online |

# Lesson 2: Tools for Measuring Performance

SQL Server provides numerous tools you can use to measure SQL Server performance. These tools enable you to conduct a general or detailed evaluation of SQL Server performance You can use the following tools to gather information about SQL Server activity: SQL Performance Monitor, SQL Trace, some DBCC statements, some SET statements, and SQL Server processes and locks.

## After this lesson you will be able to:

- Describe which Performance Monitor objects and counters can be used to measure performance.
- Describe the SQL Trace utility.
- Explain how SQL Server locking can impact performance.
- Identify DBCC statement options that can be used to measure performance.
- Identify SET statement options that can be useful in measuring performance.

## Estimated lesson time  60 minutes

## The Windows NT and SQL Performance Monitors

The Windows NT Performance Monitor is a graphical tool that you can use to measure the performance of one computer or a network of computers. It provides real-time charting, alerting, and reporting capabilities that reflect current activity and ongoing logging. You can open, browse, and chart log files at a later time.

The SQL Performance Monitor adds a set of counters to the Windows NT Performance Monitor that make it possible for you to get up-to-the-minute activity and performance statistics about SQL Server.

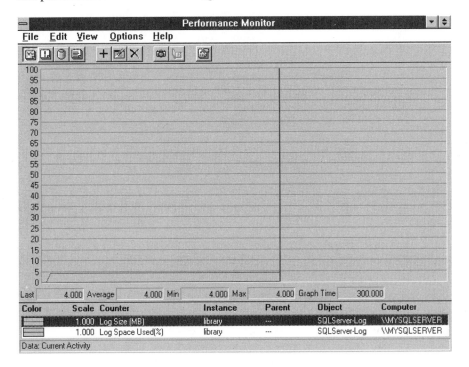

## Performance Objects and Counters

When you install SQL Server, the **setup** program automatically provides SQL Performance Monitor with eight performance objects and associated counters.

---

**Note**  When referring to objects and counters, the notation Object:Counter is used; for example, SQLServer:Cache Hit Ratio.

---

The SQL Server and Windows NT counters that you can use to measure performance can be found in the following objects: SQLServer, SQLServer-Log, SQLServer-Procedure Cache, Processor, Process, Paging File, and Memory.

### The SQLServer Object

The SQLServer object contains counters that pertain to the SQL Server service; these counters are Cache Hit Ratio, User Connections, and Max Tempdb Space Used (MB).

Cache Hit Ratio counter—Displays the percentage of time that data satisfying a query was found in the data cache, instead of being read from disk. Because reading from the cache is much faster than reading from disk, this ratio should be high. Generally, you can increase the cache hit ratio by increasing the amount of memory reserved for the data cache using the **sp_configure** system stored procedure's **memory** parameter. Some transactions can cause the cache hit ratio to be "artificially" high (80–90 percent). For example, in the course of certain transactions, a page might be requested several times, creating the possibility that, after the first request, all requests would be satisfied by the data cache.

User Connections counter—Displays the number of active user connections that are currently connected to the SQL Server. If this counter is nearing your maximum configured user connections, and you anticipate additional connections, you can increase the maximum user connections using the **user connections** parameter of **sp_configure**.

Max Tempdb Space Used (MB) counter—Displays the maximum number of MB used in the temporary database *tempdb*. Monitor Space Used (MB) to determine if you must increase the size of the *tempdb*.

### SQLServer-Log Object

The SQLServer-Log object includes counters that provide statistics for SQL Server transaction logs for the specified database: Log Size (MB) and Log Space Used (%).

Log Size (MB) counter—Displays the size of the transaction log for a given database.

Log Space Used (%) counter—Displays the percentage of the transaction log that is full. When the log is full, transactions that require logging are rejected.

### SQLServer-Procedure Cache Object

The procedure cache holds plans and trees for stored procedures, and other information for views, triggers, rules, and defaults. Each entry in the procedure cache points to one or more buffers in the procedure buffer. The procedure buffer is where the procedure instructions are stored.

Counters related to the procedure cache include: Procedure Cache Active %, Max Procedure Cache Used %, Procedure Cache Used %, and Procedure Cache Size.

Procedure Cache Active % counter—Displays the percentage of the procedure cache that is currently active. When the procedure that is associated with a procedure cache entry is currently executing, the procedure cache entry is said to be active.

Max Procedure Cache Used % counter—Displays the maximum percentage of procedure cache that has been used during the monitoring session. A procedure cache entry is considered used when it is currently allocated. A used procedure cache entry is or is not active.

Procedure Cache Used % counter—Displays the percentage of procedure cache that is currently occupied (but not necessarily active). This number indicates the percentage of slots that are currently associated with any object that uses the cache. If Procedure Cache Used % is high during normal operations, the procedure cache may not be large enough to handle additional users or new procedures.

Procedure Cache Size counter—Specifies the size, in 2K pages, of the procedure cache. The size of the procedure cache can fluctuate depending on the activity of other SQL Server processes that might require procedure cache slots.

### The Processor and Process Objects

The Processor and Process objects contain counters that allow you to monitor the percentage of processor time that is being used for each processor, and for the SQL Server process. The Processor: %Processor Time counter displays the percentage of your processor utilized by all of the processes on your computer. The Process:%Processor Time counter for the SQLServer instance displays the percentage of the processing time being used by the SQL Server service. If your total processor utilization is high, but the processor utilization due to the SQL Server process is low, then a bottleneck might be due to all of the other things your computer is doing that are unrelated to SQL Server. If that is the case, move some of the non-SQL Server processes to another computer.

If the processor utilization of SQL Server is high, then upgrade your processor, add multiple processors to your SQL Server computer, or distribute your databases among different SQL servers.

## Using Performance Object Counters

You can use performance object counters to tune your computer. For example, you can use the Windows NT counters Memory:Pages/sec and Logical Disk:Avg. Disk sec/Transfer to determine whether the level of Windows NT paging on your computer is appropriate. If Windows NT paging is occurring, your computer is spending time reading information from disk. Paging is excessive if the percentage of disk access time used by paging exceeds 10 percent on a sustained basis. If paging is excessive, your computer needs more memory. Use the following formula to determine if paging is excessive:

```
Memory:Pages/sec * Logical Disk:Avg. Disk sec/Transfer
```

(Where the Logical Disk instance is the disk that contains the PAGEFILE.SYS file.)

**Example**    `24.8 * .013 = .322`

If you detect excessive paging, determine your computer's additional memory needs by monitoring the Process:Working Set counter for each active process in the system. For more information, see the *Windows NT Resource Guide*.

---

**Note**  You must enable monitoring of disk counters to monitor logical or physical disk counters. From a command prompt, execute the following command and then restart your computer: **diskperf -y**

---

## Generating Performance Monitor Alerts

When you are running SQL Performance Monitor you can also use the alerter utility (**sqlalrtr.exe**) to notify you when an event threshold has been reached. If you also create a SQL Server alert for the threshold event and associate a task with the alert, the task will be performed automatically when the threshold is reached.

To generate a SQL Server alert at the same time you generate the Performance Monitor alert, do the following:

1.  Set a SQL Performance Monitor alert on a SQL Server counter, configuring it to run **sqlalrtr.exe** when the alert threshold is reached. **sqlalrtr.exe** loads a specific error message into the Windows NT event log.

2.  Use SQL Enterprise Manager to define an alert on the error message generated by **sqlalrtr.exe**. The SQL Executive reads the error message in the Windows NT event log, and fires a SQL Server alert. If you create and associate a task with the SQL Server alert, the task will run.

For example, you can set a SQL Performance Monitor alert based on a SQLServer:Log Space Used (%) counter threshold, and then start a task that backs up the transaction log.

The following figure illustrates the use the Add to Alert dialog box, used to add an alert in SQL Performance Monitor.

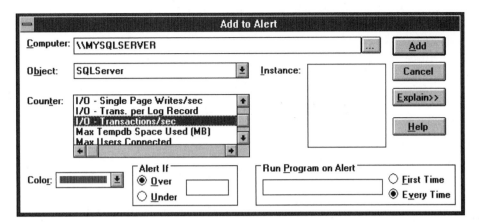

In the following procedures, you configure a SQL Performance Monitor counter and then set a SQL Performance Monitor alert on that counter's threshold event. You then define a SQL Server alert on the threshold event, create a task, and associate the task with the SQL Server alert.

▶  **To configure a SQL Performance Monitor counter**

In this procedure, you add the SQLServer-Log:Log Space Used(%) counter on the *library* database to a Performance Monitor chart. This enables you to monitor the percentage of the log space that has been used.

1.  Start SQL Performance Monitor.

2.  On the File menu, click New Chart.

3.  On the toolbar, click the Add Counter button.

    The Add to Chart dialog box appears.

4.  Verify that your computer name is displayed in the Computer box, and then in the Object box, select SQLServer-Log.

5.  In the Counter box, click Log Size (MB), and then in the Instance box, click Library.

6.  Click Add.

7.  In the Counter box, click Log Space Used (%), and then in the Instance box, click Library.

8.  Click Add.

9.  Click Done to close the Add to Chart dialog box.

10. Highlight the Log Size (MB) counter in the lower half of your screen to display the list of added counters.

11. Find the last size of the *library* transaction log using the counter information bar located in the middle of your screen. It is between the charting window (upper screen) and the list of added counters (lower screen).

---

12. Highlight the Log Space Used (%) counter, and then using the counter information bar, note the Last percentage of log space used.

---

**Note** If your log space is over 50 percent used, you must truncate the *library* transaction log to perform the following procedure.

---

▶  **To configure a SQL Performance Monitor alert**

In this procedure, you add an alert in SQL Performance Monitor that activates when the *library* log is more that 50 percent full.

1. On the toolbar, click the View the Alerts button.

2. On the toolbar, click the Add Counter button.

   The Add to Alert dialog box appears.

3. Verify that your computer name is displayed in the Computer box.

4. In the Object box, select SQLServer-Log.

5. In the Counter box, click Log Space Used (%), and then in the Instance box, click Library.

6. Under Alert If, click Over, and then type **50** in the text box.

7. In Run Program on Alert box, type the following:

   **SQLALRTR.EXE -E 1105 -M 30,'syslogs',30,'Library',15,**
   
   **'logsegment' -D Library**

8. Click Add, and then click Done.

   The Alert is added.

9. On the toolbar, click the Options button.

   The Alert Options dialog box appears.

10. Select the Switch to Alert View check box, and then under Update Time, change the Periodic Update Interval to 10 seconds.

11. Click OK.

▶ **To test the SQL Performance Monitor alert**

In this procedure, you use the alert created in the previous procedure to monitor the log space used. When the log space used exceeds 50 percent, the alert will be activated.

1. On the toolbar, click View a Chart.

2. Switch to ISQL/w and execute the FILL_LOG.SQL script file one or more times.

   This file executes an UPDATE statement that causes excess logging to occur. Depending on how full your *library* database log is, you may need to run this file one to three times.

3. Switch to SQL Performance Monitor.

   Check to see how close you are to reaching the 50% log space used marker. Once the log space used exceeds 50 percent, the SQL Performance Monitor alert activates.

4. Once the alert activates, open the Windows NT Event Viewer and view the Application log for the SQLServer error message number 1105.

5. Switch to ISQL/w and execute the DUMP_LOG.SQL script file to back up the *library* log.

Although the alert you created in Performance Monitor is useful, if you do not associate it with a SQL Server alert, you must manually check the Windows NT event log to determine whether an error has occurred. To associate the Performance Monitor alert with SQL Server, create a SQL Server alert task to back up the library transaction, and create a mail message notification to an operator.

▶ **To create an operator and a task to back up the *library* transaction log**

This procedure requires that SQL Mail be set up on your computer. If mail is not set up on your computer, see Chapter 18, "Using SQL Mail, Scheduling Tasks, and Managing Alerts," for instructions on how to set up SQL Mail.

1. Switch to SQL Enterprise Manager.

2. Create an operator that has an SQL Mail mailbox, if one does not already exist.

3. On the toolbar, click the Manage Scheduled Tasks button.

   The Manage Scheduled Tasks window appears.

4. On the Manage Scheduled Tasks window toolbar, click the New Task button.

5. In the New Task dialog box, create a task by providing the following information.

| Property | Value |
| --- | --- |
| Name | Backup Library |
| Type | TSQL |
| Database | Library |
| Command | DUMP TRAN library WITH NO_LOG |
| Schedule | On Demand |

6. Click Options, and then in the TSQL Task Options dialog box, provide the following information.

| Property | Value |
| --- | --- |
| Email Operator | The operator created in Chapter 18 |
| Write to Windows NT Application Event Log | On Success and On Failure |

▶ **To create and test an alert**

1. On the SQL Enterprise Manager toolbar, click the Manage Alerts and Operators button.

   The Manage Alerts and Operators window appears.

2. On the Manage Alerts and Operators window toolbar, click the New Alert button.

3. In the New Alert dialog box, create an alert by providing the following information.

| Property | Value |
| --- | --- |
| Name | Library Log Full |
| Error Number | 1105 |
| Database Name | Library |
| Task to Execute | Backup Library |
| Include Error Message Text in | Email |
| Operator to Notify by Email | Operator you created earlier |

4. Switch to a query window and execute the FILL_LOG.SQL script one or more times to fill the *library* transaction log.

5. Switch to SQL Enterprise Manager, and then on the Manage Alerts and Operators window toolbar, click Refresh to verify that the alert has activated.

6. On the Manage Scheduled Tasks window toolbar, click Refresh to verify that the task was executed.

7. Observe the SQL Performance Monitor counter Log Space Used (%) on the chart.

   Notice that the Log Space Used (%) is now 0 because the log has been backed up.

# SQL Trace

SQL Trace is a SQL Server 6.5 graphical utility that monitors and records database user activity, enabling you to audit your server's performance. SQL Trace can display all server activity in real time or create filters that focus on the actions of particular users, applications, or host servers. SQL Trace can display any SQL statements or RPCs that are sent to any SQL Server 6.5 server. SQL Trace also records connections and disconnections made to and from the server. SQL Trace activity can be saved to disk in a script or as an activity log. SQL Trace is installed with SQL Server 6.5 server software and, optionally, with the 32-bit client software.

SQL Trace can annotate all events with the:

- SQL Server login name.
- Windows NT domain\username.
- Application name.
- Host name (where available).
- Statistics start time, end time, and duration.
- Processor usage, reads, and synchronous writes.

For language and RPC events, SQL Trace statistics refer to the individual events. For events such as disconnection, SQL Trace statistics refer to the complete session. SQL Trace activity can also be captured in a SQL Server table or as **bcp** utility log activity information.

## SQL Trace Processing

SQL Trace is implemented directly on the server so that tracing can be dynamically turned on and off, and information can be obtained from other servers. It captures incoming statements, RPC events, and connects and disconnects. SQL Trace also provides client-side editing and creation of user-defined filters. Filter definitions are stored on the server, and filenames and the formatting definition for captured data are stored on the client. This enables users to select a predefined filter and still have individual control over how the results are stored and displayed.

## SQL Trace Filters

You can create SQL Trace filters to focus on the actions of particular users, applications, or host servers. You can start, pause, stop, or modify any filter that has been created. When you start SQL Trace, if filters exist, you can select a filter. If filters do not exist, you can create a filter. The following figure illustrates the New Filter dialog box.

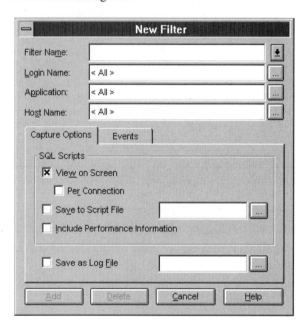

The following table lists the elements in the SQL Trace window.

| Element | Description |
|---|---|
| SQL Trace title bar | Displays the name of the connected server. |
| Active Filter pane | Displays the activity of the named filter and the requests that are coming to the server named in the SQL Trace title bar. The Active Filter pane title bar displays the filter name. |
| Filter Status pane | Lists the filters that are currently defined on the server, displays information about these filters, and provides Start, Pause, and Stop buttons. |
| Screen check box | Specifies whether to display filter activity in the Active Filter pane. |
| Script check box | Specifies whether to save filter activity as an SQL script. |
| Log check box | Specifies whether to save filter activity to a log. |
| Active Filters box (lower-right corner) | Displays the number of active filters. |

In the following procedures, you start SQL Trace and create a SQL Trace filter.

▶ **To start SQL Trace and create a SQL Trace filter**

1. Open ISQL/w and log in as SA. Leave the session running.

2. Create a subdirectory at the root of drive C called SQLTRACE.

3. Open SQL Trace.

   The Connect Server dialog box appears.

4. Connect to SQL Server as SA.

5. A message box appears to determine whether you want to create a filter. Click Yes.

   The New Filter dialog box appears.

6. Enter the following information.

| Property | Value |
| --- | --- |
| Filter Name | Sample_fltr |
| Login Name | sa |
| Application | Microsoft ISQL/w |
| Host Name | MYSQLSERVER |

**Note**  If Microsoft ISQL/w is not displayed in the Application box, you must start it.

7. Click the Capture Options tab, and then enter the following information.

| Property | Value |
| --- | --- |
| View on Screen | Selected |
| Save to Script File | Selected |

   The Save SQL Script File For 'Sample_fltr' As dialog box appears.

8. Enter the following information, and then click Save.

| Property | Value |
| --- | --- |
| Directory | C:\SQLTRACE |
| File Name | Sample_fltr |

9. Select the Include Performance Information and Save as Log File check boxes.

   The Save SQL Log File For 'Sample_fltr' As dialog box appears.

10. Enter the following information, and then click Save.

| Property | Value |
|---|---|
| Directory | C:\SQLTRACE |
| File Name | Sample_fltr |

11. Click the Events tab, and then enter the following information.

   a. Accept the default selected items (Connections, SQL Statements, RPC, and Disconnections).

   b. Under SQL Statements, select Filter.

   c. In the Filter box, type the following to specify that only Transact-SQL statements containing the key word SELECT will be monitored:

   **%SELECT%;%select%**

---

**Note**  By specifying both uppercase and lowercase, you can trace any uppercase and lowercase combination of SELECT statements.

---

12. Click Add.

   The Filter Activity window displays your new filter.

13. On the toolbar, click the Toggle Filter Status Display button.

   The Filter Status pane allows you to control filter activity in the following ways:

   - You can start a filter by clicking the right-pointing arrow Start button.

   - You can pause a filter by clicking the parallel vertical bars Pause button.

   - You can stop a filter by clicking the solid box Stop button.

   Leave the filter running.

14. Switch to ISQL/w.

15. Execute the following SELECT statement:

   ```
   SELECT * FROM library..member WHERE member_no = 4567
   ```

16. Switch to SQL Trace, and then view the trace information.

   Do you see you SELECT statement?

17. Execute the following UPDATE statement.

    ```
    UPDATE library..member SET lastname = 'Martinez' WHERE member_no =
    4567
    ```

    Do you see the UPDATE in SQL Trace?

    _____

    Why?

    _____

18. In the status area at the bottom of the screen, click the Stop Filter button for the Sample_fltr.

19. Switch back to ISQL/w.

20. Open and execute the SQL Trace script file located in C:\SQLTRACE\SAMPLE_FLTR.SQL

    What happened?

    _____

    _____

## The xp_sqltrace Extended Stored Procedure

SQL Trace provides a graphical user interface to the extended stored procedure **xp_sqltrace**. **xp_sqltrace** allows database administrators and application developers to monitor and record database activity. Multiple instances of **xp_sqltrace** can be executed simultaneously. By creating an automatically-started stored procedure that calls **xp_sqltrace**, it is possible to automatically start SQL Server monitoring.

**Syntax**

**xp_sqltrace** [[@Function = ] *function*] [, [ @EventFilter = ] *eventfilter*] [, [ @LangFilter = ] '*langfilter*'] [, [ @RPCFilter = ] '*rpcfilter*'] [, [ @UserFilter = ] *userfilter*] [, [ @AppFilter = ] *appfilter*] [, [ @HostFilter = ] *hostfilter*] [, [@BufSize = ] *bufsize*] [, [ @TimeOut = ] *timeout*] [, [ @TraceId = ] *traceid*] [, [@FullText = ] *fulltext*] [, [ @FullFilePath = ] '*outputfilename*'] [, [ @IntegerEvents = ] *integerevents*]

# DBCC

DBCC is the SQL Server database consistency checker. The DBCC statement can be used with specific parameters to check the logical and physical consistency of a database, check memory usage, and check performance statistics. The most-commonly-used DBCC parameters are MEMUSAGE, SQLPERF, PERFMON, SHOW_STATISTICS, and SHOWCONTIG.

**Syntax**

DBCC MEMUSAGE

The DBCC MEMUSAGE statement displays information about how SQL Server uses memory, and it provides a snapshot of both the data cache and the procedure cache. It is the only way to accurately determine the size of the SQL Server executable code.

The output from DBCC MEMUSAGE provides three types of information:

- How the SQL Server memory was allocated at startup.

- How much memory is used by the 20 largest objects in the data cache.

- How much memory is used by the 20 largest objects (stored procedures, triggers, views, rules, and defaults) in the procedure cache.

  Multiple copies of an object can be in the procedure cache—both precompiled versions of the object (trees), and compiled versions (plans). DBCC MEMUSAGE sums the total memory the copies are using and lists the sizes of both the trees and plans.

**Syntax**

DBCC SQLPERF ({IOSTATS | LRUSTATS | NETSTATS | RASTATS [, CLEAR]} | {THREADS} | {LOGSPACE})

The DBCC SQLPERF statement provides information about performance statistics. The following options are available for this statement: IOSTATS, LRUSTATS, NETSTATS, RASTATS, and CLEAR.

- IOSTATS generates the I/O statistics since the server was last started or since the statistics were last cleared.

- LRUSTATS generates statistics about cache use since the server was last started or since the statistics were last cleared. LRU stands for "least recently used" and is the algorithm used by the SQL Server cache manager.

- NETSTATS provides statistics about network use.

- RASTATS provides statistics about Read Ahead.

  Read ahead or "parallel data scan" capabilities enable asynchronous read ahead of data when SQL Server determines that pages are being retrieved in sequential order. With read ahead (RA), separate background threads will be used to pre-fetch pages for a given results set.

- CLEAR clears the statistics.

The other DBCC SQLPERF options are THREADS and LOGSPACE.

- THREADS provides a mechanism to map the Windows NT system thread ID to a SQL Server system process identification number (*spid*). Because of thread pooling, many different Windows NT threads will service a single SQL Server *spid* over time, so this Windows NT system thread ID is usually not useful.

- LOGSPACE generates statistics about the percentage of log space used at the time the statement is executed. This statement can be used only on a log that is on a separate device from its database.

**Syntax**          DBCC PERFMON

The DBCC PERFMON statement provides a way to view all four types of SQLPERF statistics in order (IOSTATS, LRUSTATS, NETSTATS, and RASTATS). It takes no parameters.

**Syntax**          DBCC SHOW_STATISTICS (*table_name*, *index_name*)

The DBCC SHOW_STATISTICS option displays all of the statistical information in the distribution page for an index (*index_name*) on a specified table (*table_name*). The results returned indicate the selectivity of an index (the lower the density returned, the higher the selectivity) and provide the basis for determining whether or not an index would be useful to the optimizer. The results returned are based on distribution steps of the index.

To see the last date the statistics were updated, use the STATS_DATE system function.

**Syntax**          DBCC SHOWCONTIG (*table_id*, [*index_id*])

The SHOWCONTIG option determines whether a table is heavily fragmented. Table fragmentation occurs through the process of data modifications (INSERT, UPDATE, and DELETE statements) made against the table. Because the normal distribution of these modifications is not usually equally distributed among the records of a table, the "fullness" of each page will begin to vary over time. For queries that scan part or all of a table, this can cause additional page reads. When a table is heavily fragmented, you can reduce fragmentation and improve read-ahead (parallel data scan) performance by dropping and recreating a clustered index (without using the SORTED_DATA option). Recreating a clustered index will "compact" the data such that data pages are essentially full again; however, the level of "fullness" can also be configured with the FILLFACTOR option.

Use the following query to find the *index_id* of a nonclustered index, specify the nonclustered index name (*nc_index_name*):

```
SELECT indid FROM sysindexes
   WHERE name = 'nc_index_name'
```

▶ **To calculate the number of pages**

In this procedure, you manually estimate the row size, rows per page, and size of the *member* table in the *library* database. You then use DBCC CHECKTABLE to verify your estimate.

1. Open a query window and drop any constraint or clustered index on the *member* table of the *library* database.

   - To find any constraints or clustered indexes, use the **sp_help** stored procedure.

   - To drop an index, use the DROP INDEX command.

   - To drop a constraint, use the ALTER TABLE command. See the DROPCNST.SQL script file.

2. For the *library* database, estimate the row size for the *member* table using the following formula:

Fixed row overhead (4 bytes)

+ Sum of bytes in all columns

+ Number of variable-length columns

= Row size

Because the *member* table columns *lastname* and *firstname* are variable-length, assume those fields are on average just under half full. This means if *lastname* is *varchar(15)* you would use the value of 7 bytes as the average field size. The *member* table contains three user-defined datatypes: *member_no*, *shortstring*, and *letter*. Use **sp_help** *<user defined datatype>* to find out the system datatype of the user-defined datatype, and then execute **sp_help** on *member* to find the rest of the information you need.

*member* table

| Columns | Datatypes | System datatypes | Size | Size used | Allow NULL or variable-length |
|---|---|---|---|---|---|
| *member_no* | *member_no* | *smallint* | 2 | 2 | no (0) |
| *lastname* | *shortstring* | *varchar(15)* | 15 | 7 | yes (1) |
| *firstname* | *shortstring* | *varchar(15)* | 15 | 7 | yes (1) |
| *middleinitial* | *letter* | *char(1)* | 1 | 1 | yes (1) |
| *photograph* | *image* | *image* | 16 | 16 | yes (1) |
| **Totals** | | | | **33** | **4** |

What is the row size for the *member* table?

How many rows fit per page?

_____

Assuming there are 10,000 rows, approximately how large is the *member* table in terms of pages?

_____

3.  Check the actual number of pages used by the *member* table by executing the following statement:

```
DBCC CHECKTABLE (member)
```

What was the total number of pages reported for the *member* table?

_____

The page estimate is only off by a few pages. Remember that it is almost impossible to calculate an exact row size when using variable-length fields. There is also the possibility that the rows per page can be dramatically affected by FILLFACTOR when an index or constraint was created.

## The SET Statement

The SET statement sets SQL Server query-processing options for the duration of a user's work session. The SET options that are important when measuring query performance are SHOWPLAN and STATISTICS IO.

**Syntax**

SET SHOWPLAN {ON | OFF}

SET SHOWPLAN describes the method chosen by the SQL Server query optimizer to retrieve data. The optimizer is an intelligent, cost-based query optimizer that attempts to determine the best method for retrieving the data requested through ad hoc queries. The optimizer attempts to choose the access method that incurs the lowest estimated cost in terms of page I/O. The chosen method is known as the plan. To see the plan, you must set the SHOWPLAN option ON. You can set SHOWPLAN to ON using the SET statement in a query window, or you can select Show Query Plan in the Query Options dialog box.

**Syntax**

SET STATISTICS IO {ON | OFF}

SET STATISTICS IO displays the number of scans, the number of logical reads (pages accessed in cache), and the number of physical reads (number of times the disk was accessed) for each table referenced in the statement. SET STATISTICS IO enables you to examine the I/O consumed by a query. Note the count of logical page I/Os because the optimizer's goal is to minimize I/O count. This forms a baseline against which to measure improvement.

You can use the SET statement to improve performance once you have a baseline and performance seems slow. First isolate the query or queries that are slow (often it appears that an entire application is slow, when only a few of the queries are slow). It is often more effective to focus exclusively on the STATISTICS IO output and experiment with different query and index types than to use SET SHOWPLAN ON. Interpreting and effectively applying the output of SHOWPLAN can require some study, and it can unnecessarily consume time.

▶ **To use SET STATISTICS IO and SET SHOWPLAN**

In this procedure, you execute a SELECT statement on the *member* table two times. The first time the query does not use an index. The second time the query uses an index. Compare SHOWPLAN and STATISTICS IO output between the two queries.

1. Open ISQL/w, set SHOWPLAN and STATISTICS IO on.

```
SET SHOWPLAN on
SET STATISTICS IO on
GO
```

2. Execute the following SELECT statement using the *library* database:

```
SELECT member_no, lastname FROM member WHERE member_no = 1234
```

Did this query use an index? What happened?

_____

What was the total logical reads cost to process this query? What does that cost represent?

_____

_____

_____

3. Type and execute the following statement to create a PRIMARY KEY constraint with a clustered index on the *member_no* column of the *member* table.

```
ALTER TABLE member ADD CONSTRAINT pk_member_no PRIMARY KEY CLUSTERED
(member_no)
```

4. Execute the same SELECT query again.

```
SELECT member_no, lastname FROM member WHERE member_no = 1234
```

Did this query use an index? What happened?

_____

What was the total logical reads cost to process this query? What does that cost represent?

_____

_____

_____

# SQL Server Processes and Locks

Each client connecting to SQL Server opens one or more connections to the server. Each client connection might cause locking to occur, depending on the activities each client is performing.

## SQL Server Processes

A process is a task being carried out by SQL Server. Processes can be initiated either by a user executing a statement or by SQL Server.

Each process is assigned a unique (but not necessarily consecutive) *spid* when it starts. Each *spid* identifies a connection to SQL Server. Some client applications establish several connections. A process can determine its own *spid* by executing SELECT @@SPID. Process identification numbers and other information about each process are stored in the *sysprocesses* table in the *master* database.

### The sp_who System Stored Procedure

You can check ongoing processes regularly with the **sp_who** system stored procedure. **sp_who** provides information about current SQL Server users and processes. The information returned can be filtered to return only those processes that are not idle.

**Syntax**          SP_WHO [*login_name* | '*spid*' | **active**]

This procedure reports information about a specific process identified by *login_name* or *spid*, or all processes currently running (active). Executing **sp_who** without parameters reports all processes on the server. Using parameters with **sp_who** allows you to limit the number of processes (rows) you see in the results set, but the information reported on each process is the same amount of detail.

In the following example, **sp_who** is executed without any parameters. By not using any parameters, all of the *spids* currently active on the server are returned.

**Example**          `EXEC sp_who`

**Results**

| spid | status | loginame | hostname | blk | dbname | cmd |
|------|--------|----------|----------|-----|--------|-----|
| 1 | sleeping | sa | | 0 | master | MIRROR HANDLER |
| 2 | runnable | sa | | 0 | master | LAZY WRITER |
| 3 | sleeping | sa | | 0 | master | CHECKPOINT SLEEP |
| 4 | sleeping | sa | | 0 | master | RA MANAGER |
| 10 | sleeping | sa | MYSQLSERVER | 0 | master | AWAITING COMMAND |
| 11 | sleeping | sa | MYSQLSERVER | 0 | master | AWAITING COMMAND |
| 12 | runnable | sa | MYSQLSERVER | 0 | master | SELECT |

`(1 row(s) affected)`

The results of **sp_who** always display *spids* 1–4. These are SQL Server processes that are used for maintaining the server. Notice that in the previous example, at the time **sp_who** was executed the lazy writer process (*spid* 2) was running. The SQLExecutive Service *spids* are numbers 10 and 11. Depending on the activity on your computer, you might see more rows (activity) from **sp_who**. On a final note, notice that *spid* 12 is the process that was used to execute **sp_who**.

### The KILL Statement

The KILL statement is used to terminate an ongoing process. Only the SA can issue the KILL statement (permission to use it cannot be transferred). The most frequent reason for stopping a process is that it interferes with other users. A KILL statement is not reversible and cannot be put inside a user-defined transaction. You can stop only one process at a time.

**Syntax**          KILL *spid*

You cannot stop the SQL Server processes (*spids* 1–4). Any other process can be stopped with the KILL statement. You can get a list of process ID numbers using the **sp_who** system stored procedure.

## Locks

When two or more users access a database concurrently, SQL Server uses locking to ensure that their actions do not interfere with one another. Locking prevents users from reading data that is being changed by other users, and it prevents different users from making more than one change to a record at any one time.

### The sp_lock System Stored Procedure

Another system stored procedure, **sp_lock**, also reports on processes. It gives information about all of the locks currently held on SQL Server, including the *spid* of the process holding each one.

**Syntax**

sp_lock [*spid1* [, *spid2*]]

The parameters *spid1* and *spid2* are the SQL Server process ID numbers from *master.dbo.sysprocesses*. Execute **sp_who** to get the *spid* of the lock. If parameters are not supplied, information about all locks is displayed. When reading **sp_lock** information, use the OBJECT_NAME( ) function to get a table's name from its ID number.

**Example**

```
SELECT object_name(16003088)
EXEC sp_lock
```

**Results**

| spid | locktype | table_id | page | dbname |
|------|----------|----------|------|--------|
| 12 | Sh_intent | 704005539 | 0 | master |

(1 row(s) affected)

Results of **sp_lock** vary from server to server because the more queries you have running, the more locking information there is to report.

### The Current Activity Window

SQL Enterprise Manager also provides an easier way to view server activity by combining the information from **sp_who**, **sp_lock,** and the KILL statement in the Current Activity window.

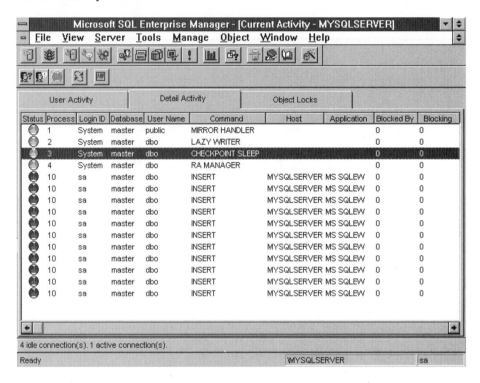

▶ **To use the Current Activity window to view server activity**

1. Start SQL Enterprise Manager, and then select your server.

2. On the Server menu, click Current Activity.

   The Current Activity window appears.

3. Maximize the Current Activity window.

   What users are shown under the User Activity tab?

   _____

   _____

4. Click the Detail Activity tab.

5. Click the Process ID column heading so that information is now sorted by Process ID.

Notice that the process IDs are displayed in ascending order.

6. On the Current Activity window toolbar, click the Display Legend button.

With the legend displayed, which processes are currently active (runnable)?

_____

7. On the Current Activity window toolbar, click the Refresh button.

You may see some new processes displayed or a current process detail change.

### Types of Locks

The *locktype* column in the Current Activity window's Detail Activity tab indicates whether the lock is a shared lock (Sh), an exclusive lock (Ex), or an update lock (Update_page). This column also indicates whether the lock is held on a table (table or intent), a page, or an extent. The blk suffix in the *locktype* column indicates that this process is blocking another process that needs to acquire a lock. As soon as this process finishes, the other processes move forward.

In general, read operations acquire shared locks, and write operations acquire exclusive locks. Update locks are created at the page level and are acquired during the initial portion of an update operation when the pages are being read. Update locks are compatible with shared locks. Later, if the pages are changed, the update locks are promoted to exclusive locks.

An intent lock indicates the intention to acquire a shared or exclusive page-level lock. An intent lock prevents another transaction from acquiring a table lock for that table. An extent lock is held on a group of eight database pages while they are being allocated or freed. Extent locks are set while a CREATE or DROP statement is running or while an INSERT or UPDATE statement that requires new data or index pages is running.

When reading **sp_lock** information, use the OBJECT_NAME( ) function to get a table's name from its ID number.

**Example**

```
SELECT object_name(16003088)
```

Given the *spid* returned from **sp_lock** you can also retrieve other information using the Windows NT Performance Monitor, and the DBCC statements OPENTRAN, OUTPUTBUFFER, and INPUTBUFFER.

### Monitoring for Blocking Conditions

In a multiuser environment, there are times when a user or process may hold a resource for an extended period of time. When resources are unavailable, the users cannot complete their transactions; therefore, it is important to be able to identify blocking locks. Factors that may cause resources to be held too long are poor client application design, a mixed on-line transaction process (OLTP) and Decision Support server environment, or a high number of concurrent users. These factors can cause resources to be blocked from other users.

A process that blocks a resource can cause a chain of blocked locks, in which one user or process blocks resources from another user or process that is waiting to access the resource. Users or processes that are blocked can also block other users that are also waiting to access the same data. The correct way to resolve chains of blocked resources is to follow the chain to the initial blocking lock and remove the lock, typically by killing the process. Once the initial blocked resource is removed, the other processes or users waiting for the resource can process their tasks.

You can use the following Current Activity window Detail Activity tab columns to obtain information on a lock chain:

Blocked By—Displays the *spid* of any processes that are blocking your process.

Blocking—Displays whether your process is blocking any other processes. A zero in the column indicates that it is not blocking. Any number other than zero indicates the server process ID that it is blocking.

The **sp_who** system stored procedure also returns information about blocking processes. The *blk* column is the equivalent of Blocked By in the Current Activity window. The *blk* column contains the *spid* of any blocking processes.

**Example**

If User1 holds a lock on a table (*resource*) and User2 tries to gain access to the *resource* table, User1 will block User2. If a third user, User3, tries to gain access to the same table that User1 has locked and that User2 is waiting for, User 2 is both blocked by User 1 and blocking User3. To resolve blocked locks, you must identify the first blocking user in the chain of blocked locks. In this case, User1 is the problem. In most cases, if User1's locks are released, all of the other waiting processes can then proceed.

### Transactions Not Committed Due to Blocking

In a multiuser environment, it is possible for an open transaction to become blocked on locks held by another process. In this situation, the transaction remains open, preventing log truncation. Well-designed transactions should complete quickly and rarely block others. If a transaction does block another transaction, the blocking transaction can be terminated with the KILL statement. To detect a blocked transaction, the programmer or database administrator can use **sp_who**, **sp_lock**, the Current Activity window, or other tools to analyze the concurrency environment. In most cases, blocking problems can be reduced or eliminated through proper query, index, and database design.

▶ **To use SQL Enterprise Manager to resolve blocked locks**

In this procedure, you create blocked locks and use the SQL Enterprise Manager Current Activity window to view server activity.

1. Open SQL Enterprise Manager.

2. On the Server menu, click Current Activity.

   The Current Activity window appears.

3. Maximize the Current Activity window, click the Detail Activity tab, and then click the Process ID column to list the activity in ascending order.

4. Optional: Adjust the columns so you can view as far as the Locked Object column.

   This step is not required, but can make it easier to read the activity information.

5. On the Current Activity window toolbar, click Display Legend. Make note of the Blocking, Blocked, and Blocked/Blocking icons in the legend.

6. Switch to ISQL/w, and then execute the following statements in the *pubs* database:

```
USE pubs
BEGIN TRANSACTION one
    UPDATE pubs..authors SET au_lname = 'User1'
```

   This transaction executes an UPDATE statement that creates an exclusive table-level lock on the *authors* table. No other users will be able to read or modify this information until this transaction is committed or rolled back. This transaction has been intentionally left uncommitted to hold the lock.

7. Switch to SQL Enterprise Manager, and then click Refresh on the Current Activity window toolbar to update the list of processes in the Detail Activity window.

   You should see a new process ID with an application name of Microsoft ISQL/w with an exclusive table lock on the *pubs..authors* table.

8. Switch back to ISQL/w and on the toolbar, and then click New Query.

   You should have two query windows open.

9. In the new query window, execute the following statements:

```
USE pubs
BEGIN TRANSACTION two
    UPDATE pubs..authors SET au_lname = 'User2'
COMMIT TRAN two
```

   Transaction two executes an UPDATE statement similar to the Transaction one. For this update to execute, Transaction two must be able to obtain an exclusive table-level lock on the *authors* table. Because Transaction one currently has an exclusive table lock on the *authors* table, Transaction two is not able to execute.

10. Switch to SQL Enterprise Manager, and then click Refresh.

    You should see a new process that is showing as being *blocked*. You should also see that Transaction one is *blocking*.

    Transaction one is *blocking* Transaction two (Transaction two is *blocked by* Transaction one). Transaction two must wait until the first transaction is committed or rolled back. Transaction two is not holding any locks.

11. Switch back to ISQL/w, and then on the toolbar, click New Query.

    You should have three query windows open.

12. In the new Query Window, execute the following statements:

```
USE pubs
BEGIN TRANSACTION three
    UPDATE pubs..authors SET au_fname = 'User3'
COMMIT TRAN three
```

    Transaction three executes an UPDATE statement similar to the first two transactions. For this update to execute, Transaction three must be able to obtain an exclusive table-level lock on the *authors* table. Because Transaction one currently has an exclusive table lock on the *authors* table, Transaction three is not able to execute. The first transaction is *blocking* Transaction Two, and Transaction two is blocking Transaction Three.

13. Switch to SQL Enterprise Manager, and then click Refresh on the toolbar.

    You should see a new process that is showing as being *blocked*. The second process is *blocked/blocking*, and the first transaction is *blocking*.

    Transaction two is *blocked by* the first transaction and is *blocking* transaction three. Transaction three must wait until the Transactions one and two are committed or rolled back. Transaction three is not holding any locks.

14. In the Detail Activity window, double-click the process (Transaction one) that is holding the exclusive table lock on the *pubs..authors* table.

The Process Details dialog box appears. In the Last TSQL Command Batch section the transaction commands that are holding the locks appear.

15. Click Kill Process to terminate the first transaction.

Killing the transaction that started the chain of blocking locks, immediately releases the locks, so that the blocked transactions execute. Notice that all of the blocked or blocking locks are gone.

### Deadlocks

A deadlock results when both of the following occur:

- Two (or more) processes attempt to access a resource that the other process holds a lock on.

- Each process has a request for each others resource, and neither process can be completed.

Deadlocks can happen at any time. They are more prevalent in high-volume applications and in poorly designed applications. Every application should be prepared to deal with them. Deadlocks cannot be completely eliminated, but, the probability or frequency of them occurring can be greatly reduced in many ways.

SQL Server detects and resolves deadlocks automatically. When a deadlock is detected, SQL Server chooses the process with the least amount of processing time and breaks the deadlock. SQL Server rolls back the transaction of the selected process and returns error message 1205 to the client application. This error is not "fatal" and may not cause the batch containing the transaction to be terminated.

Client applications should be written to handle deadlocks to increase the throughput and efficiency of SQL Server. Client applications can check for error 1205 (deadlock) and then resubmit the query.

To reduce the chance of a deadlock, minimize indexing (and the possibility of index locking) on appropriate tables, shorten transactions and transaction times, and use resources in the same order in all transactions. The client application can also set a deadlock priority in which a process can "volunteer" to be terminated in the event of a deadlock.

In some instances, a deadlock condition causes a DB-Library function (such as dbsqlexec, dbsqlok, dbresults, or dbnextrow) to return FAIL. It is always the responsibility of the application to check the return codes from each DB-Library function. If FAIL is returned by one of these DB-Library functions, the application should cancel the batch and not attempt to continue. In some cases, it is possible to continue execution of subsequent functions in the batch. However, because a deadlock situation occurred and the functions that caused it were rolled back, later functions in the batch will probably fail with a more serious error, such as "Object Not Found."

In other instances, a deadlock condition does not cause a DB-Library function to return FAIL. In these cases, the application must check for error message 1205 in the message handler and use the dbsetuserdata function to communicate the deadlock to the client application. The application must then check for the deadlock indicator after every DB-Library call and should cancel the batch if a deadlock is detected.

While it may seem unnecessary to cancel a batch after receiving a 1205 deadlock message, it is necessary because the server does not always terminate the batch in a deadlock situation. If the batch is not canceled, any attempt to submit a new batch can result in a DB-Library error 10038 "Results Pending."

You can also use the SET statement with the DEADLOCKPRIORITY option. SET DEADLOCKPRIORITY controls how the session reacts when in a deadlock situation. If set to LOW, the specified process is the first eliminated in a deadlock situation. If set to NORMAL, the session will use the default deadlock-handling method.

## Lesson Summary

The tools that you can use to troubleshoot SQL Server are:

- SQL Performance Monitor—SQL Performance Monitor provides eight performance objects and associated counters that enable you to get up-to-the-minute activity and performance statistics about SQL Server.

- SQL Trace—You can use SQL Trace to display all server activity in real time, or to create filters that focus on the actions of particular users, applications, or host servers.

- The DBCC statement—You can use certain DBCC options to check several aspects of the database, including the logical and physical consistency of a database, memory usage, and performance statistics.

- The SET statement—You can use the SET statement's SHOWPLAN and STATISTICS IO options to measure query performance.

- The **sp_who** system stored procedure—**sp_who** enables you to check ongoing procedures regularly.

- The **sp_lock** system stored procedure—**sp_lock** provides you with information about all of the locks currently held on SQL Server.

| For more information on | See |
|---|---|
| Performance Monitor | "Performance Monitor" in SQL Server Books Online |
| SQL Trace | "SQL Trace" in SQL Server Books Online |
| **xp_sqltrace** | "xp_sqltrace" in SQL Server Books Online |
| DBCC | "DBCC Statement" in SQL Server Books Online |
| SHOWPLAN | "Understanding SHOWPLAN Output" and "SHOWPLAN Output" in SQL Server Books Online |
| STATISTICS IO | "Analyzing Queries" in SQL Server Books Online |
| **sp_who** | "sp_who System Stored Procedure" in SQL Server Books Online |
| **sp_lock** | "sp_lock System Stored Procedure" in SQL Server Books Online |
| Process Counter Object | Either the *Windows NT Resource Guide* or the *Windows NT Training: Hands-On, Self-Paced Training Kit* |

# Lesson 3: Tools for Performance Tuning

Once you have determined your system's baselines, you can tune the performance of your SQL server. You can change your configuration options and you can run DBCC to check the consistency of your data.

---

### After this lesson you will be able to:

- Understand which server configuration options should be changed.
- Change appropriate server configuration options.
- Execute appropriate DBCC options to verify database consistency.

### Estimated lesson time  30 minutes

---

## Server Configuration Options

SQL Server's configuration options allow you to manage and control much of the server environment. After installing SQL Server, you might decide to adjust some configuration options. Before you change any configuration options, you should first understand the impact the options can have on the server environment.

You can use SQL Enterprise Manager or the **sp_configure** system stored procedure to display and manage configuration options.

---

**Note**  If you set a configuration option incorrectly and it prevents SQL Server from starting, you can start SQL Server using the **-f** parameter. This starts the server with all of the configuration options at the default settings.

---

### Configuration Options to Change for Optimal Performance

There are four server configuration options that you can change to optimize the performance of SQL Server: memory, user connections, *tempdb* in RAM, and procedure cache.

### Memory

When you install SQL Server, the **setup** program adjusts the amount of memory available to SQL Server based on the amount of physical memory on your computer. If your computer has less than 32 MB of RAM, SQL Server is assigned 8 MB; if the computer has 32 MB or more, SQL Server is assigned 16 MB.

Change the memory value only after one of the following events:

- The initial installation has been performed.
- Memory has been added to the computer.
- Memory has been removed from the computer.
- The use of your system has changed.

Once the total memory for SQL Server has been configured, that memory is divided between several components in an ordered fashion. Memory is allocated first to the SQL Server kernel and resource structures. The remaining memory is divided between the procedure cache and the data cache, in that order. You can configure the size of the procedure cache, and then the data cache is allocated the remaining memory.

It is important to know when to change the memory value. It is also important to know what the appropriate value for memory should be.

The following table provides figures to give you an idea of appropriate values for SQL Server memory allocation over different amounts of RAM. These values are intended for use on a dedicated server.

| RAM (MB) | SQL Server memory allocation (in MB) | SQL Server memory allocation (in 2K units) |
|---|---|---|
| 16 | 4 | 2048 |
| 24 | 8 | 4096 |
| 32 | 16 | 8192 |
| 64 | 40 | 20,480 |
| 128 | 100 | 51,210 |
| 256 | 216 | 110,592 |
| 512 | 464 | 237,568 |

For more exact figures, you can use statistics from the SQL Performance Monitor to determine your system memory behavior and to help you determine appropriate values for the memory.

A computer with $x$86 processors must have at least 16 MB of RAM. However, adding more RAM is usually a wise investment. 32 MB of RAM are preferred, and it is not uncommon for servers to be configured with 128 MB RAM or more. The maximum amount of RAM is 2 GB.

Before adding or allocating more memory, you should determine whether it will help solve the problem. The easiest way to determine your memory needs is to use SQL Performance Monitor to check the SQL Server cache hit ratio while SQL Server is under a typical load. If the cache hit ratio is relatively high (over 90 percent), adding or allocating more memory is unlikely to be beneficial because additional memory is mainly used for additional SQL Server data cache, which increases the hit ratio. If the hit ratio is already high, then the maximum available improvement is small. If the hit ratio is consistently lower than 90 percent, adding more memory may improve the hit ratio and thereby performance, if the added memory is proportionally significant compared to the current amounts.

In determining whether it is beneficial to add more RAM to your computer or allocate more memory to SQL, consider the following:

- Increases in memory that are a small percentage of total memory rarely afford any significant benefit.
- Allocating excessive memory to SQL Server can result in poor performance because of excessive Windows NT paging.
- You should add RAM to the computer in significant amounts before allocating additional memory to SQL Server.

### SQL Server Memory Configuration and the Windows NT Virtual Memory Page File

Installing SQL Server can cause the Windows NT virtual memory page file (PAGEFILE.SYS) to grow. For SQL Server installation, the initial configured size of PAGEFILE.SYS file must be at least 12 MB greater than the amount of memory installed on the computer, and the maximum configured size must be larger. Before you install SQL Server, make sure that you have enough free disk space to allow PAGEFILE.SYS to grow to its maximum configured size. Use the System application in the Windows NT Control Panel to check the configuration of your Windows NT PAGEFILE.SYS.

The minimal Windows NT operating system memory requirement is approximately 12 MB with some variation depending on application-induced overhead. As SQL Server parameters are configured upward, the system overhead requirement can grow as Windows NT needs more resident memory to support additional threads, page tables, and so on.

When memory is configured for SQL Server, Windows NT allocates that memory from its physical RAM. As you increase the SQL Server memory configuration, check to ensure that Windows NT still has enough memory, both physical and virtual, to continue to run efficiently. If you allocate too much RAM to SQL Server, Windows NT will not have enough physical RAM to operate, which can increase its use of virtual memory. If the virtual memory file can not grow, either because of limited disk space or poor configuration, performance will be severely compromised because eventually Windows NT will incur excessive paging.

Ideally, you want to allocate as much memory as possible to SQL Server without causing Windows NT to page. You can use the SQL Performance Monitor to help determine what the threshold is for your system—the Memory: Page Faults/sec counter indicates whether you are generating page faults. If you are generating page faults, SQL Server could be configured to run with too much memory for the existing physical memory on the computer. The threshold varies depending on your system. For example, on a 32-MB system, 16 MB might be appropriate for SQL Server; on a 64-MB system, 48 MB might be appropriate.

## User Connections

The dynamic user connections option specifies the maximum number of simultaneous connections to SQL Server. If the number of dynamic user connections is too low, your users can receive error messages stating that they cannot be connected to SQL Server. If the number of dynamic user connections is too high, you could be wasting SQL Server memory that would otherwise be given to data and procedure cache.

Each configured user connection requires approximately 40K of memory, whether or not the connection is used. When you configure additional user connections and restart SQL Server, the additional overhead reduces the amount of memory for data and procedure caches, unless you also increase the memory. Do not configure more user connections than necessary.

### *tempdb* in RAM

The temporary database *tempdb* is used as a workspace for creating temporary tables. *tempdb's* default size is 2 MB. It can be made to reside entirely in RAM. When SQL Server is configured to store *tempdb* in RAM, *tempdb* resides in the physical RAM of your Windows NT server, rather than as a physical disk file. The physical RAM allocated to *tempdb* is taken from Windows NT, which in turn makes less physical RAM available to SQL Server. You must ensure that there is enough physical RAM to provide efficient functioning for the way you are configuring your computer.

In some specific situations (listed below), *tempdb* in RAM can provide a performance advantage. However, if *tempdb* in RAM is used inappropriately, it can damage performance by consuming memory that could be better used for the SQL Server cache buffer system. Using available RAM for the SQL Server cache buffer system is often better than using a large chunk of it for *tempdb* in RAM.

There are some cases where storing *tempdb* in RAM can be beneficial. If all of the following conditions are true, using *tempdb* in RAM might be beneficial:

- You have a significant amount of available system RAM. This ordinarily would equate to more than 64 MB, with amounts of 128 MB and above more typical.

- Your applications have a locality of reference such that the SQL Server cache hit ratio is poor, even with a lot of available buffer cache. This hit ratio can be monitored with Performance Monitor as SQLServer:Cache Hit Ratio.

- Your applications perform numerous *tempdb* operations. Rather than guess whether this is the case, you can monitor *tempdb* by using **sp_lock** to observe the lock activity in *tempdb* while queries are executing. Also, you can use **sp_lock** or a similar query, SELECT SUM(DPAGES) FROM TEMPDB..SYSINDEXES, either interactively or from a looping batch file to monitor *tempdb* space consumption.

- The *tempdb* operations are sized such that they will fit on the *tempdb* made possible by your RAM configuration.

Regardless of whether *tempdb* is stored on disk or in RAM, *tempdb* is altered in the same way as any other database. When *tempdb* resides in RAM, it can only be altered 10 times without requiring the server to be shut down and restarted. If you alter *tempdb* while it is in RAM, each alteration of the database is allocated a new chunk of contiguous memory in *tempdb*. This "chunk" of memory, although it is contiguous, is not necessarily located next to the existing portion(s) of *tempdb* in RAM. In order to obtain maximum performance, the server should be stopped and restarted after *tempdb* is altered.

**Determining an Appropriate Size for *tempdb***   Before you can determine whether *tempdb* should reside on disk or in RAM, you must first determine the appropriate size of the temporary database. A good estimate of the maximum space used in *tempdb* can be found using the SQL Performance Monitor counter Max Tempdb Space Used (MB). To determine what the size of *tempdb* should be, evaluate the following factors:

- The number of concurrent users
- The number of concurrently executing SQL statements that include the following:
  - GROUP BY
  - ORDER BY
  - SELECT DISTINCT
  - SELECT INTO
  - Join operations requiring temporary tables
  - Cursors

When considering the size of *tempdb*, consider the combination of all of the above factors. For example, when you have determined the number of users, you also need to look at those users and determine how many may be creating temporary tables at the same time and what the largest size of the temporary tables might be. If the size of *tempdb* is too small, SQL Server will display an error message (1105) stating you have run out of room in *tempdb* during an operation. If the size of *tempdb* is too large no error message is generated. Instead, your computer can suffer from a performance degradation or you can just end up wasting disk space or memory.

**Data Cache vs. *tempdb* in RAM**    In most cases, the available RAM is best used as a data cache rather than as the location of *tempdb*. Data in *tempdb* is cached using the SQL Server cache buffer system's LRU algorithm. SQL Server always uses the data cache. It does not always use *tempdb*.

Using *tempdb* in RAM can speed up *tempdb* operations but will deplete memory available for the SQL Server cache buffer, which can lower the cache hit ratio. Memory used for *tempdb* in RAM is allocated separately from the pool seen in **sp_configure** memory, so the server must be configured appropriately. For example, if you use 10 MB for *tempdb* in RAM, the SQL Server **sp_configure** memory setting must be reduced by 10 MB to free up memory. By contrast, giving all available memory to SQL Server (as opposed to setting some aside for *tempdb* in RAM) can increase the cache hit ratio. The cache buffer system will cache all disk I/O operations, including *tempdb*.

The limited amount of RAM available on some servers can constrain the available size of *tempdb* when used in RAM. If unforeseen growth requirements for *tempdb* materialize, size could become an issues. It is not possible to have *tempdb* partially in RAM and partially on disk. It does no good to exceed the available amount of physical memory when using *tempdb* in RAM; *tempdb* references would be simply be paged to disk, eliminating any possible benefit.

**Testing Performance Benefits of *tempdb* in RAM**    If you decide to place *tempdb* in RAM, you should verify the performance benefits you have obtained. Select a query or small set of queries that typify your most frequently performed *tempdb*-intensive operations. Execute these several times, noting the execution time. Then, reconfigure for *tempdb* in RAM, execute the same queries, and note the difference. If the amount of improvement is not significant, it is probably best to give the RAM back to the SQL Server cache system.

### Procedure Cache

The procedure cache is the area of memory where the most recently used procedures are stored. The procedure cache is also used when a procedure is being created and when a query is being compiled. If SQL Server finds a procedure or a compilation already in the cache, it does not read it from the disk.

The percentage of SQL Server memory allocated to the procedure cache is set with the **procedure cache** configuration option. The default for this configuration option is 30, which gives the procedure cache 30 percent of the remaining memory after the SQL Server memory needs are met.

SQL Server memory needs are the sum of memory necessary for locks, user connections, the code itself (which varies slightly from release to release), and so on. The remaining memory is divided between the procedure cache and the data cache according to the percentage given by this configuration option. What is left over goes to the data cache.

The data cache is the area of memory where the most recently used data pages and index pages are stored. If SQL Server finds a data page or index page that has already been called by a user in the cache, it does not read it from the disk.

You can use DBCC MEMUSAGE and statistics from the Performance Monitor to help you adjust the procedure cache value. Change this value only when you add or remove memory, or when you change how you use your system.

When determining the size of the procedure cache, you should look at the number of procedures that are executed concurrently and the size of each plan. While still maintaining enough data cache, it is optimal to have enough memory in the procedure cache to hold the plans of the most commonly use stored procedures.

Because the optimum value for the procedure cache is different from application to application, resetting it can improve performance. For example, if you execute a large number of stored procedures compared to ad hoc queries, your application may use the procedure cache more, so you might want to increase this value. Many applications use more stored procedures while they are being developed. You might want to set the procedure cache to 50 while developing an application, and then reset it to 30 when your application has stabilized.

## Configuration Options That Should Rarely Be Changed

There are four server configuration options that you should rarely change: **max worker threads, max async io, priority boost,** and **SMP concurrency.**

### max worker threads

The **max worker threads** option configures the number of worker threads that are available to SQL Server processes. This pool of threads handles all user connections.

When the number of user connections is less than **max worker threads**, one thread handles each client connection. However, when the number of connections exceeds the configured **max worker threads**, new connections share the existing pool of worker threads. Because there are then more connections than threads, each new request is handled by the next worker thread that completes its current task, in a process called *thread pooling*.

By default the worker thread limit is 255 and can be viewed or changed with **sp_configure**. When 255 worker threads are used, the SQL Server kernel message, "The working thread limit of 255 has been reached" is printed in the error log. The message means that thread pooling is occurring because the number of user connections is greater than the number of worker threads.

Although you can reset the maximum value for worker threads as high as 1024, it is not recommended. SQL Server makes use of the native thread services of Windows NT Server. Thread pooling is desirable when there are a high number of user connections (usually several hundred). Using a single thread per connection can create undesirable operating system overhead.

### max async io

The maximum asynchronous IO (**max async io**) parameter controls the number of outstanding asynchronous disk input/output (I/O) requests, which the server checkpoint and lazywriter threads use. *Asynchronous*, or overlapped, *I/O* refers to the ability of a calling application to issue an I/O request and, without waiting for completion, to continue with another activity. When the I/O finishes, the operating system notifies the application by a callback or other Win32® application programming interface synchronization mechanism. SQL Server uses the asynchronous IO capability of the Windows NT operating system.

Asynchronous IO:

- Makes implementation easier for an application designer, because the operating system can be used to perform asynchronous I/O rather than having to simulate this capability in the application.

- Multiple outstanding I/O requests can drive certain high-performance disk subsystems at greater performance levels than would be otherwise possible.

  This is generally only possible with high-performance intelligent disk subsystems. On these systems increasing the **max async io** parameter for SQL Server can result in performance improvements during disk-intensive operations. The actual setting used for this parameter and the resultant performance increase vary depending on the exact hardware and database I/O profile. It should not be set arbitrarily high, because inordinate asynchronous IO consumes system resources.

The default setting is 8, which is adequate for most systems. However, high-performance servers with intelligent disk subsystems might gain some performance benefit by increasing this number. Nonspecialized disk subsystems will not benefit from increasing this parameter, and the default setting is adequate.

It is recommended that the optimum value for the **max async IO** parameter be determined by conducting controlled testing for a given situation using either the Microsoft TPC-B Benchmark Kit or a customer-specific benchmark. To determine the optimum value for async IO, run using the baseline setting of 8, and then increase the parameter slowly over subsequent test runs. When no further performance increase is noted, the optimum value has been found. In the absence of any empirical testing, the parameter should be left at the default setting.

### priority boost

**priority boost** determines whether SQL Server should run at a higher priority in the Windows NT scheduler than other processes on the same computer. The default is 0, indicating that SQL Server should run at the same priority as other processes (thread priority 8). A configured value of 1 indicates that SQL Server should run at a higher priority (thread priority 13).

If this option is set to 1 on a non-dedicated SQL Server computer, other processes running on the server computer can suffer from poor response time because Window NT is running SQL Server threads at a higher priority.

### SMP concurrency

**SMP concurrency** controls the number of threads that SQL Server releases to Windows NT for execution. **SMP concurrency** in effect, limits the number of processors used by SQL Server. On a uniprocessor computer, the optimal value is 1. On a symmetric multiprocessor (SMP) computer, the limit depends on whether or not the server is a dedicated SQL Server. If the server is not dedicated, reconfiguring this value can cause poor response time from other applications running on the same server. If response time for other applications is not an issue, set SMP concurrency to -1, "Dedicated SMP Support," which means that there is no limit to the number of processors.

When SQL Server is installed, **SMP concurrency** will be set to 0, which means auto configure. In auto configure mode, the limit is set to N-1, where N is the number of processors detected at SQL Server startup. On a uniprocessor computer this value will be set to 1. If "Dedicated SMP Support" is chosen, **SMP concurrency** will be set to -1.

### thread affinity

Generally, Windows NT does not guarantee that any thread in a process will run on a given processor. A thread may migrate from processor to processor, causing the processor's cache to reload. Under heavy system loads, specifying which processor should run which thread can improve performance by reducing the reloading of the processor cache.

**thread affinity** has been introduced into SQL Server to increase and tune performance on SMP systems with four or more processors. **thread affinity** allows you to specify which processors are used by SQL Server. Because moving the thread structures and thread data between processors is minimized, the threads that handle the network interrupts are masked off. This can result in an increase in throughput of heavy loads when using the affinity mask configuration option to specify on which processors SQL Server threads run.

Before applying the affinity mask option to a computer system, however, consider that Windows NT assigns all I/O handling to processor 0, the first processor in the system. Changes in disk I/O, for example, will be reflected in the usage level of processor 0. Windows NT assigns delayed process call (DPC) activity associated with network interface cards to the highest numbered processor in the system. In systems with more than one installed and active network interface card, each additional card's activity is assigned to the next higher numbered processor. For example, in an eight-processor system with one network interface card, Windows NT assigns I/O to processor 0 and DPCs to processor 7. The same eight-processor system with two network interface cards will have I/O assigned to processor 0 and DPCs for each network interface card assigned to processor 7 and to processor 6.

# DBCC

DBCC helps ensure the physical and logical consistency of a database. It is recommended that you make periodic checks to verify the logical and physical consistency of your data.

**Syntax**

DBCC CHECKTABLE (*table_name* [, NOINDEX | *index_id*])

CHECKTABLE checks the specified table to see that index and data pages are correctly linked, that indexes are in proper sorted order, that all pointers are consistent, that the data information on each page is reasonable, and that page offsets are reasonable. If the log segment is on its own device, executing DBCC CHECKTABLE on the *syslogs* table reports the log's used and free space.

DBCC CHECKTABLE spawns multiple threads to automatically check nonclustered indexes in parallel. Because the table is loaded in the data cache, each of the simultaneous threads see an improvement because of an increase in the cache hit ratio.

If an *index_id* is specified, CHECKTABLE checks only that index.

**Syntax**

DBCC CHECKDB [(*database_name* [, NOINDEX])]

Executes the same checks as CHECKTABLE, but on every table in the specified database. If *database_name* is not supplied, CHECKDB checks the current database.

**Syntax**   DBCC NEWALLOC [(*database_name* [, NOINDEX])]

Checks data and index pages against corresponding extent structures. DBCC NEWALLOC details all table information as well as provides summary information. DBCC NEWALLOC will not stop processing if it encounters an error.

---

**Important**  DBCC NEWALLOC should be executed while minimal database activity is occurring. If DBCC NEWALLOC is executed while transactions are in progress, the output may return errors. To ensure that no other users have transactions in progress, set the database to **read-only** or **single user** with the **sp_dboption** system stored procedure before executing DBCC NEWALLOC.

---

**Syntax**   DBCC...[,NOINDEX]...

The NOINDEX option of CHECKDB, CHECKTABLE, and NEWALLOC specifies that only the clustered index (the B-tree and the data itself) is to be checked for user-defined tables. If no clustered index exists, only the data is checked. The NOINDEX option decreases the overall execution time of CHECKDB, CHECKTABLE, and NEWALLOC because it does not check nonclustered indexes for user-defined tables. The NOINDEX option does not affect a check made against the system tables. When used against a system table(s), all clustered and nonclustered indexes are checked.

**Syntax**   DBCC DBREINDEX ([*'table_name'* [, *index_name*
[, *fillfactor* [, {SORTED_DATA | SORTED_DATA_REORG}]]]])
[WITH NOINFOMSGS]

The DBCC DBREINDEX statement rebuilds an index for a table or all indexes defined for a table. By allowing an index to be rebuilt dynamically, indexes that enforce PRIMARY KEY or UNIQUE constraints can be rebuilt without having to drop and recreate constraints. This means that an index can be rebuilt without having to know the table's structure or constraints.

If the index is a clustered index, all nonclustered indexes are also reindexed with the same supplied fillfactor. This statement is completely recoverable as a unit of work for all of the indexes being rebuilt.

If you specify one of the optional parameters (ind_name, fillfactor, or SORTED_DATA), you must specify all of the parameters preceding it in the parameter list.

## Lesson Summary

You can use configuration options and some DBCC statement options to tune SQL Server. Configuration options allow you to manage and control most of the server environment. However, before you change configuration options you should know what the configuration options do, and how to use them. Some of the most common configuration options to change are memory, user connections, *tempdb* in RAM, and procedure cache. Some options that you would rarely change include **max worker threads**, **max asynch i/o**, **priority boost**, and **SMP concurrency**.

| For more information on | See |
| --- | --- |
| Advanced configuration options | "sp_configure" in SQL Server Books Online |
| Tuning SQL Server | "Frequently Asked Questions About Microsoft SQL Server" in /KB on the compact disc |
| DBCC | "How to Improve DBCC Performance on SQL Server" in /KB on the compact disc |
| *tempdb* in RAM | "When to Use *tempdb* in RAM" in /KB on the compact disc |
| Worker threads | "SQL Server and Windows NT Thread Scheduling" in /KB on the compact disc |

# Review

The following questions are intended to reinforce key information presented in this chapter. If you are unable to answer a question, review the lesson and then try the question again.

1.  When tuning a server, what information should you have before you begin?

_____

2.  You have noticed that your server has been slowing down over time. Your server environment has consistently been changing. What tool or utility would you use to determine what the general problem is and when it is occurring?

_____

3.  Your server runs well when no client applications are running, but when client applications are processing, performance is significantly degraded. You are unable to determine which Transact-SQL statements being executed by the client applications are causing the problem. Which tool or utility would you use to determine what the problem is?

_____

4.  You have been experiencing long wait times and even complete halts in client application operations. Some clients are even receiving the error 1205. What tool or utility would you use to determine deadlocks and blocked locks? How can you terminate the offending process?

_____

_____

# Questions and Answers

Page 824

▶ **To calculate row size and I/O requirements**

2. Calculate the row size and I/O.

What is the sum of bytes for all columns?

**75 bytes (4+25+46=75 bytes)**

What is the number of columns that allow NULL or are variable-length?

**1**

What is the row size?

**80 bytes**

4 + (_____) + (_____) = _____

**4+75+1=80 bytes**

3. Calculate the missing information.

Number of rows per page in the database.

**25 rows per page (2,016 page /80 bytes per row)**

Total number of pages in the table.

**400 pages (10,000 rows / 25 rows per page)**

I/O to retrieve expected 150 rows?

**6 pages (150 rows per results set / 25 rows per page)**

Page 831

▶ **To configure a SQL Performance Monitor counter**

11. Find the last size of the *library* transaction log using the counter information bar located in the middle of your screen. It is between the charting window (upper screen) and the list of added counters (lower screen).

**Your answer will vary, depending on your computer.**

12. Highlight the Log Space Used (%) counter, and then using the counter information bar, note the Last percentage of log space used.

**Your answer will vary, depending on the system.**

Page 837

▶ **To start SQL Trace and create a SQL Trace filter**

16. Switch to SQL Trace, and then view the trace information.

Do you see you SELECT statement?

**Yes.**

17. Execute the following UPDATE statement.

```
UPDATE library..member SET lastname = 'Martinez' WHERE member_no =
4567
```

Do you see the UPDATE in SQL Trace?

**No.**

Why?

**You are only tracing SELECT statements.**

20. Open and execute the SQL Trace script file located in C:\SQLTRACE\SAMPLE_FLTR.SQL

What happened?

**The script file executes all of the statements that were traced using SQL Trace.**

Page 842

▶ **To calculate the number of pages**

2. For the *library* database, estimate the row size for the *member* table using the following formula:

Fixed row overhead (4 bytes)

+ Sum of bytes in all columns

+ Number of variable-length columns
_____

= Row size

What is the row size for the *member* table?

**4 + (33) + (4) = 41 (row size)**

How many rows fit per page?

**2016 / 41 = 49 (rows per page)**

Assuming there are 10,000 rows, approximately how large is the *member* table in terms of pages?

**10000 / 49 = 204 (Approximate number of pages for the *member* table)**

3. Check the actual number of pages used by the *member* table by executing the following statement:

```
DBCC CHECKTABLE (member)
```

What was the total number of pages reported for the *member* table?

**178 data pages. Your answer may vary.**

Page 844

▶ **To use SET STATISTICS IO and SET SHOWPLAN**

2. Execute the following SELECT statement using the *library* database:

```
SELECT member_no, lastname FROM member WHERE member_no = 1234
```

Did this query use an index? What happened?

**No. When an index is not used to retrieve data rows you will always do a table scan.**

What was the total logical reads cost to process this query? What does that cost represent?

**About 178 I/O. The 178 I/O represents the number of data pages read for the member table. To retrieve one row SQL Server had to read all ten thousand rows in the table.**

4. Execute the same SELECT query again.

```
SELECT member_no, lastname FROM member WHERE member_no = 1234
```

Did this query use an index? What happened?

**Yes. It used the clustered index.**

What was the total logical reads cost to process this query? What does that cost represent?

**Two I/O. The two I/O represents the data pages read to retrieve the one row using the index. Using the index to retrieve one row, SQL Server only had to read two pages in the table.**

Page 848

▶ **To use the Current Activity window to view server activity**

3. Maximize the Current Activity window.

What users are shown under the User Activity tab?

**The two most common users are sa and System. You might also see additional users.**

6. On the Current Activity window toolbar, click the Display Legend button.

With the legend displayed, which processes are currently active (runnable)?

**The processes that are currently active will vary.**

Page 868

## Review Questions

1. When tuning a server, what information should you have before you begin?

   **A performance baseline.**

2. You have noticed that your server has been slowing down over time. Your server environment has consistently been changing. What tool or utility would you use to determine what the general problem is and when it is occurring?

   **SQL Performance Monitor.**

3. Your server runs well when no client applications are running, but when client applications are processing, performance is significantly degraded. You are unable to determine which Transact-SQL statements being executed by the client applications are causing the problem. Which tool or utility would you use to determine what the problem is?

   **SQL Trace.**

4. You have been experiencing long wait times and even complete halts in client application operations. Some clients are even receiving the error 1205. What tool or utility would you use to determine deadlocks and blocked locks? How can you terminate the offending process?

   **The SQL Enterprise Manager Current Activity window or sp_who and sp_lock. Use the KILL statement.**

C H A P T E R   2 0

# Distributed Data Overview

## About This Chapter

This chapter provides an overview of a distributed data environment and the various components and tools that go into making the environment work effectively and efficiently. The main focus of this chapter is on the need for distributed data, its advantages, and how it works. Various methods are discussed for distributing data. This chapter provides information and procedures for creating interactive, and database-driven World Wide Web (WWW) sites using the Microsoft SQL Server Web Assistant. You also look at replication models and learn how to determine the most appropriate replication scenario to fit your business needs.

## Before You Begin

To complete the lessons in this chapter, you must have:

- Installed SQL Server on your computer. Installation procedures are covered in Chapter 2, "Installing SQL Server."

- The *pubs* database installed. To update the *pubs* database, see \SCRIPTS\BLD_PUBS\INSTPUBS.SQL.

# Lesson 1: Overview

A distributed data environment is one in which multiple copies of the same information reside on multiple servers. The primary advantage of this type of network environment is that the information is made available to many users.

### After this lesson you will be able to:

- Explain the need for distributed data.
- Describe applications of tight and loose data consistency.
- Determine which methods to use when implementing distributed data in your environment.

### Estimated lesson time  10 minutes

## The Need for Distributed Data

In an environment where users are updating and reading data at the same time, access to data can get unnecessarily complicated. In a distributed data environment, component partitions of data are distributed over various nodes (stations of the network), reducing conflicts during user requests.

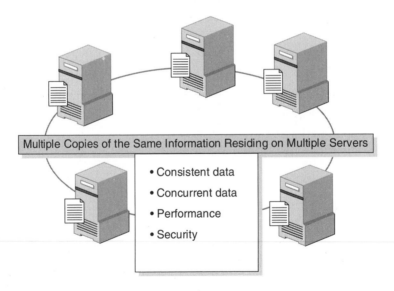

Multiple Copies of the Same Information Residing on Multiple Servers

- Consistent data
- Concurrent data
- Performance
- Security

Depending on the volume of update and retrieval activity, distributing data can significantly enhance overall server performance. However, you still have to provide adequate performance for users, as well as checks for data consistency, data concurrency, and database security. When multiple copies of the same data exist, such as in a distributed environment, getting up-to-the-minute, accurate information when you need it is a primary concern.

### Distributed Transactions and Replication

There are two models to ensure the consistency of data: *distributed transactions,* which ensure that data at all sites is in sync 100 percent of the time, and *replication,* which provides recent replicas of data. How current your data must be determines which model you use. Some environments, such as on-line transaction processing (OLTP), require that data be synchronized at all times. Other environments, such as decision support, require less frequent synchronization of data.

### Tight and Loose Consistency

Data consistency is often referred to as being either tight or loose. *Tight consistency*, implemented through the use of distributed transactions, guarantees that all updates to copies of data are consistently identical. It requires a high-speed local area network (LAN), reduces database availability, and is a less scalable model than one based on loose consistency. An appropriate use for this is a stock market transaction.

*Loose consistency* is a replication model that allows a time lag between the moment when original data is changed and when the replicated copies of that data are changed. It *does not* guarantee that all copies are consistently identical to the original at an exact point in time. An advantage of loose consistency is that it supports LANs, wide area networks (WANs), fast and slow communication links, and intermittently connected databases. It allows better database availability and is much more scalable than a tight consistency model. An example of a loose consistency model is credit card billing that you receive on a monthly basis (though the credit card company keeps its own data on a tight consistency basis). SQL Server replication is based on a loose consistency model.

## Methods for Distributing Data

Under the umbrella of distributed transactions and replication, there are many methods for implementing distributed data. Some of the tools that can be used in SQL Server are: the Microsoft Distributed Transaction Coordinator (MS DTC), replication, the SQL Server Web Assistant, remote stored procedures, removable media, and the Bulk Copy Program (**bcp**). Several of these methods were covered in other chapters in this book.

These tools for distributing data take many forms: they can be automatic or manual, dynamic or static. Each tool has varying degrees of data consistency and concurrency. As you can see in the following figure, a gain in one value means a decrease in the other. For example, DTC has the greatest consistency but the lowest concurrency. You should select the method that best meets the requirements of your system and your business environment.

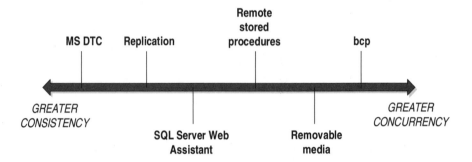

### Distributed Transaction Coordinator (DTC)

Distributed transactions update data on two or more network-connected computer systems and are available as part of Microsoft Distributed Transaction Coordinator (MS DTC), a built-in feature of SQL Server. DTC provides an interface to applications that update distributed data.

Distributed transactions are an essential tool for building robust, scalable, distributed applications. Distributed applications can be vulnerable to hardware and network failure. DTC creates a lower level of concurrency because a transaction cannot occur if one computer is offline or unavailable. However, distributed transactions permit distributed data to be updated while providing data integrity and consistency to the application.

**Note**  For a demonstration of how MS DTC processes transactions, see SQLMOD3.EXE in \DEMO on the compact disc.

### Replication

Replication can be used to automatically distribute read-only copies of transactional data. Data can be replicated continuously or at specified intervals. It can be replicated in its entirety or as filtered subsets. Each destination server can receive some or all of the replicated data. Any number of source and destination servers can exist in an enterprise, and servers can perform both source and destination roles.

You can keep multiple copies of a table up-to-date, keep multiple databases closely synchronized, intermittently update data on multiple databases, and resynchronize data following a system outage or failure. You can easily configure, manage, and monitor replication using SQL Enterprise Manager.

## SQL Server Web Assistant

SQL Server simplifies the creation and management of intranet and Internet applications. Microsoft SQL Server Web Assistant uses a step-by-step interface to assist you in the process of publishing Microsoft SQL Server data on the World Wide Web, making it easier to create interactive, database-driven Web sites.

The SQL Server Web Assistant automatically generates HTML pages or populates HTML templates with data from SQL Server when data changes or when it is a scheduled task.

When SQL Server is used in combination with Microsoft Internet Information Server (IIS), users can access Web browsers, including Microsoft Internet Explorer, to query data stored in SQL Server.

## Remote Stored Procedures

Remote stored procedures allow a client application to extend its reach—in a controlled environment—across multiple SQL servers to minimize the impact on the client, on the servers, and on the total number of open connections required. Remote stored procedure events can originate with clients or with SQL Server, and they can run either on the connected server or on another server on the network.

SQL Enterprise Manager manages both remote servers and remote logins. With the Remote Servers and Logins Manager interface, one person can manage many servers and centralize administrative tasks. With this interface, you can also set distribution options for replication and configure ODBC subscribers.

## Removable Media

With Microsoft SQL Server, you can create databases for distribution on removable media. You can distribute these databases on read-only removable media, such as a compact disc, or you can distribute on read/write, removable media, such as disks, WORM drives, or optical drives.

Removable media is one method for distributing large amounts of read-only data that is updated periodically, such as once a month or once a quarter. One disadvantage of using removable media is that you have to physically distribute a new compact disc each time you want to distribute new or updated data.

## Bulk Copy Program (bcp)

Using the Bulk Copy Program (**bcp**), you can import (insert) data into a new or existing table or export (select) data to an operating system file. For example, you can transfer large amounts of data to and from the SQL server, transfer data from another DBMS, or transfer data from one SQL server to another SQL server. However, **bcp** is not used frequently because its "picture" of the data is static. In a sense, it is like a snapshot that records a point in time.

You can use **bcp** to transfer:

- Large amounts of data to and from SQL Server.
- Selected columns or data with customized file format definitions.
- Data into SQL Server that was previously associated with another application, usually another DBMS.
- Data from one SQL server to another through an intermediate file.
- Data to other applications, such as a spreadsheet application or mainframe application.

Whether to use **bcp** depends on a number of factors including: the type of destination server you are using, the interface and types of source servers, and the amount of data you are transferring.

## Lesson Summary

A distributed data environment makes information available to many users. Copies of information are made available on multiple servers. In a distributed data environment, you can have significant improvement in overall data modification activity; however, you must pay additional attention to other issues, such as database security and data consistency. There are various methods to distribute data that provide varying degrees of consistency and concurrency.

| For more information on | See |
| --- | --- |
| The Bulk Copy Program (**bcp**) utility | Chapter 17, "Transferring Data" |
| The SQL Transfer Manager Interface | Chapter 17, "Transferring Data" |
| Removable media | Chapter 17, "Transferring Data" |

# Lesson 2: SQL Server and the World Wide Web

SQL Server makes it possible to publish database information on the World Wide Web. SQL Server contains both graphical tools and syntax-based tools to create Web pages. These Web pages contain the results of database queries.

### After this lesson you will be able to:

- Describe how SQL Server can interact with the Internet.
- Describe the *pull* and *push* models for publishing SQL Server data on the World Wide Web.
- Create and update Web pages using the SQL Server Web Assistant.

### Estimated lesson time  25 minutes

## World Wide Web (WWW) Pages

Web pages are also called HTML files. HTML commands or *tags* are added to a document using a text editor or using a specialized Web page editor such as the Microsoft Word Internet Assistant document authoring and viewing tool for Microsoft Windows, or the Microsoft FrontPage™ Web authoring and management tool. HTML tags are used to present and format simple text, tables, graphics, and database query results. HTML files form the basis for the Web pages that display on the World Wide Web. These files can be viewed with any HTML (or Web page) browser.

## The Microsoft Internet Information Server (IIS)

When you connect to the Internet, you communicate with other computers using servers and clients. The information and services resources of the Internet are on host computers called servers. An Internet server contains the Web pages, as well as other services including communication tools and methods for exchanging information with a database system. When a client computer connects to an Internet server, the client can view or retrieve files stored on the server.

Microsoft Internet Information Server (IIS) provides the software necessary to publish information on the Internet. IIS is available to run on any Microsoft Windows NT Server-based computer. With IIS you can publish Web documents, communicate with an ODBC database (such as SQL Server or Microsoft Access), and track Web use with built-in SQL Server analysis tools.

## Two Distribution Models

There are two ways to distribute data on the Internet: with the *data push* model or with the *data pull* model. With the *data push* model, you build a Web page and post it on an Internet server in the same way as you post information on a bulletin board. With this model, those who access the information cannot manipulate the data; they can only read it. Initially, Internet distribution followed this model almost exclusively. When you use the SQL Server tool for publishing data, the SQL Server Web Assistant, you are automatically using the *data push* model.

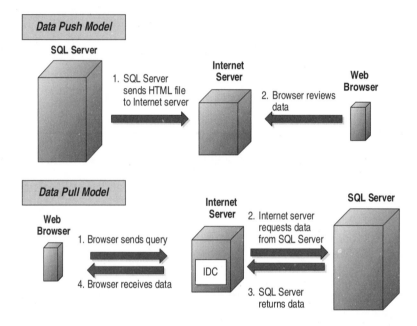

With the *data pull* model, a client opens a Web page posted on an Internet server and interacts with the page. Then the Internet server queries SQL Server for the requested information, pulls that information back, generates a new Web page, and sends the new Web page to the client. The key to this model is a component that can modify and retrieve information from SQL Server as well as create new Web pages. This component, the Internet Database Connector (IDC), is built into the Microsoft Internet Information Server, making it easy to use.

As more businesses use the Internet for operations such as making order forms available to their potential customers, this model will become the norm for interacting with customers over the Internet. However, because of its high level of interactivity, the *data pull* model is a much more complex way to distribute data. Also, its use is dependent on having a mechanism in place that allows a Web server to communicate with the database.

**Note**  You can download the Microsoft Internet Information Server from http://www.microsoft.com.

## SQL Server Web Assistant

The SQL Server Web Assistant is an easy-to-use graphical tool for creating HTML files (Web pages) from SQL Server data. This is the tool you use to implement the *data push* model. With SQL Server Web Assistant, you can generate pages on a one-time basis or as a regularly scheduled SQL Server task. A Web page can also be updated using a trigger when the supporting data changes.

SQL Server Web Assistant is automatically installed with SQL Server and can be installed on 32-bit clients. In order to use SQL Server Web Assistant, you must have CREATE PROCEDURE privileges in the database and SELECT privileges on the columns accessed by the query.

**Note**  SQL Server Web Assistant is only available on Intel-based computers. Internet capabilities are available on other platforms using system stored procedures.

▶   **To run the SQL Server Web Assistant**

- From the SQL Server program group, double-click the SQL Server Web Assistant icon.

The SQL Server Web Assistant - Login dialog box appears. The login settings are identical to those for SQL Server logins.

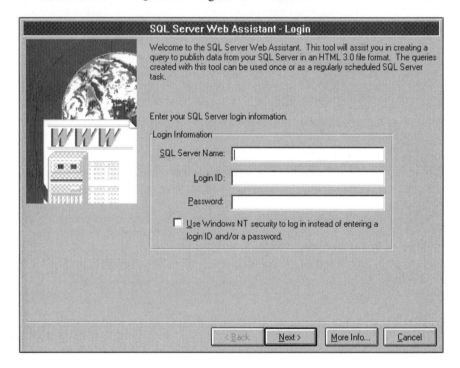

## SQL Server Web Assistant Options

When you have connected to Web Assistant, you supply certain information and make selections from other options in a series of dialog boxes.

### Specifying the Query

Using SQL Server Web Assistant, you can build queries from a graphical database/table hierarchy, enter queries directly as text, or use an existing stored procedure. The Query page asks you to select how to supply the query, then to type the query.

**Note**  The graphical query builder requires you to specify joins (ORDER BY and GROUP BY) separately. It performs Cartesian products when you select multiple tables without explicitly specifying a join.

### Scheduling

You can schedule the creation of Web pages as is listed in the following table.

| Scheduling option | Description |
| --- | --- |
| Now | Immediate, one time execution. |
| Later | Scheduled task, one time execution for a specific date and time. |
| When Data Changes | Automatic, triggered execution. You specify that changes to certain tables and columns cause the Web page to be updated. |
| On Certain Days of the Week | Scheduled task, execution at a day and time; for example, Wednesday at noon. |
| On a Regular basis | Scheduled task, execution every $n$ minutes, hours, days, or weeks; for example, every 5 minutes. |

### File Options

SQL Server Web Assistant allows you to specify the following file options:

- The filename and path of the Web page to be created.

  This is either on a local or a remote computer. The default is C:\WEB.HTML.

- A template file.

  This optional file can be used as a template for the Web page. The template can contain any static text, Universal Resource Locator (URL) links, or other features that you want to include. You can create your template with any text editor or Web page editor and insert the following tag where you want SQL Server to merge the result of the query into the document.

  ```
  <%insert_data_here%>
  ```

- The title of the Web page.

  This title is inserted and formats a heading at the top of the HTML file.

- The title for the query results.

  This title is inserted just before the results set in the HTML file.

- Any URL links to be included on the Web page.

  You can specify one or more URL links, or you can specify a database query that returns URL links as the result.

### Formatting Options

HTML offers a limited variety of fonts and formatting options. You can specify which HTML heading styles to use for titles of the Web page and data sections. Additionally, you can choose fixed or proportional fonts as well as bold and italic typefaces for the data portion of the Web page. A timestamp and column headers can be added. You can also limit the query results to a certain number of rows. Keep in mind that if you use a template file, several of these options will already be determined. After the page is generated, you can manually edit it to enhance the formatting and presentation of the data with additional HTML tags.

## A Sample HTML File Generated by SQL Server Web Assistant

The following options were used to generate an HTML file. Other options were left at their default settings.

| Option | Selection |
| --- | --- |
| Database | Pubs |
| SQL Statement | SELECT distinct au_lname as 'Author', title as 'Title' FROM authors, titles, titleauthor WHERE authors.au_id = titleauthor.au_id AND titleauthor.title_id = titles.title_id |
| Template | no template used |
| Web page title | West Overshoe Library |
| Title for query results | Available New Books |
| Insert a timestamp | selected |
| Include column names | selected |

**Example**                The following example shows how an HTML file appears.

```
<HTML>
<HEAD>
<TITLE>West Overshoe Library</TITLE>
</HEAD>
<BODY>
<H2>Available New Books</H2>
<HR>
<PRE><B>Last updated: Apr 4 1996  1:58PM</B></PRE>
<P>
<P><TABLE BORDER=1>
<TR><TH ALIGN=LEFT>Author</TH><TH ALIGN=LEFT>Title</TH></TR>
<TR><TD NOWRAP><B>Bennet</B></TD><TD NOWRAP><B>The Busy Executive's
Database Guide</B></TD></TR>
<TR><TD NOWRAP><B>Blotchet-Halls</B></TD><TD NOWRAP><B>Fifty Years in
Buckingham Palace Kitchens</B></TD></TR>
<TR><TD NOWRAP><B>Carson</B></TD><TD NOWRAP><B>But Is It User
Friendly?</B></TD></TR>
        .
        .
        .

<TR><TD NOWRAP><B>Hunter</B></TD><TD NOWRAP><B>Secrets of Silicon
Valley</B></TD></TR>
</TABLE>
<HR>
</BODY>
</HTML>
```

After the HTML file has been generated, you can view it with any Web browser. The following figure shows the Web page viewed through Microsoft Internet Explorer.

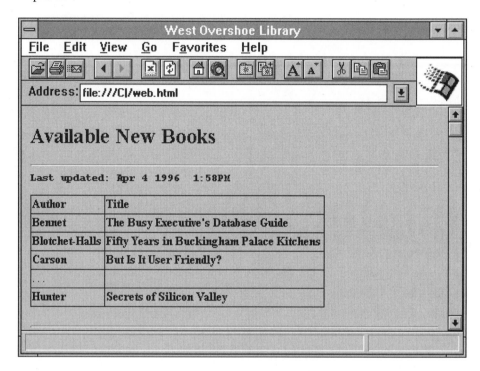

## Creating and Updating a Web Page with SQL Server Web Assistant

In the following procedures, you create a simple static Web page, view the Web page, create a trigger to update the Web page when data changes in the database, view the trigger, test the trigger, create a task to update the Web page on a regular basis, and then view the task.

▶ **To create a Web page**

1. Open the SQL Server Web Assistant.

2. Log in to SQL Server as SA with your SA password.

3. In the SQL Server Web Assistant - Query dialog box, select Enter a Query as Free Form Text.

4. Select the *pubs* database, and then type the following query:

   **SELECT au_fname, au_lname FROM authors**

5. Click Next.

   The Scheduling Option dialog box appears.

6. Confirm that the Scheduling Option dialog box specifies to create the task **Now**.

7. Click Next.

   The File Options dialog box appears.

8. In the File Options dialog box, enter the following options.

   | Option | Value |
   | --- | --- |
   | Filename | C:\AUTHORS.HTML |
   | Title of the Web page | West Overshoe Library |
   | Title for the query results | Authors in the Libraries Collection |
   | URL links | none |

9. Click Next.

   The Formatting dialog box appears.

10. Accept the default options by clicking Finish.

▶ **To view the created Web page**

In this procedure, you view the Web page source first with Notepad, and then with a Web browser.

1. Open Notepad.

2. Open the C:\AUTHORS.HTML file.

3. Review the contents of this file.

4. Open your Web browser.

5. Open the Authors.HTML file.

6. Notice how the HTML code is displayed by your Web browser.

▶ **To create a trigger to update a Web page**

In this procedure, you create a trigger at the same time that you create a Web page.

1. Open the SQL Server Web Assistant.

2. Log in to SQL Server as SA with your SA password.

3. In the SQL Server Web Assistant-Query dialog box, select Enter a Query as Free Form Text.

4. Select the *pubs* database, and then type the following query:

   **SELECT au_fname, au_lname FROM authors**

5. Click Next.

   The Scheduling dialog box appears.

6. In the Scheduling dialog box, select When Data Changes from the list.

7. Select the *authors* table, the *au_id, au_fname,* and *au_lname* columns from the tree.

8. Use the default options to complete the rest of the steps that create the Web page.

▶ **To view the trigger**

1. In the SQL Enterprise Manager Server Manager window, open the Databases folder.

2. Expand the *pubs* database to the *tables* folder.

3. Click the secondary mouse button on the *authors* table.

4. Click Triggers.

   The Manage Triggers dialog box appears.

5. Examine the SQL statement that creates the trigger.

6. Close the window when finished.

▶ **To test the trigger**

In this procedure you insert new information into the *pubs..authors* table.

1. Open a query window, and then type the following SQL statement:

   **USE PUBS**
   **INSERT INTO authors (au_id, au_fname, au_lname, contract)**
   **VALUES ('111-22-3333', 'Johann', 'Bach', 2**

   Inserting a new row into the *authors* table causes the trigger to fire and a new version of the Web page to be created.

2. Using either Notepad or a Web browser, view the resulting C:\AUTHORS.HTML file.

▶ **To create a task to update the Web page**

1. Start SQL Server Web Assistant and create a new page. When the Scheduling Option dialog box appears, select On a Regular Basis from the list.

2. Set the task to be done every 5 minutes.

3. Use the default options to complete the rest of the steps that create the Web page.

▶  **To view the task**

1. Switch to SQL Enterprise Manager.

2. Select your server in the Server Manager Window.

3. On the Server menu, click Scheduled Tasks.

   The Manage Scheduled Tasks window appears.

4. Confirm that your Web task appears on the Task List.

5. Select your Web task from the list.

6. On the toolbar, click Run Task (the clock with green arrow icon).

7. On the toolbar, click Task History to confirm that the Web page was created.

8. Click Delete Task to remove this task from the schedule.

9. Close the Manage Scheduled Tasks window.

## Using System Stored Procedures for Web Pages

In addition to the graphical SQL Server Web Assistant, the system stored procedures, **sp_makewebtask**, **sp_runwebtask**, and **sp_dropwebtask**, can be used to create and manage the generation of Web pages from SQL Server data. These procedures provide the same options as SQL Server Web Assistant, but they also allow you to build this functionality into your own scripts and triggers. Because SQL Server Web Assistant is only available on the Intel platform, you must use these system stored procedures on Power PC™, MIPS, or Alpha installations.

**Syntax**

**sp_makewebtask** {@outputfile = '*outputfile*', @query = '*query*'}
[, [@fixedfont = *fixedfont*,] [@bold = *bold*,] [@italic = *italic*,]
[@colheaders = *colheaders*,] [@lastupdated = *lastupdated*,]
[@HTMLHeader = *HTMLHeader*,] [@username = *username*,]
[@dbname = *dbname*,] [@templatefile = '*templatefile*',]
[@webpagetitle = '*webpagetitle*',] [@resultstitle = '*resultstitle*',]
[[@URL = '*URL*', @reftext = '*reftext*'] |
[@table_urls = *table_urls*, @url_query = '*url_query*',]]
[@whentype = *whentype*,] [@targetdate = *targetdate*,] [@targettime = *targettime*,]
[@dayflags = *dayflags*,] [@numunits = *numunits*,] [@unittype = *unittype*,]
[@procname = *procname*, ] [@maketask = *maketask*,] [@rowcnt = *rowcnt*,]
[@tabborder = *tabborder*,] [@singlerow = *singlerow*,] [@blobfmt = *blobfmt*]]

After the task is created, it can be executed with **sp_runwebtask** or deleted with **sp_dropwebtask**. The output of **sp_runwebtask** is the HTML file containing the query results.

**Syntax**

**sp_runwebtask** { @procname = procname | @outputfile = outputfile | @procname = procname, @outputfile = outputfile }

**Example**

```
sp_runwebtask @procname = MYHTMLTASK, @outputfile =
'C:\Web\Availbks.html'
```

## Lesson Summary

You can create a World Wide Web page to publish SQL Server database information using SQL Server Web Assistant. The Web pages are published over the Internet or a corporate intranet. There are two models used to distribute data on the Internet: the *data pull* and the *data push* models. SQL Server Web Assistant implements the data push model.

| For more information on | See |
| --- | --- |
| SQL Server Web Assistant | "SQL Server Web Assistant" in SQL Server Books Online |
| Microsoft Internet Explorer | www.microsoft.com |
| Microsoft Internet Information Server (IIS) | www.microsoft.com |

# Lesson 3: Replication Overview

Replication is a duplication of table data from a source database to a destination database, usually (but not necessarily) on separate servers. This lesson provides an introduction to SQL Server replication, describing its essential features, components, and capabilities.

## After this lesson you will be able to:

- Describe the publisher/subscriber metaphor used in SQL Server replication.
- Explain the roles of the publication, distribution, and subscription servers.
- Describe the types of replication models.
- Determine the appropriate replication scenario to fit a specific business environment.
- Explain publication rules and *push* and *pull* subscriptions.

## Estimated lesson time  15 minutes

## What Is Replication?

Replication allows you to automatically distribute read-only copies of transactional data from a single source server to one or more destination servers at one or more remote locations. Data can be replicated continuously or at specified intervals. It can be replicated in its entirety or as filtered subsets. Each destination server can receive some or all of the replicated data. Any number of source and destination servers can exist in an enterprise, and servers can perform both source and destination roles.

### Characteristics of SQL Server Replication

The following lists the primary characteristics of SQL Server replication.

- It is transaction log-based—transactions marked for replication are read from the transaction log of the source database and are applied to the destination databases.
- It uses a publisher/subscriber metaphor to easily replicate SQL Server data to various servers.
- It places servers in different roles—publisher, distributor, and subscriber.
- It uses a dedicated SQL Server database—a queue for replicated data.
- It offers flexibility when selecting data that is replicated to other databases.
- It provides easy, graphical tools for set up and administration.
- It enhances security by limiting which users can set up and administer replication and which destination servers can receive (or even see) tables available for replication.

# Replication Goals

The goals of SQL Server replication are: continuous distribution of transactions, a minimal amount of time for the replication process (minimal transaction latency), maximum concurrency, transaction consistency, an ability to replicate at the row level and column level, replication to different (heterogeneous) data sources such as Microsoft Access and ORACLE, and fault-tolerant design.

*Continuous distribution of transactions* is managed by the distribution task. This task can be configured to execute in varying degrees of frequency from immediate to once every two months, or on demand. The time it takes for the distribution task to deliver the changes to a subscription server is known as *transaction latency*.

By implementing replication, many copies of data are maintained from one data source. Replicating data minimizes user conflicts on the data. This is beneficial in an environment where there is both OLTP and decision support (DS) activity on the same server. By separating this activity, *maximum concurrency* can be achieved. When a transaction affects several tables, those changes are replicated as a single transaction on the subscriber so the data remains consistent. *Transaction consistency* is maintained through the distribution server.

The data to be replicated can be specified at row and column levels. This allows flexibility in specifying only the data you want to replicate. After the data is defined, only changes to that data are replicated to the subscriber, thus allowing replication to other (*heterogeneous*) database environments in the future.

*Fault-tolerant design* refers to the distribution database. Replication does not actually replicate the data; it replicates the Transact-SQL statements (UPDATE, INSERT, and DELETE) as transactions.

# Replication Benefits

The benefits of replication are:

- Improved data availability through autonomous site operations.
- Improved performance.
- Distribution of the workload across multiple servers.
- Physical separation of online transaction processing environments from decision support systems.
- Reduction of network traffic through the decentralization of data.
- Support of a range of organizational models by providing a flexible and scalable model.

# How Replication Works

For data to be made available for replication, a publication must be created. The following publisher/subscriber metaphor describes how SQL Server replication works in a publishing environment.

## The Publisher/Subscriber Metaphor

In a publishing environment, a publisher disseminates information and a subscriber receives information. In SQL Server replication a server can perform these roles: publication server, distribution server, and subscription server. A server can play one of these roles or any combination of these roles.

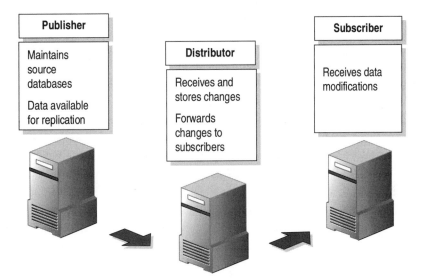

### Publisher (Publication Server)

A publication server maintains the source database, makes published data from those databases available for replication, and disseminates all changes made to published data to the distribution server.

### Distributor (Distribution Server)

The distribution server is the server where the distribution database, also known as the store-and-forward database, is located. The distribution server receives all of the changes to the published data, stores the changes in the distribution database, and then forwards the changes to the appropriate subscription servers. The publisher and the distributor can be on the same server, but in heavy use, you should put the distributor on its own server.

### Subscriber (Subscription Server)

The subscription server holds a copy of the data and receives the changes from the modified published data.

### Data On Subscriber Should Be Treated As Read-Only

In SQL Server replication, published data moves in only one direction—from the publishing server to the subscribing servers. Data should be modified only on the publishing server. The replicated data copied to a subscribing server should be treated as read-only and should *not* be updated on the subscriber. This does not mean that the database option should be set to read-only. Setting the database to read-only limits the ability to apply replicated inserts, updates, and deletes. While SQL Server does not restrict the ability to update replicated data on the subscribers, doing this can cause future replicated transactions to fail. Give only SELECT permissions on the replicated table. When designing complex replication scenarios, it becomes critical to uniquely identify data from multiple sources to ensure that only local data, not replicated data, can be updated on the local server.

## Transaction Log-Based Replication

SQL Server uses transaction log-based replication. This implementation means that only the transactions or changes to the data are replicated, not the entire table. The transaction log marks modifications designated for replication. All changes to a replicated table are applied to destination tables residing on multiple destination servers asynchronously, allowing the main database processing to continue.

After the servers are configured for replication and the source and destination data tables are synchronized, SQL Server replication on the publisher monitors the transaction log of each database that has been set up for replication, searching for transactions marked for replication. The transactions are copied to the *distribution* database where they are held until they can be distributed to the appropriate destination servers and applied to the destination databases.

This solution is based on delivering individual transactions intact to the destination database. Replication can be accomplished without completely excluding user access to tables during the associated inserts, deletes, and updates.

## Synchronization

Synchronization allows for entire databases or individual tables to be synchronized before replication of data modifications begins. Synchronization of new subscribers happens at time intervals defined by an administrator. A scheduled synchronization event for tables or databases is required as the first step for initiating replication. This is accomplished by providing a snapshot of the table schema and the data in the table to ensure data integrity. Then, modifications to the published data can be replicated to the subscribing servers.

## Types of Replication Models

There are four basic replication models. These models provide examples of how the server roles can be implemented in replication.

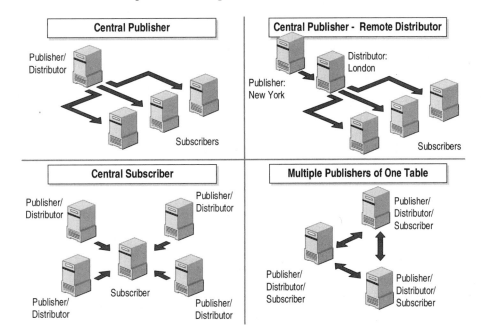

### Central Publisher

In this model, one server is defined as the publisher. The publisher distributes data to any number of servers that are set up as subscribers. This model is the default option for replication in SQL Server. The publication server is the primary owner or source of all replicated data. Subscription sites should treat replicated data as read-only.

### Central Publisher Using a Remote Distributor

This scenario is similar to the central publisher model except that a separate distribution server is established to store data before it is published to the subscribing servers. This offloads much of the replication work from the publisher to the distributor.

### Central Subscriber

In this model, multiple publishers replicate data to a single subscriber. This scenario addresses the need for consolidating data at a centralized site and providing the local site with only the local data. Because multiple publishers are writing to the same subscription table, precautions must be taken to ensure that all data has a unique local owner and is not overwritten by any other publisher.

## Multiple Publishers of One Table

In this model, multiple publication servers and multiple subscription servers each potentially play a dual role. This model is the closest implementation to fully distributed data processing. Care must be taken in designing both the schema and update methods to ensure that the data at all sites remains consistent.

## Examples of Replication Models

The following scenarios describe how two of the models are implemented to fit different environments and to solve specific replication problems.

### Central Subscriber Example

An Australian company sells automobile parts. The company has four independent distributors that have warehouses in different regions of Australia. All warehouses manage their own inventories. Low inventory levels are not noticed until a warehouse is unable to completely fill a customer's order. Then the inventory control manager at the warehouse places an order with the supplier. This procedure requires that each warehouse manually monitor and place orders because there is no centralized inventory monitoring.

As illustrated in the following figure, this problem can be solved by implementing a central subscriber replication scenario that rolls up the inventory information from all of the regional sites to a master inventory database at the central site.

*region1 orders (Publication server)*

| PK | | | |
|---|---|---|---|
| reg_code | id | order_no | qty |
| 1 | 1000 | ~ | ~ |
| 1 | 3100 | ~ | ~ |

*region2 orders (Publication server)*

| PK | | | |
|---|---|---|---|
| reg_code | id | order_no | qty |
| 2 | 1000 | ~ | ~ |
| 2 | 2380 | ~ | ~ |

*master orders (Subscriber server)*

| PK | | | |
|---|---|---|---|
| reg_code | id | order_no | qty |
| 1 | 1000 | ~ | ~ |
| 1 | 3100 | ~ | ~ |
| 2 | 1000 | ~ | ~ |
| 2 | 2380 | ~ | ~ |
| 3 | 1000 | ~ | ~ |
| 3 | 1070 | ~ | ~ |
| 4 | 1000 | ~ | ~ |
| 4 | 2000 | ~ | ~ |

*region3 orders (Publication server)*

| PK | | | |
|---|---|---|---|
| reg_code | id | order_no | qty |
| 3 | 1000 | ~ | ~ |
| 3 | 1070 | ~ | ~ |

*region4 orders (Publication server)*

| PK | | | |
|---|---|---|---|
| reg_code | id | order_no | qty |
| 4 | 1000 | ~ | ~ |
| 4 | 2000 | ~ | ~ |

To successfully configure this replication scenario, consider these design issues:

- At present, the id number for the auto parts is the same in all regions. To uniquely identify information from the different regional warehouses, create a separate region code column. This identifies data from a particular region when it is viewed at the central site.

- Create a composite primary key of the location-specific column and the part id column. In this example, the *reg_code* and *id* columns comprise the primary key.

By taking these steps, records from one site will be uniquely identified; they will not conflict with records from the other sites.

### Multiple Publishers of One Table Example

A Parisian pastry company has three shops located in different areas of Paris. When one shop runs out of a necessary ingredient, that shop must contact one or both of the other shops to find out if it is in stock, and then separately arrange to have it ordered. A more efficient approach uses the multiple publishers of one table model.

In the following figure, Servers A, B, and C—representing each of the three shops—have a copy of the *orders* table. Each server publishes the rows of the *orders* table that it owns to the other two servers, and it also subscribes to the rows of the *orders* table owned by the other two servers. Each server has responsibility for only a portion of the data. The *orders* table is horizontally partitioned by region. For example, Server A is responsible for updating the data in region 1 and treats the remaining rows as read-only. For this scenario to work, each server should only update the data for its own region.

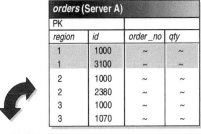

*orders* (Server A)

| PK | | | |
|---|---|---|---|
| region | id | order_no | qty |
| 1 | 1000 | ~ | ~ |
| 1 | 3100 | ~ | ~ |
| 2 | 1000 | ~ | ~ |
| 2 | 2380 | ~ | ~ |
| 3 | 1000 | ~ | ~ |
| 3 | 1070 | ~ | ~ |

*orders* (Server B)

| PK | | | |
|---|---|---|---|
| region | id | order_no | qty |
| 1 | 1000 | ~ | ~ |
| 1 | 3100 | ~ | ~ |
| 2 | 1000 | ~ | ~ |
| 2 | 2380 | ~ | ~ |
| 3 | 1000 | ~ | ~ |
| 3 | 1070 | ~ | ~ |

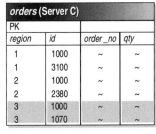

*orders* (Server C)

| PK | | | |
|---|---|---|---|
| region | id | order_no | qty |
| 1 | 1000 | ~ | ~ |
| 1 | 3100 | ~ | ~ |
| 2 | 1000 | ~ | ~ |
| 2 | 2380 | ~ | ~ |
| 3 | 1000 | ~ | ~ |
| 3 | 1070 | ~ | ~ |

Using this model, a pastry shop that runs out of chocolate for its *pains au chocolat* can immediately identify the shop that has surplus chocolate and order it.

---

**Note**  Only the data changed for the local region is replicated, not the entire table.

---

## Articles and Publications

In keeping with the publisher/subscriber metaphor, data to be published is referred to as either an article or a publication. An *article* is a single table or subset of data in a table. It is the basic unit of replication. An article is always part of a publication; it cannot be published by itself.

A *publication* contains one or more articles (individual tables) marked for replication. One or more publications can be created from each user database on a publication server. If a publication is subscribed to, then all of the articles within the publication are subscribed to. It is not necessary to subscribe to articles individually, although it is possible to do so. There is an advantage to subscribing to an entire publication rather than to individual articles: SQL Server replication synchronizes all articles in the publication as a group, preserving referential integrity between the underlying tables.

## Publishing Rules

In a user-defined database, any table or subset of data in a table can be published. There are some restrictions in terms of system tables and certain datatypes. An important criteria for all published tables is that they must contain a primary key.

### What Can Be Published

You can publish all SQL Server columns, including *text* and *image* columns. You can also publish groups of tables, individual tables, or partitions of tables. Tables can be partitioned vertically, horizontally, or vertically and horizontally. You can vertically partition a table so that only selected columns are published and subscription servers receive only that subset of the columns of the source table. When vertically partitioning data for replication, the replicated columns must contain the primary key.

In the following figure showing *vertical partitioning*, note that only the replicated columns appear in the subscription server.

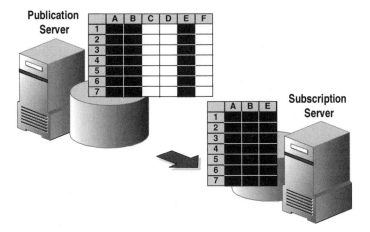

You can also horizontally partition a table by limiting the *rows* to be published. Providing a WHERE clause for the article makes this possible. In the following figure that shows *horizontal partitioning*, note that subscription servers receive only the subset of the rows in the table.

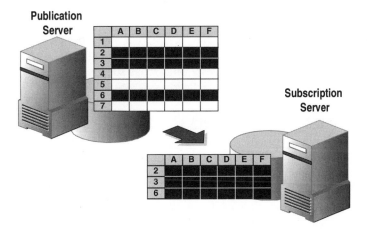

**Note**  Each instance of a partitioned table is a separate article and appears as such in the publication list.

It is possible to combine vertical and horizontal partitioning to publish only certain columns and certain rows.

### What Cannot Be Published

You cannot publish *model*, *tempdb*, *msdb*, and *system* tables in the *master* database; tables lacking a primary key; *timestamp* columns, they are converted to *binary*(8) columns; and *identity* columns. (An *identity* column does not carry the IDENTITY property with it, but it does replicate the data.)

## Subscription Options

You have the option to subscribe to entire publications or to individual articles within a publication.

### Initiating a Subscription

The process of initiating a subscription can occur from either the publishing side (a push subscription) or from the subscribing side (a pull subscription).

### Push Subscription

With a push subscription, the publication server performs all of the administration of setting up subscriptions during the process of defining a publication. The advantage of a push subscription is that it simplifies and centralizes administration. You can set up multiple subscribers at the same time. Push subscriptions are possible only when the user who administers and manages the publication server also has SA rights on the subscription servers.

### Pull Subscription

With a pull subscription, the subscription server performs all of the administration of setting up the subscription after the initial publication has been created. The advantage of a pull subscription is that a subscriber can browse a list of available publications to determine what data to subscribe to.

## Heterogeneous Data Replication

SQL Server has extended replication capabilities. SQL Server information can now be replicated to Oracle and Microsoft Access databases, as well as other ODBC-compliant databases. This allows SQL Server to easily operate in mixed database environments and is particularly useful in distributed environments for moving information closer to the users who need it.

## Lesson Summary

Replication is a duplication of table data from a source to a destination database. It uses a publisher/subscriber metaphor. There are four basic replication models. SQL Server replication maintains transaction consistency and allows replication to other databases.

| For more information on | See |
| --- | --- |
| *text* and *image* columns | "*text* and *image* Replication" in SQL Server Books Online |
| Replication | "Replication Terminology," and "Frequently Asked Questions," in SQL Server Books Online |

# Lesson 4: Replication Processing

In the previous lesson, you were introduced to SQL Server replication. This lesson takes a more detailed look at how replication works.

## After this lesson you will be able to:

- Identify replication components.
- Describe the log reader, synchronization, and replication distribution processes.
- Describe the four methods of synchronization.

## Estimated lesson time  10 minutes

A server can be configured to play a single role, or any combination of roles, in the publisher/subscriber metaphor. For simplicity, these roles are referred to separately in this section. The following figure shows an overview of replication processing. The steps in the process are outlined in greater detail in the following pages.

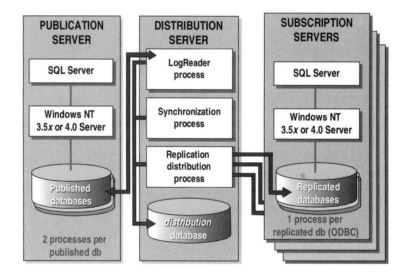

## Replication Components

There are replication components specific to each of the server roles. These replication components are listed in the following table.

| Publication server | Distribution server | Subscription server |
| --- | --- | --- |
| Published databases | Log reader process | Subscription server administration |
| Transaction log | Synchronization process | Subscription event processing |
| | Distribution process | Replicated tables |
| | *distribution* database | |

## The Log Reader Process

The log reader process is the mechanism used by SQL Server to monitor the transaction log of a published database to see if any changes have occurred that must be replicated.

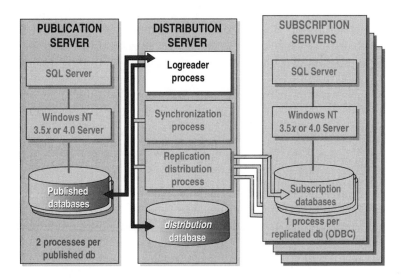

Each published database has its own separate process to monitor the log. The log reader uses two processes per published database: one process monitors the published database and another process moves the replicated data from the publisher to the distributor. This takes place in the following order:

1. The published database transaction log marks the transaction for replication.
2. The log reader monitors the transaction log of each database enabled for publication and at scheduled intervals checks for marked log records.
3. The log reader copies the marked transaction from the publication server transaction log into the *distribution* database and constructs a SQL statement or stored procedure that will be used to recreate changes at the subscription server.

   The *distribution* database holds all of the replicated publication transactions that must be distributed to subscription servers. The transaction log of the *distribution* database is maintained in the same manner as any transaction log.

---

**Note** Transactions are applied at the subscription server in the same order that they occur in the publication server.

---

During normal operation, transactions marked for replication are preserved in the transaction log of the publication database until they have been moved into the *distribution* database by the log reader. After this occurs, log entries will be truncated or removed using normal procedures.

## The Synchronization Process

Before replication can begin, synchronization must occur. This ensures that the data in the replicated table is identical to the data in the source table at a point in time. It also guarantees that replication transactions will succeed.

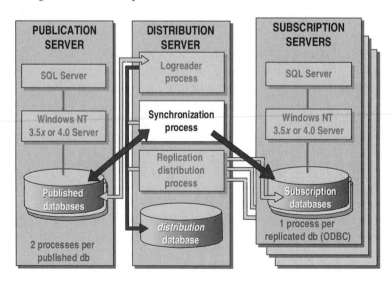

Synchronization is performed to ensure that the schema and data located on each subscription server are exact replicas of the article or publication in the publication database. Synchronization applies to new subscribers only. After a subscriber is initially synchronized, all changes are applied through the distribution process and additional synchronization is no longer required.

The synchronization process is initiated automatically for each subscription at scheduled intervals. At periodic intervals, the process checks to see if any new subscribers have been added. If there are no new subscribers, nothing occurs until the next scheduled synchronization. If there are new subscribers, the following steps are performed:

1. A synchronization set is created from the schema and the data. Each article within a publication has a synchronization set.

   A script (.SCH) file is created from the table schema. This script is stored in the default directory \MSSQL\REPLDATA on the server with the *distribution* database. The script file includes indexes, if requested.

   A data (.TMP) file is created from the data. It is stored in the same directory. The file is a **bcp** output file. Native mode **bcp** is used only for SQL Server subscribers. Character mode is used for an ODBC destination.

2. A synchronization job is added to the *distribution* database.

3. All modifications to the published data that have occurred since the start of the synchronization process are placed as transactions into the *distribution* database after the initial synchronization job.

4. The synchronization set of files is applied on the subscription server to create the table replicas.

5. The distribution server is notified that synchronization is completed (if manual synchronization was not specified).

6. Transactions that have accumulated in the *distribution* database are then applied to the subscriber at scheduled intervals.

7. After all of the subscriptions have acknowledged successful synchronization, all data (.TMP) files are deleted from the working directory when the cleanup task is executed. This task is automatically created when replication is installed.

## Methods of Synchronization

Four synchronization methods are available for replication: automatic, manual, no synchronization, and scheduled table refresh.

### Automatic

This synchronization method is the default. It is useful when the table being published is not too large. Automatic synchronization:

- Is initiated by SQL Server.
- Creates the synchronization set (.SCH and .TMP files). Synchronization automatically occurs.
- Automatically creates the tables on the subscriber and bulk copies in the data. No interaction on the part of the user is required.
- Can occur at scheduled intervals.
- Can be scheduled for a low-activity period on the publication server.
- Occurs only for those subscribers that have requested synchronization (not subscribers that are already synchronized).

Scheduled synchronization occurs based on the date and time of the distribution server, not the subscription servers.

### Manual

Manual synchronization is useful when the table being published is large and the publication and subscription servers are connected by a slow, expensive, or poor quality network connection. The following takes place with manual synchronization:

- It creates the synchronization set (.SCH and .TMP files) from the working directory of the distribution database (by default, \MSSQL\REPLDATA). This is automatic.
- It is implemented by the administrator moving the .SCH and .TMP files to the subscriber and executing the scripts and/or **bcp** to set up the replica tables.
- It is moved to the subscriber server using tape backup or another medium.

You must inform SQL Server that the manual synchronization is complete by using SQL Enterprise Manger or by incrementing the *MSlast_job_info* table in the subscribing database.

### No Synchronization

The no synchronization option method bypasses the creation and application of the synchronization set. SQL Server assumes that the schema and data in the destination tables are a snapshot of the published article at the time of the creation of the publication. It is the responsibility of the user to ensure that the schema and data are synchronized. Replication can begin immediately after the user acknowledges that synchronization has occurred. This option is useful when the administrator can guarantee that the data is synchronized; for example, after a standard dump and load has occurred on the subscriber.

### Scheduled Table Refresh

The Scheduled Table Refresh option provides the means to periodically replicate a snapshot of the data. The synchronization set is created periodically and applied to the subscriber. Subsequent modifications to the published data are not applied transaction-by-transaction to the subscribers. A table refresh can be scheduled to occur at defined intervals. This option is available when initially setting up the subscription: you can choose either Transaction Based or Scheduled Table Refresh.

## The Replication Distribution Process

The replication distribution process distributes replicated publication transactions held in the *distribution* database to each subscription server.

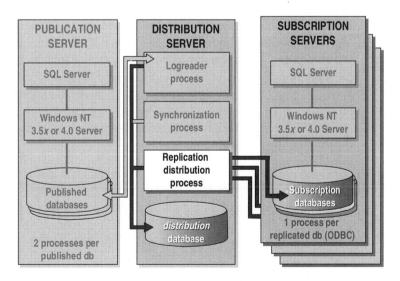

The replication distribution process performs the following:

1. It distributes transactions to all subscribers at scheduled intervals. This is set up as one task for each subscribing database. The process starts from the last received job.

2. After a replication transaction is committed, the event entry is either removed from the *distribution* database or set to hold the entry for statistics and recovery purposes. This only happens if the transaction has been distributed to all subscribers.

3. It updates the *jobid* column in the *MSlast_job_info* table in the subscription server's database.

---

**Note** Each subscriber has a separate distribution process. An ODBC connection is made to each subscriber.

---

## Subscription Server

The subscription server is set up to receive replicated data. Before a subscription server can receive logged transactions for any replicated object, the object must first be synchronized between the two servers. Synchronization can occur automatically, or the subscription server can request manual synchronization.

The subscription server:

- Receives updates (replicated transactions) as SQL statements or stored procedures. Note that stored procedures might improve performance.

- Stores the most recent sequence number in the subscription (*MSlast_job_info*) table. Note that each publisher database has a separate entry.

---

**Note** Constraints and triggers are enforced at the publisher, and should not be declared at the subscriber.

---

## Lesson Summary

Replication begins with the synchronization of data. After data is synchronized, the log reader process begins reading changes recorded in the published database log. Then the distribution process delivers those changes to all subscribers.

| For more information on | See |
| --- | --- |
| Cleanup task | "Replication Cleanup" in SQL Server Books Online |
| Distribution database tables | "System Tables—Replication Tables" in SQL Server Books Online |
| Manual synchronization | "Manual Synchronization" in SQL Server Books Online |

# Review

The following questions are intended to reinforce key information presented in this chapter. If you are unable to answer a question, review the lesson and then try the question again.

### Distributed Data Scenario

Your company has been experiencing locking problems. This occurs when the Sales and Marketing department runs its daily reports while the Order Processing department is processing orders. Because of this, your company has decided to implement some form of data replication. In order to choose the appropriate method or tool for making copies of the company data, which features and characteristics should be considered when defining your requirements?

_____

_____

_____

_____

### SQL Server and the World Wide Web Scenario

Your company sells tickets to major sporting events and concerts. How can you use the *push* model to publish information about upcoming events onto the World Wide Web?

_____

_____

_____

_____

### Replication Scenario

Your company has decided to replicate data using Microsoft SQL Server replication. You are currently in the planning and design phase of your replication strategy. Your company is a large international manufacturer that has a large number of distributors around the world. Your goal is to receive all of the distributors' sales information on a daily basis at the company headquarters. Because most of your distributors are remote, you are concerned about the high cost of all of the telephone lines that will be used to receive the information from all of the distributors. With this in mind, which replication model(s) would you implement? Why?

_____

_____

_____

_____

# Questions and Answers

Page 910

### Review Questions

#### Distributed Data Scenario

Your company has been experiencing locking problems. This occurs when the Sales and Marketing department runs its daily reports while the Order Processing department is processing orders. Because of this, your company has decided to implement some form of data replication. In order to choose the appropriate method or tool for making copies of the company data, which features and characteristics should be considered when defining your requirements?

**At the minimum, you should consider the following: transaction integrity, consistency of data (tight or loose), concurrency, security, existing data sources, data update frequency, performance, automation/administration, and update capabilities.**

#### SQL Server and the World Wide Web Scenario

Your company sells tickets to major sporting events and concerts. How can you use the *push* model to publish information about upcoming events onto the World Wide Web?

**You can use SQL Server Web Assistant to generate a task which automatically uses a template to rebuild a Web page calendar of sporting events and concerts each day. These pages are posted using an Internet server such as IIS.**

#### Replication Scenario

Your company has decided to replicate data using Microsoft SQL Server replication. You are currently in the planning and design phase of your replication strategy. Your company is a large international manufacturer that has a large number of distributors around the world. Your goal is to receive all of the distributors' sales information on a daily basis at the company headquarters. Because most of your distributors are remote, you are concerned about the high cost of all of the telephone lines that will be used to receive the information from all of the distributors. With this in mind, which replication model(s) would you implement? Why?

**The best approach to address these requirements would be to combine two of the replication models. One approach has a central subscriber in each region that would act as a remote distributor, which could then replicate the daily sales information to headquarters at night. By using regional remote distributors, you minimize the number of telephone lines required.**

C H A P T E R   2 1

# Implementing SQL Server Replication

## About This Chapter

The conceptual aspects of what replication is and how it can be used are covered in Chapter 20, "Distributed Data Overview." This chapter explains how to plan and design replication, the tasks that must be performed before you can implement replication, and the tasks involved in setting up replication. This chapter also describes how to view all of the servers that participate in a replication scenario. After you implement the replication scenario, you learn how to publish publications and articles, and how to manage subscriptions.

## Before You Begin

To complete the lessons in this chapter, you must have:

- Installed SQL Server on your computer. Installation procedures are covered in Chapter 2, "Installing SQL Server."

- The *testpubs* database installed. To update the *testpubs* database, see \SCRIPTS\BLD_TPUBS\INSTTP.SQL.

# Lesson 1: Planning Replication

Planning replication is similar to planning a logical database design because it is necessary to have a working model before you can successfully implement replication.

## After this lesson you will be able to:

- Describe the factors that should be considered prior to implementing replication.
- Describe the issues to consider when planning a replication scenario.

## Estimated lesson time  10 minutes

## Initial Planning

Planning replication takes time. There are several issues which should be addressed, including deciding what to replicate, who needs the replicated data, and how to replicate it. Consider the following questions when planning replication.

### What Data Is Replicated?

When distributing data, your subscribing servers typically require only a subset of the data from the database. It is important to replicate only necessary data and not the whole database.

### Who Receives the Data?

How are the sites going to use the replicated data? If sites are read-only and require only specific information from the database, then use replication. If sites must have update capabilities, you probably should not consider using replication.

### How Often Is Data Replicated?

How current must information be for the replicated site? If a site uses data for summary reporting or trend reporting on sales activity for the current year, it is not critical for that data to be 100 percent up-to-date. A marketing department (decision support) is a good example of a site that would not require the most up-to-the-minute information.

### Who Should Distribute the Data?

The database server that serves as the central point for data modifications is the best candidate for distributing information.

### Is Replication the Appropriate Tool?

Replication, like any tool, must be used correctly. The following are a few ways in which SQL Server replication might be used:

- To separate decision support (DS) activity from OLTP. Replication can maintain several decision support servers by removing the report generation and ad hoc query impact from the source (OLTP) server.

- To distribute and update read-only copies of data from a master price list on a source server to several regional servers supporting field offices.

- To distribute location-specific data from a centralized master table.

- To support asynchronous order processing during a communications outage.

There are some situations when it is best not to use replication. Consider not using replication when:

- The data is volatile.

- The data must be up-to-date with no delays.

- Business requires update-anywhere capabilities.

- Business requires multiserver transactions.

# Planning a Replication Scenario

Setting up a replication scenario with multiple publishers and multiple subscribers can be complex. Using the SQL Enterprise Manager graphical tools make the physical implementation easy, but the design warrants almost the same attention as is necessary to develop the original database schema. When planning a replication scenario, address the following issues.

### Determine the Appropriate Replication Scenario

Consider the following:

- Determine the purpose of the replicated data (corporate rollup, report generation, decision support systems, master list updating, and so on).

- Assess network connections. Note if there is a slow link that would benefit from having a separate distribution server.

- Determine if it is necessary to offload traffic on the OLTP server.

### Estimate the Number of Subscribers

Estimating the number of subscribers helps to determine:

- The load on the server.
- The appropriate size for the transaction log for each database marked for publication.

### Estimate the Frequency of Replication

Estimating the frequency of replication helps to determine:

- The appropriate time for each subscriber to receive replicated data.
- The appropriate backup strategy.
- The appropriate size for the *distribution* database and transaction log.
- Load balancing requirements.

### Determine the Maintenance Issues

Consider the following:

- The frequency and method to clean up old jobs.
- Database and transaction log backup strategies.

### Plan the Implementation

Determine the following:

- The size of databases and transaction logs.
- A schedule for replication (frequency).
- A schedule for synchronization (frequency).
- The synchronization method—automatic, manual, no synchronization, or Scheduled Table Refresh (also known as a snapshot).
- If local data needs to be updated, then establish a method to uniquely differentiate local data from data that is replicated:
  - Set up location-specific codes so that data is not overwritten.
  - Create a composite primary key with location code.

## Lesson Summary

Good planning is the key to successful replication. Planning includes considering what data to replicate, where the data is going, how often you plan to replicate the data, and who distributes it. If you determine that replication is the appropriate method to distribute data, it is necessary to plan the replication scenario.

# Lesson 2: Preliminary Tasks

Before you start to implement a replication scenario, you must ensure that certain requirements are met.

## After this lesson you will be able to:

- Identify the tasks that must be performed prior to implementing replication.

## Estimated lesson time  10 minutes

To enable replication, tasks must be performed that involve the network, servers, devices, databases, users, data sources, and data.

## Network and Servers

It is necessary to identify servers for replication and establish communication to those servers. For communication to take place, you should verify network protocols and the trust relationships between domains.

❑ **Ensure that adequate memory is available for the distribution server.**

The server designated as the distribution server requires at least 32 MB of RAM with 16 MB dedicated to SQL Server. The publication server and the subscription servers require at least 16 MB of RAM. If the *distribution* database is on the publication server, then 32 MB of RAM is required.

❑ **Ensure that the working directory is available to the publication server.**

The working directory for the synchronization task must be available to the publication server. The default is \MSSQL\REPLDATA.

❑ **Register all servers that are in the replication scenario.**

You can register servers prior to or as part of configuring replication. You can do this using SQL Enterprise Manager.

❑ **Set the default network to use Named Pipes or Multiprotocol**

To replicate across domains, you must use either Named Pipes or Multiprotocol because they allow trusted connections.

❑ **Trust relationships between domains must be established (if appropriate).**

If servers participate in replication but reside within separate Microsoft Windows NT Server domains, trust relationships must be established between those domains. Note that if servers are in the same domain, trust relationships are set up automatically.

**Note**  To have consistent query results on replicated data between all servers, it is recommended that servers that participate together in replication use the same character set and sort order. However, this is not required.

## Devices and Databases

You should make sure that there is enough space allocated to each database and log for the publisher, the distributor, and the subscriber. Factors that impact space allocation include: the number of publishers, the number of publications and articles, replication frequency, replication latency, and data activity.

❑ **Verify that adequate disk space is available for the transaction log.**

Ensure that the transaction log for each published database on the publication server has adequate device space. Also ensure that the transaction log of the *distribution* database has adequate disk space.

❑ **Verify that adequate disk space is available for the destination database.**

Ensure that the destination database on each subscription server has adequate disk space for the data that will be replicated. If the destination database does not exist, you must create it.

---

**Tip**  Create all of the databases you require for replication *before* you start to set up replication. Then all of the databases are listed in SQL Enterprise Manager and you can mark them as authorized to publish or subscribe at the same time that you configure the server replication options.

---

## Users

Before replication can take place, certain user accounts with appropriate privileges must exist. User connections are also required to replicate data.

❑ **Create one user account in Windows NT for the SQL Executive service.**

Create a user account with administrative privileges in Windows NT for the SQL Server Executive service. The account should be a member of the Administrator group and granted the right to "Log on as a service." You should also set the following options for this user account:

- User Cannot Change Password
- Password Never Expires

❑ **Increase the number of user connections.**

Increase the number of user connections to allow the log reader to access the transaction log of each database enabled for publishing and each of the subscription servers.

- On the publisher (if the *distribution* database is on a different server), increase the number of user connections by the number of user databases that are enabled for publishing.
- On each subscription server, increase the number of user connections by the number of subscription databases.

## Data Sources and Data

The destination data must be defined with certain characteristics. Also, if you are replicating to a mixed (heterogeneous) environment, it is necessary to have the appropriate ODBC driver.

❑ **Add declared primary keys to tables that will be published.**

All published tables *must* contain a declared primary key except for Scheduled Table Refresh (snapshots). Existing tables can be prepared for publishing by adding a declared primary key using the Manage Tables functionality of SQL Enterprise Manager or by using the ALTER TABLE statement.

❑ **Ensure that drivers for ODBC subscribers conform to the Microsoft SQL Server replication requirements for generic ODBC subscribers.**

The ODBC driver:

- Must be ODBC Level 1-compliant.

- Must be 32-bit and thread-safe.

- Must be able to run on one of the following platforms for the distribution process: Intel, Power PC, MIPS, or Alpha.

- Must have transaction capability.

- Must support the data definition language (DDL).

- Cannot be read-only.

## Lesson Summary

A number of preliminary tasks must be performed before implementing replication. These include: configuring your servers to communicate, verifying that there is enough database and log space for replication, establishing user accounts, and verifying that destination data is configured properly.

| For more information on | See |
|---|---|
| Domains | "Domains" in Windows NT Books Online and the *Windows NT Resource Kit* |

# Lesson 3: Setting the Replication Scenario

After you have addressed all of the requirements necessary for implementation, the next step is to set up the replication scenario. When setting up replication, you must install or select the *distribution* database, set options for the publication servers, and set options for the subscription servers.

## After this lesson you will be able to:

- Install the *distribution* database.

- Configure a publication server.

- Configure a database for publishing.

- Set options for the subscription server.

- Access the Replication Topology window to see a graphical view of all servers participating in the replication scenario.

## Estimated lesson time  20 minutes

## Installing or Selecting the *distribution* Database

The *distribution* database is a key component of replication. It stores replicated Transact-SQL statements and distributes them to the appropriate subscribers at intervals defined by the distribution task. If a server participates in replication as a publisher, you must either install a *distribution* database on that server or use a remote distribution server. A *distribution* database must exist before you can begin any other replication tasks.

### Considerations for the *distribution* Database Size

The *distribution* database must be able to store replicated information for all of the publication and subscription servers. To determine the size of the *distribution* database, consider the following:

- The total number of tables that are published

- Estimated transaction rate per hour

- Average transaction size

- Maximum time that a subscriber can be offline

- Maximum retention

## How to Install the *distribution* Database

When you set up the *distribution* database, on the Server menu, select Replication Configuration, and then click Install Publishing. The Install Replication Publishing dialog box appears. After you install the *distribution* database using SQL Enterprise Manager, you can continue to set up publishing.

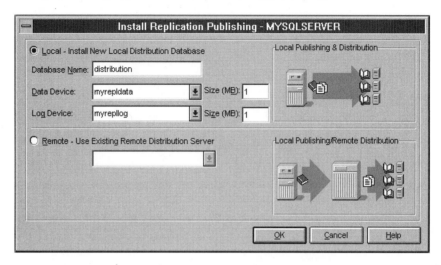

As part of the Install Replication process, you must create the *distribution* database using separate devices for the database and the transaction log. The *distribution* database can be installed locally on the same server as the publication server or on a different server; or you can specify an existing remote distribution server. Then SQL Server automatically truncates the log of the *distribution* database and defines the server as the distribution server.

# Setting Options for the Publication Server

After you install the *distribution* database, you must establish which servers will be publication servers. You also must enable your databases for publishing.

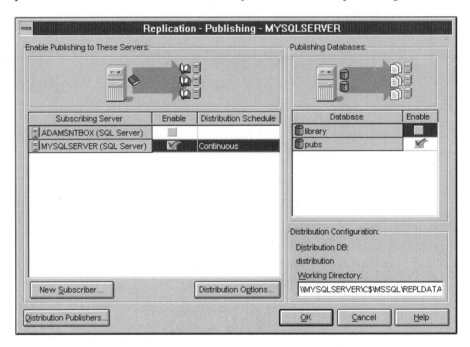

## How to Set Options for the Publication Server

When you set options for the publication server, on the Server menu, select Replication Configuration, and then click Publishing. The Replication – Publishing dialog box appears. To continue setting options, do the following:

- Define the servers that will be permitted to subscribe to this server's publications.

- Set the distribution options for each subscription server (the default is Continuous Replication).

- Set the maximum number of transactions per batch to be committed to each subscriber.

- Set the distribution schedule (replication frequency) so that transactions are replicated on a continuous basis or scheduled for a specific time for each subscriber.

- Determine the length of time that transaction information is retained in the *distribution* database after it is applied to the last subscriber.

- Specify the databases that will publish or replicate data.

- Specify the servers that will be allowed to use this server as their remote distribution server.

### ODBC Subscribers

You must set up ODBC subscriptions by administering the publisher, that is, by using the push subscription model. You cannot set up ODBC subscriptions by administering a subscriber (the pull subscription model). For ODBC subscribers, the subscribing database has no administrative capabilities regarding the replication being performed.

### How to Set Up ODBC Subscriptions

When setting up ODBC subscriptions, do the following: On the Server menu, select Replication, and then click Publishing. The Replication – Publishing window appears. Click New Subscriber. The New Subscriber dialog box appears. Next, click ODBC Subscriber. The New ODBC Subscriber dialog box appears. Specify the Distributor's DSN (data source name), Description, User Name, and Password. Then click OK.

## Enabling Publishing

For the purpose of this self-study book, it is understood that you have one server. In the following procedures, you configure your server to have the roles of publication server, distribution server, and subscription server. You use SQL Enterprise Manager to install the *distribution* database and configure the publishing server.

▶ **To create the *receiverx* database**

In this procedure, you create the *receiverx* database on the subscription server (your server).

1. Create a device that is 3 MB in size named RECEIVERDEV.

2. Create a 3 MB database with the name *receiverx* on the RECEIVERDEV device.

▶ **To install the *distribution* database on the publication server**

In this procedure, you enable your server to publish data.

1. In the Server Manager window, select your server.

2. On the Server menu, select Replication Configuration, and then click Install Publishing.

   The Install Replication Publishing dialog box appears. Verify that Local-Install New Local Distribution Database is selected.

   ---
   **Note**  If you receive an error message indicating that SQL Server has not been configured with enough memory, change the memory setting now.

   ---

3. In the Database Name box, confirm that distribution displays as the default.

4. In the Data Device box, select <new>.

   The New Database Device window appears.

5. Create a 5 MB database device named DISTRIBUTIONDATA in your C:\MSSQL\DATA directory.

6. Click Create Now.

   A confirmation box appears.

7. Click OK.

8. In the Log Device box, select <new>.

   The New Database Device window appears.

9. Create a 5 MB database device named DISTRIBUTIONLOG in your C:\MSSQL\DATA directory.

10. Click Create Now.

    A confirmation box appears.

11. Click OK.

    The Install Replication Publishing dialog box appears.

12. Click OK.

You receive a message stating that replication publishing is successfully installed. You are also asked if you want to install Publishing Databases and Subscribers at this time.

13. Click Yes.

The Replication-Publishing dialog box appears.

---

**Note**  Once you have successfully installed replication publishing the menu item "Install Publishing" will dynamically change to "Uninstall Publishing..." which can be found on the Server menu by selecting Replication Configuration.

---

▶ **To configure a publication server**

In this procedure, you set up your local server to publish to other servers and specify the subscription server.

1. In the Replication - Publishing dialog box, under Enable Publishing to These Servers, select the Enable box for the subscribing server (your local server). This allows your server to publish data to a subscription server.

2. Click Distribution Options.

The Distribution Options dialog box appears

What is the default number of transactions before a commit is sent to the server?

_____

After transactions have been distributed to the subscription server, what is the default retention period for keeping them?

_____

3. To exit without making any changes, click Cancel.

▶ **To configure a database for publishing**

In this procedure, you enable a database to publish data.

1. Under Publishing Databases, select the Enable box for the *testpubs* database.

2. Click OK.

# Setting Options for the Subscription Server

To subscribe to other servers, you must first select the option that enables subscribing from the servers. Using SQL Enterprise Manager, there are two ways to make a server display as a server option: on the Server menu, select Register Servers or select Remote Servers.

---

**Note**  When servers are added as remote servers, those servers will not display in the Server Manager window.

---

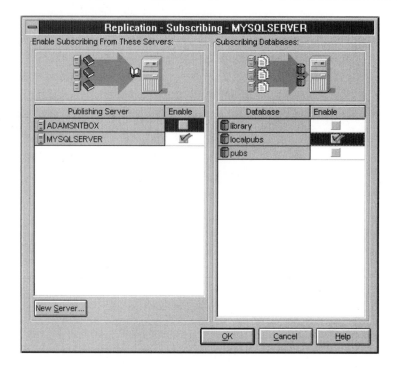

▶  **To set up a subscription server**

In the following procedure, you use SQL Enterprise Manager to select the publication server that will replicate to the subscription server. (In this case, your server functions in both roles.) You also select the destination database for replicated publications.

1. On the Server menu, select Replication Configuration, and then click Subscribing.

   The Replication-Subscribing dialog box appears.

2. Under Enable Subscribing From These Servers, select the Enable box for the selected Publishing Server.

3. Under Subscribing Databases, select the Enable box for *receiverx*. This enables the subscribing *receiverx* database to receive data from the Publishing Server.

4. Click OK.

# The Replication Topology Window

The Replication Topology window in SQL Enterprise Manager provides a graphical view of all servers that are participating in a replication scenario. Each server is labeled according to the role that it plays in replication; whether it is a publication, distribution, or subscription server. Each server can be configured from within the Replication Topology window.

---

**Note**  If a subscriber initiates a subscription, it appears as a remote server in the Replication Topology window.

---

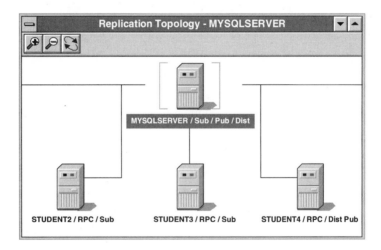

## How to Access the Replication Topology Window

There are two ways to access the Replication Topology window: on the toolbar, click Replication Topology; or on the Server menu, select Replication Configuration, and then click Topology.

## Managing Replication

To manage replication for any of the depicted servers, use the secondary mouse button to click the server, and then select from the commands on the menu that appears.

- Click *Replication Configuration* to install or select a *distribution* database, or to set server publication and subscription options. It is the equivalent of the same command on the Server menu.

- Click *Publications* to publish data. It is the equivalent of the Manage Replication/Publications command from the Manage menu, or Manage Publications on the toolbar. This command is unavailable if this server's publication options are not set up to allow publishing.

- Click *Subscriptions* to subscribe to published data. It is the equivalent of the Manage Replication/Subscriptions command from the Manage menu, or Manage Subscriptions on the toolbar. This command is unavailable if this server's subscription options are not set up to allow subscribing.

# Lesson Summary

It is necessary to have all three server roles established, whether these roles are defined separately, combined, or are on the same server. The distribution server is the first server that must be in place. When this is created, the *distribution* database must also be created. After this you configure a database for publishing on the publication server, and set options on the subscription server. You can view the replication scenario using the Replication Topology window.

| For more information on | See |
|---|---|
| ODBC subscribers | "Publishing to ODBC Subscribers" in SQL Server Books Online |

# Lesson 4: Publishing

After you have configured your servers, you can create publications and articles.

## After this lesson you will be able to:

- Create a publication on a publishing server.
- Create an article with and without partitioning.
- Choose and schedule a synchronization method.
- Describe how to set up and manage subscriptions.
- Set up a pull subscription.
- View the progress of replication.

## Estimated lesson time  30 minutes

## Defining Publications and Articles

You can create one or more publications from each user database on a publication server. Publications cannot span databases; each publication can contain articles from only one database.

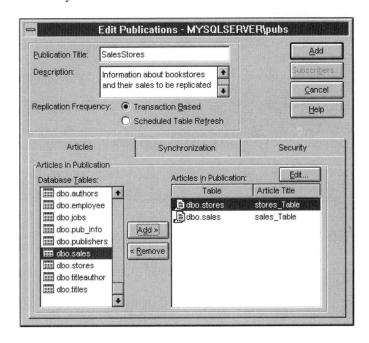

Articles are defined by choosing the tables to include for replication. If you must maintain referential integrity between published tables, you must include all of the tables involved in the relationship in one publication. This guarantees that transactions are applied at the same time and that integrity is maintained. You can further define an article by creating filters or scripts to specify the columns or rows to be included. To create a vertical partition, you can select only the columns that you want to be replicated. To create a horizontal partition, use a WHERE clause to restrict the set of rows to be replicated.

# Editing an Article

You can edit an article using the Manage Article dialog box. To go to this dialog box, on the Manage menu, select Replication, and then click Publications. The Manage Publications dialog box appears. Double-click your publication, and the Edit Publications dialog box appears. Click Edit, and the Manage Article dialog box appears.

The Manage Article dialog box allows you to specify the article name, description, and destination table. You can also customize filters and scripts for the article. You can also select one or both article characteristics: Owner Qualify Table Name and Use Column Names in SQL Statements.

## Owner Qualify Table Name

Users other than database owners (DBOs) can replicate tables between databases and maintain their ownership of the tables. A table that is replicated from a publisher to a subscriber can be owned by the owner of the published table. It is then referred to as an owner-qualified table. This feature is useful for users who want to maintain ownership of their replicated tables in the subscriber database.

---

**Note**  When using the owner-qualified option, automatic synchronization is not supported.

---

## Use Column Names in SQL Statements

In SQL Server, the replication INSERT statements can include a column list. This column list guarantees that inserted data will populate the correct columns in the subscriber's table.

---

**Important**  This functionality should be enabled only if you suspect problems will occur with replication. Enabling the column list increases the length of the generated INSERT statements, resulting in higher storage requirements for the distribution database and increased network traffic.

---

## Setting Publishing Methods

The following publishing methods can be set using the SQL Enterprise Manager-Edit Publications dialog box.

### Replication Frequency

You can choose the method to replicate this publication, either Transaction Based or Scheduled Table Refresh.

### Synchronization

You must determine the method for initial synchronization. The synchronization methods include bulk data copy using native format or character format. You can also schedule how often to perform initial synchronizations. This applies to new subscribers only. After a subscriber is synchronized, this subscriber does not have to be resynchronized unless a problem occurs.

### Security

You have the option to restrict replication to only selected servers. A publication marked Restricted To is visible only to those subscription servers that have been marked for access. A publication marked Unrestricted is visible to any subscription server, and it can be subscribed to by any subscription server.

## Creating Publications and Articles

In the following procedures, you create a publication and two articles for publishing. You also define the synchronization method on the publishing server.

▶ **To create a publication on the publishing server**

1. Using SQL Enterprise Manager, in the Server Manager window, select the Publishing server.
2. On the Manage menu, select Replication, and then click Publications.

   The Manage Publications dialog box appears.
3. Select the *testpubs* database.
4. Click New.

   The Edit Publications dialog box appears.
5. In the Publication Title box, type:

   **sample_publication**

   The Publication Title must be unique for this database and match the rules for identifiers.
6. In the Description box, type a short description of the publication.
7. Verify that the Transaction Based default option is selected.

▶  **To create an article**

1. In the Edit Publications dialog box, verify that the Articles tab is selected.

2. In the Database Tables box, select the *dbo.publishers* table.

3. Click Add.

   The *dbo.publishers* table appears in the Articles in Publication box.

▶  **To create an article and apply partitioning**

In this procedure, you create another article and then apply horizontal and vertical partitioning of the original data.

1. In the Database Tables box, select the *dbo.titles* table.

2. Click Add.

   The *dbo.titles* table appears in the Articles in Publication box.

3. Select *dbo.titles* in the Articles in Publications box.

4. Click Edit. The Manage Article dialog box appears.

5. On the Filters tab, verify that *title_id*, *title*, and *price* columns are selected for replication. Clear all other columns.

6. In the Restriction Clause box, type:

   **PRICE > 15**

7. Click OK.

▶  **To select and schedule the synchronization method**

1. In the Edit Publications dialog box, select the Synchronization tab.

2. Verify that the Bulk Data Copy-Native Format is selected.

3. Click Change.

   The Task Schedule dialog box appears.

4. Under Daily Frequency, change the Occurs Every value so that replication occurs every minute.

5. Click OK.

   The Edit Publications dialog box reappears.

6. Verify that the Articles tab is selected, and then click Add in the upper right.

   The Manage Publications dialog box appears. Note that the new publication appears under Publications.

7. Expand Testpubs.

8. Click Close.

# Setting Up and Managing Subscriptions

In the previous lesson, you learned how to set up your server as a subscription server. In this section you will learn how to subscribe to publications and articles.

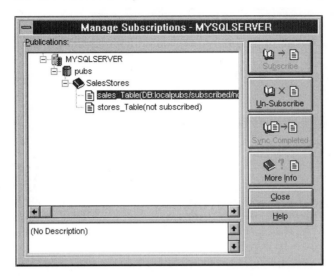

As stated earlier in this chapter, there are two methods for subscribing to publications: pull subscriptions and push subscriptions. You specify a push subscription from the publication server; you specify a pull subscription from the subscription server.

## How to Set Up a Subscription from the Publishing Server (Push Subscription)

You can set up subscriptions at the same time you create or edit an article on the publishing server. This is known as a *push subscription*.

When setting up a push subscription, you create or edit the publication and you can also select subscribers that will subscribe to that publication.

1. Create or edit the publication as described earlier in this chapter. (On the Manage menu, click Replication, and then from the drop-down menu that appears, click Publications.)

2. In the Manage Publications dialog box, highlight the publication, and then click the Change button. The Edit Publications dialog box appears.

3. In the Edit Publications dialog box, click Subscribers.

4. From the Subscriptions Server list, select a server, and then click Subscribe.

5. Follow the remaining steps on the screen.

6. Repeat the process for additional subscribers.

**Note**  Push subscriptions can only be specified at the article level. Pull subscriptions can be accomplished at both the publication and article levels.

## Setting Up a Subscription (Pull)

In the following procedures, the subscription server subscribes to a publication on the publication server and enables the destination (*receiverx*) database to receive replicated data. (For the purpose of these procedures, your server functions in both server roles.)

▶  **To subscribe to a publication**

1. In the Server Manager window, select the subscription server.
2. On the Manage menu, select Replication, and then click Subscriptions.

   The Manage Subscriptions dialog box appears. You should see your local server also as a publication server.
3. Click the "+" signs in the publication box until you see the *publishers_table* article.

   What is the state of the *publishers_table* article?

   _____

4. Select the *publishers_table* article, and then click Subscribe.

   The Subscription Options dialog box appears.

   What is the source database?

   _____

5. In the Destination Database box, select the *receiverx* database.
6. Under Sync Method, accept the default: Data Synchronization Automatically Applied.
7. Click OK.

   What is the state of the *publishers_table* article?

   _____

8. Subscribe to the *titles_table* article using the previous steps in this procedure.
9. Click Close.

## Verifying Replication

In the following procedure, you execute a script that adds and updates rows to the *publishers* table. This data automatically replicates to the subscribing server within a few seconds. You then check the progress of your replication by executing queries on both the *testpubs* and the *receiverx* databases.

▶  **To view the progress of replication**

In this procedure, your server functions as both the publication server and the subscription server.

1. Open a query window and use *testpubs*.

2. Type and execute the following query to check the number of rows in the *testpubs..publishers* table on the publication server:

   ```
   SELECT * FROM testpubs..publishers
   ```

   Write the number of rows here.

3. Type and execute the following query to check the number of rows in the *receiverx..publishers* table on the subscription server:

   ```
   SELECT * FROM receiverx..publishers
   ```

   Write the number of rows here.

4. Review the script and execute ADDDATA.SQL on the *testpubs* database in the publication server. This script inserts a new row and updates the row where *pub_id* = 1756 to *city* = San Francisco.

5. Using the *testpubs* database on the publication server, type and execute the following query to check that the row was added and the update was successful:

   ```
   SELECT * FROM testpubs..publishers
   ```

   Write the number of rows here. Was the new row inserted? Was the update successful?

6. Execute the same query in the *receiverx* database on the subscription server to see how many rows have been successfully replicated.

```
SELECT * FROM receiverx..publishers
```

Write the number of rows here. Was the replication successful?

7. Review the script and execute DELDATA.SQL in the *testpubs* database on the publication server. This script deletes the row added in Step 3.

8. Using the *testpubs* database, type and execute the following query to check that a row was deleted successfully in the publication server.

```
SELECT * FROM testpubs..publishers
```

Write the number of rows here. Was the delete successful?

9. Execute the same query in the *receiverx* database on the subscription server to see how many rows have been successfully replicated.

```
SELECT * FROM receiverx..publishers
```

Write the number of rows here. Was the replication successful?

## Lesson Summary

Publications and articles are created on the publication server. On this server you specify what data is replicated, the data format, and the replication frequency. You subscribe to publications using either the push subscription or the pull subscription method. Replication can be tested by executing INSERT, UPDATE, or DELETE statements in the publishing database.

| For more information on | See |
| --- | --- |
| Articles | "Defining Articles" in SQL Server Books Online |
| Replication | "Getting Started with Microsoft SQL Server Replication" and "Manual Replication Setup with a Remote Distributor" in \KB on the compact disc |

# Review

The following questions are intended to reinforce key information presented in this chapter. If you are unable to answer a question, review the lesson and then try the question again.

1. You have finished implementing replication. You issue an UPDATE statement to see if the update is replicated to a subscriber. After waiting several minutes you discover that your update was not replicated. What three key replication items would you check to help you determine what is wrong?

2. The decision has been made to separate the activity in the Marketing department (Decision Support) from the activity in the Sales department (Online Transaction Processing) because conflicting queries from each department cause locking contention. To separate this activity you must maintain multiple copies of some of the tables in the *sales* database. You have determined that you can do this using replication provided you comply with these requirements: you must allow the highest level of throughput to the server for the Marketing department, and the data on the *marketing* database can be no more than one day old. What replication frequency would you choose for the Marketing subscriber?

# Questions and Answers

Page 925

▶ **To configure a publication server**

2. Click Distribution Options.

The Distribution Options dialog box appears

What is the default number of transactions before a commit is sent to the server?

**100.**

After transactions have been distributed to the subscription server, what is the default retention period for keeping them?

**0 hours.**

Page 934

▶ **To subscribe to a publication**

3. Click the "+" signs in the publication box until you see the *publishers_table* article.

What is the state of the *publishers_table* article?

**(not subscribed)**

4. Select the *publishers_table* article, and then click Subscribe.

The Subscription Options dialog box appears.

What is the source database?

**testpubs**

7. Click OK.

What is the state of the *publishers_table* article?

**(DB: receiverx/subscribed/not synched/Automatic)**

Page 935

▶ **To view the progress of replication**

2. Type and execute the following query to check the number of rows in the *testpubs..publishers* table on the publication server:

```
SELECT * FROM testpubs..publishers
```

Write the number of rows here.

**8 rows.**

3. Type and execute the following query to check the number of rows in the *receiverx..publishers* table on the subscription server:

```
SELECT * FROM receiverx..publishers
```

Write the number of rows here.

**8 rows.**

5. Using the *testpubs* database on the publication server, type and execute the following query to check that the row was added and the update was successful:

```
SELECT * FROM testpubs..publishers
```

Write the number of rows here. Was the new row inserted? Was the update successful?

**9 rows, yes, yes.**

6. Execute the same query in the *receiverx* database on the subscription server to see how many rows have been successfully replicated.

```
SELECT * FROM receiverx..publishers
```

Write the number of rows here. Was the replication successful?

**9 rows, yes.**

8. Using the *testpubs* database, type and execute the following query to check that a row was deleted successfully in the publication server.

```
SELECT * FROM testpubs..publishers
```

Write the number of rows here. Was the delete successful?

**8 rows, yes.**

9. Execute the same query in the *receiverx* database on the subscription server to see how many rows have been successfully replicated.

```
SELECT * FROM receiverx..publishers
```

Write the number of rows here. Was the replication successful?

**8 rows, yes.**

Page 937

## Review Questions

1.  You have finished implementing replication. You issue an UPDATE statement to see if the update is replicated to a subscriber. After waiting several minutes you discover that your update was not replicated. What three key replication items would you check to help you determine what is wrong?

    **The log reader, Sync, and Distribution tasks. For each task, check the Last Run and Last Run Status and view the Task History. Also check to see how often the task is scheduled to run.**

2.  The decision has been made to separate the activity in the Marketing department (Decision Support) from the activity in the Sales department (Online Transaction Processing) because conflicting queries from each department cause locking contention. To separate this activity you must maintain multiple copies of some of the tables in the *sales* database. You have determined that you can do this using replication provided you comply with these requirements: you must allow the highest level of throughput to the server for the Marketing department, and the data on the *marketing* database can be no more than one day old. What replication frequency would you choose for the Marketing subscriber?

    **Scheduled Table Refresh. This allows you to execute queries on the marketing database without running into locking conflicts that can be produced by replicated updates done on a continuous frequency.**

C H A P T E R   2 2

# Extensions and Interfaces to SQL Server

## About This Chapter

SQL Server extended stored procedures, the SQL Server Distributed Management Objects, and interfaces for data management are explained in this chapter. SQL Server contains several components that allow it to extend beyond its environment. Extended stored procedures, Messaging Application Programming Interface (MAPI), and SQL Distributed Management Objects (SQL-DMO) give SQL Server the ability to exchange information with other servers and clients, and to share information with other applications, such as Microsoft Excel and Microsoft C++. Distributed Management Objects make it possible for developers to manage SQL Server database objects directly. Open Database Connectivity (ODBC), DB-Library, Open Data Services (ODS), and Application Programming Interfaces (APIs) also are covered in this chapter.

## Before You Begin

To complete the lessons in this chapter, you must have:

- Microsoft Excel 5.0 for Microsoft Windows NT (32-bit version) installed on your computer.
- Created the *library* database. If you must create *library*, execute \SCRIPTS\BLD_LIB\BLDLIB.CMD on the compact disc.

# Lesson 1: SQL Server Extension and Interface Overview

SQL Server contains several components that make it capable of extending beyond its environment. These include extended stored procedures, the Messaging Application Programming Interface (MAPI), SQL Distributed Management Objects (SQL-DMO), Open Database Connectivity (ODBC), DB-Library, and Open Data Services (ODS).

### After this lesson you will be able to:

- Describe two or more components used to expand the SQL Server environment.

### Estimated lesson time  5 minutes

Each of the following components makes it possible for SQL Server to load and execute functions, communicate with messaging applications, be accessed through other applications, or act as an interface between client and server requests.

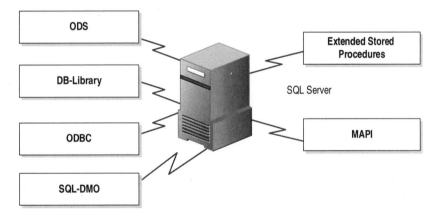

- Extended Stored Procedures—Used to dynamically load and execute a function within a dynamic-link library (DLL) in a manner similar to that of a stored procedure.
- Messaging Application Programming Interface (MAPI)—Enables SQL Server to communicate with MAPI-enabled electronic messaging applications in which SQL Server can send and receive messages and results sets through an electronic mail system.
- SQL Distributed Management Objects (SQL-DMO)—32-bit OLE Automation objects for Microsoft operating systems. SQL-DMO objects can be used by a range of applications, such as Microsoft Excel, Microsoft Visual FoxPro™, Microsoft Visual Basic 4.0, and Microsoft C++, to manage objects in SQL Server.

- Open Database Connectivity (ODBC)—A generic set of client APIs that uses product-specific drivers for use and development of client-side applications that require database access.
- DB-Library—A set of APIs used specifically to develop client-side applications for SQL Server.
- Open Data Services (ODS)—Defines a server-side API that acts as the interface between client and server requests that are made to the Open Data Services library.

## Lesson Summary

SQL Server uses several components to extend its capabilities beyond its normal operating environment. These include extensions accessed from within SQL Server (extended procedures), a collection of OLE objects used to program SQL Server remotely, client-side APIs (ODBC and DB-Library), as well as the server-side APIs (Open Data Services).

| For more information on | See |
|---|---|
| Open Data Services and extended stored procedures | Programming Open Data Services 6.0 in Chapter 1, "Overview," in SQL Server Books Online |
| MAPI | Administrator's Companion 6.0, Part 7 "SQLMail Overview," in SQL Server Books Online |
| SQL-DMO | Programming SQL Distributed Management Objects in Chapter 1, "Getting Started," in SQL Server Books Online |
| ODBC | Programming ODBC for SQL Server in Chapter 1, "Overview," in SQL Server Books Online |

# Lesson 2: Extended Stored Procedures

Extended stored procedures can extend SQL Server functionality. They provide a way to dynamically load and execute a function stored in a DLL. Actions outside SQL Server can be triggered easily, and external information returned to SQL Server. Return status codes and output parameters—identical to their counterparts in regular stored procedures—are also supported.

## After this lesson you will be able to:

- Define the function and purpose of extended stored procedures.

## Estimated lesson time  15 minutes

Extended stored procedures are:

- Executed in the same way as stored procedures.

- Used to integrate security between Microsoft Windows NT and SQL Server.

- Defined as functions that you develop using the Open Data Services API. These functions can be integrated into SQL Server.

- Created by using your own C application code with the Open Data Services API.

Extended stored procedures generally execute faster than stored procedures because they consist of fully compiled C code. By storing them as a DLL, the dynamic linking and loading improve efficiency.

SQL Server provides some predefined extended stored procedures. The following table lists some common SQL Server extended stored procedures.

| Extended stored procedure | Description |
| --- | --- |
| xp_cmdshell | Executes a given command string in an operating system command shell and returns output as rows of text. |
| xp_logevent | Logs a user-defined message in the SQL Server log file or in Windows NT Event Viewer. |
| xp_logininfo | Reports the account, the type of account, the privilege level of the account, the mapped name of the account, and the permission path for the account's access to SQL Server. |
| xp_msver | Returns SQL Server version information, the actual build number of the server, and environment information. This information can be used within Transact-SQL statements, batches, and stored procedures to enhance logic for platform-independent code. |
| xp_enumgroups | Provides a list of local Windows NT–based groups or a list of groups defined in a specified Windows NT domain. |

# Using and Managing Extended Stored Procedures

You can issue the EXECUTE command followed by the name of the extended stored procedure and any required parameters. In addition, SQL Server can call an extended stored procedure as the result of a trigger.

## Using Extended Stored Procedures

Extended stored procedures are categorized by their use. There are five categories of extended stored procedures as shown in the following table.

| Category | Extended stored procedures |
| --- | --- |
| Integrated Security | xp_enumgroups, xp_grantlogin, xp_loginconfig, xp_loginfo, xp_revokelogin |
| General System Administration | xp_cmdshell, xp_logevent, xp_msver, xp_sprintf, xp_sscanf |
| SQLMail | xp_deletemail, xp_findnextmsg, xp_readmail, xp_sendmail, xp_startmail, xp_stopmail |
| Internal | These extended stored procedures are used by the other stored procedures, such as system replication and catalog. They are not intended to be executed separately. |
| User Defined | You can create custom extended stored procedures by using Microsoft Open Data Services. |

Many of the extended stored procedures handle general administrative tasks and integrated security with Windows NT.

### Using xp_cmdshell

A commonly-used extended stored procedure is **xp_cmdshell**. This extended stored procedure executes operating system commands and returns the output as text. By default, when you grant execute permission for **xp_cmdshell**, users can execute any Windows NT operating system command that the account running SQL Server has privileges to execute. Granting such permission is not recommended because of the potential for data loss due to a lack of system security. To address the lack of system security, restrict **xp_cmdshell** access to users who have administrator permission on the Windows NT–based computer where SQL Server is running.

You can use SQL Setup or SQL Enterprise Manager to set the following option: xp_cmdshell - Use SQLExecutiveCmdExec Account for Non SA's. With this option selected, **xp_cmdshell** commands issued by users other than the SA run in the security context of the SQLExecutiveCmdExec account. The SA can adjust the permissions of this account to prevent unauthorized actions.

**Syntax**

**xp_cmdshell** *command_string* [, NO_OUTPUT]

With the NO OUTPUT parameter, the command executes, but it does not return any information to the client.

▶   **To return a list of executable files from inside a SQL script**

1. Open a query window.

2. Type and execute:

```
EXEC master..xp_cmdshell "dir *.exe"
```

### Using xp_logevent

The **xp_logevent** extended procedure logs a user-defined message in the SQL Server log file and in the Windows NT Event Log. Procedures, triggers, and batches use the RAISERROR statement when you send messages from Transact-SQL. To raise an error without sending a message to the client, use **xp_logevent**.

**Syntax**

**xp_logevent** *error_number*, *message*, *[severity]*

▶ **To log a user-defined message in the SQL Server log file and in the Windows NT event log**

1. Open a Query window.

2. Type and execute:

```
xp_logevent 60000, 'Invalid Member number', informational
```

3. Open the Windows NT Event Viewer - Application Log.

4. Confirm that the message was posted to the log.

▶ **To grant SQL Server access to a Windows NT group or user**

In this procedure, you list all defined Windows NT groups and grant administrator privileges to members of the Windows NT SQLAdmins group.

1. Open a Query window.

2. Type and execute:

```
xp_enumgroups
```

3. Confirm that the SQLAdmins group appears in the list.

If it does not exist, use the User Manager tool to create the group for Domains.

4. Type and execute:

```
xp_grantlogin 'sqladmins', 'admin'
```

## Managing Extended Stored Procedures

When you create new extended stored procedures, you must inform SQL Server by using **sp_addextendedproc** before you can use the new extended stored procedure. This procedure adds entries to the *sysobjects* table and registers the name of the new extended stored procedure in the *master* database. In addition, the procedure adds the name of the DLL as an entry into the *syscomments* table.

**Syntax**    **sp_addextendedproc** *function_name*, *dll_name*

**Example**
```
sp_addextendedproc xp_diskfree, 'xp'
```

Use **sp_dropextendedproc** to drop an extended stored procedure from the *sysobjects* table.

**Syntax**    **sp_dropextendedproc** *function_name*

**Example**
```
sp_dropextendedproc xp_diskfree
```

Use **sp_helpextendedproc** to display the currently defined extended functions and the name of the DLL to which the function belongs. If a function name is given, information about that function only is displayed.

**Syntax**    **sp_helpextendedproc** [*function_name*]

**Note**  Only the system administrator can add or drop extended stored procedures. New extended stored procedures must be registered in the *master* database.

# Extended Stored Procedures and Messaging Application Program Interface (MAPI)

SQL Server provides a group of extended stored procedures and one system stored procedure that enable it to receive and respond to queries using any Messaging Application Program Interface (MAPI)-complaint mail system.

## Connecting to Mail

You can use two extended stored procedures to manage the mail session for which SQL Server is a client. Those extended stored procedures are:

- **xp_startmail** ['user'][,'password']
- **xp_stopmail**

The extended stored procedure **xp_startmail** attempts to log on to a mail client using either the supplied username and password or, if none are supplied, the ones specified in the Mail login dialog box under Server Options during SQL Server setup. Alternatively, you can use SQL Enterprise Manager to set the default Mail logon ID and password by using the SQL Mail Configuration dialog box from the Server-SQL Mail-Configure menu. Before you use **xp_startmail**, the mail client must be started. You can configure the mail client to start automatically either by setting the Auto Start Mail Client server options or by using the **setup** program. If an existing mail session is running when **xp_startmail** is executed, a new session will not be started.

## Interacting with a MAPI-Compliant Mail System

SQL Server provides several extended procedures and one system stored procedure that enable queries to be received and processed. The results of those queries can then be returned using the mail system. Additionally, these actions can be scheduled to occur on a regular basis as a task. Once the mail session is established, you can link SQL Server with any MAPI-compliant mail system by using **xp_deletemail**, **xp_findnextmsg**, **xp_readmail**, and **xp_sendmail** in scripts. For example, the administrator may want to mail the results of a query to a group of users. In this case, the administrator uses **xp_sendmail** to send a message, a query results set, and an attachment to the specified recipients.

**Syntax**

**xp_sendmail** @recipient = recipient [; recipient2; [...; recipientn]]
[, @message = message]
[, @query = query]
[, @attachments = attachments]
[, @copy_recipients = recipient [; recipient2; [...; recipientn]]]
[, @blind_copy_recipients = recipient [; recipient2; [...; recipientn]]]
[, @subject = subject]
[, @type = type]
[, @attach_results = {'true' | 'false'}]
[, @no_output = {'true' | 'false'}]
[, @no_header = {'true' | 'false'}]
[, @width = width]
[, @separator = separator]
[, @echo_error = {'true' | 'false'}]
[, @set_user = user]
[, @dbuse = dbname]

**Example**

```
xp_sendmail 'Tom', @query = 'Select au_fname,au_lname from authors',
@dbuse = 'Pubs'
```

### Using sp_processmail

The system stored procedure **sp_processmail** uses extended stored procedures (**xp_findnextmsg**, **xp_readmail**, and **xp_deletemail**) to process incoming mail from the inbox for SQL Server. The messages should contain only a single query. After the message is received, **sp_processmail** uses the **xp_sendmail** extended stored procedure to return the results set to the message sender.

**Syntax**

**sp_processmail** [@subject = *subject*] [[,] @filetype = *filetype*]
[[,] @separator = *separator*] [[,] @set_user = *user*] [[,] @dbuse = *dbname*]

The **sp_processmail** procedure expects the incoming electronic mail (e-mail) to contain a single valid SQL query as the message text. Results of the query are returned to the message sender and copied to any e-mail users on the CC: list of the original message. After messages are processed, they are deleted from the inbox. If e-mail is sent often to the server, you should execute **sp_processmail** frequently. To set up regular e-mail processing, you can use the SQL Executive to schedule an **sp_processmail** task. This stored procedure then processes mail at the specified frequency and provides a record of the number of queries processed in the task history. Results are sent as an attached file. You can set up several different **sp_processmail** tasks for queries in different databases.

You can execute the query in the security context of the message sender. If the e-mail usernames are the same as your SQL Server usernames, change the call to **xp_sendmail** to use @set_user = @originator. If your mail usernames are not valid SQL Server usernames (for example, if they contain embedded blanks), use a table lookup or character substitution to get the appropriate SQL Server username to pass to **xp_sendmail**.

The following example processes all messages in the *pubs* database with results sets returned to the client in comma separated values (CSV) format.

**Example**

```
sp_processmail @filetype = 'CSV', @separator = ',', @dbuse = 'pubs'
```

## Lesson Summary

Extended stored procedures provide a way to dynamically load and execute functions stored in a dynamic-link library. SQL Server calls extended procedures as the result of a trigger or an EXECUTE command. SQL Server also provides extended stored procedures to receive and respond to queries using any MAPI-compliant mail system.

# Lesson 3: Using the SQL Distributed Management Objects Interface for System Management

The SQL Distributed Management Objects (SQL-DMO) interface provides controller applications with the ability to reference the SQL Server object library. These applications can then communicate with SQL Server objects.

SQL-DMO are 32-bit OLE Automation objects for the Microsoft Windows 95 and Microsoft Windows NT operating systems. They can be accessed from Microsoft Excel 5.0 (32-bit), Microsoft Visual FoxPro, and Microsoft Visual Basic 4.0, all using Visual Basic for Applications.

### After this lesson you will be able to:

- Describe the components of SQL Server Distributed Management Objects.
- Program the SQL Distributed Management Object model.

### Estimated lesson time  25 minutes

## Distributed Management Objects Overview

OLE is a programming technology that allows applications to share objects for either administration or data access. The Distributed Management Objects (DMO) model was developed using OLE architecture. DMO makes it possible for developers to access SQL Server database objects directly. This library of objects extends full control over both SQL Server and SQL Executive. Although you are accessing system data by referencing these objects, they are not designed for query results set retrieval. You might use them in a Microsoft Excel application that shows a list of available databases and a list of users for each database.

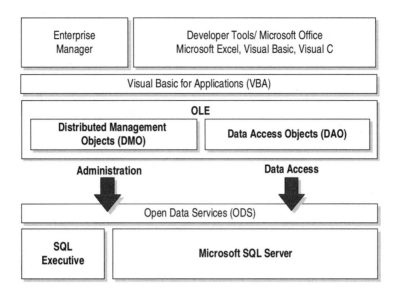

As shown in the preceding figure, Microsoft Excel uses Visual Basic for Applications to manipulate SQL-DMO objects which in turn communicate with SQL Server. For example, an administrator could build an application that automates the bulk copy process. Although it is possible to use SQL-DMO to issue a query directly against databases and tables, the SQL-DMO interface was not designed to return query results sets to clients. To build applications that perform queries against user databases, use another interface, such as DAO (Data Access Objects), DB-Library, or ODBC. SQL-DMO is designed to expose object interfaces for all SQL Server management functions. In fact, SQL Enterprise Manager itself is built using the SQL-DMO as components.

# OLE Automation

OLE Automation allows an application to expose objects, properties, and methods to other applications, as shown in the following figure. Controller applications can then program the object application. The applications can interact without specific user intervention. For example, if you need to perform a spreadsheet-like calculation in your Microsoft Visual Basic application, you can send the information to Microsoft Excel and display the returned value to the user. The user does not have to know how to use Microsoft Excel.

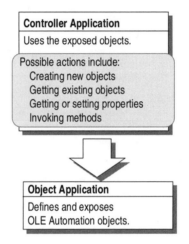

**Controller Application**

Uses the exposed objects.

Possible actions include:
    Creating new objects
    Getting existing objects
    Getting or setting properties
    Invoking methods

**Object Application**

Defines and exposes
OLE Automation objects.

OLE Automation has two main functions:

**Expose objects**  Exposed objects can be used in applications and macros. An application can expose many objects, depending on its internal complexity. But simply exposing an object is not enough; something must be done with the object.

**Manipulate objects**  An OLE Automation controller application uses OLE Automation objects exposed by other applications. Microsoft Visual Basic is an example of a general-purpose OLE Automation controller.

# OLE Automation Controller and OLE Automation Server

An application can use OLE Automation in two ways: as a controller and as a server. OLE Automation controllers are applications and programming tools that access OLE Automation objects. OLE Automation controllers can create OLE Automation objects that reside in another application, and the controllers can manipulate those objects by using the properties and methods that the OLE Automation object supports.

An OLE Automation server is an application that exposes OLE Automation objects for use by OLE Automation controllers such as Visual Basic, Microsoft Excel, or Visual C ++. SQL Server is only an OLE Automation server. SQL Server cannot call OLE automation objects from scripts on the server.

# SQL Distributed Management Objects

The purpose of the SQL Distributed Management Object (SQL-DMO) model is to allow any 32-bit controller application to reference the SQL Server object library and communicate with SQL Server objects. All SQL Server administrative functions are currently accessible by a number of different interfaces (such as DB-Library, ODBC, and Transact-SQL). These functions are now exposed in a consistent format as OLE objects, methods, and properties. Within SQL-DMO, there are more than 40 distinct objects and more than 1000 interfaces (properties and methods). DMO is not intended to support data access.

The complete SQL-DMO type library is contained in the SQLOLE65.TLB file, which by default is in the C:\MSSQL\BINN directory. The type library contains information about all SQL-DMO objects, properties, and methods. It is generally used by OLE Automation controllers, such as Visual Basic.

## Capabilities of DMO

Distributed Management Objects provide support for tuning, security, administration, scheduled maintenance, and backup and restore operations. The following are the general requirements for DMO:

- Provide OLE interfaces for all SQL Server administration functions.
- Provide a caching mechanism to buffer results, list objects, and reduce communication traffic with the server.
- Provide embedded Help for each function.
- Support OLE Automation interfaces.

In providing a consistent OLE interface to all SQL Server administration functions and services, DMO includes commands and tasks that are currently implemented in the following ways:

- SQL Server system stored procedures (such as **sp_addtype** and **sp_spaceused**)
- Open Data Services extended stored procedures (such as **xp_sendmail**)
- Transact-SQL statements (such as CREATE TABLE and DUMP DATABASE)
- SQL Performance Monitor scheduled events (such as Backup, Transaction Log, and Backups)
- Windows NT Registry entries
- SQL Server system catalog contents
- Multiserver administration

## SQL Server DMO Model

The object hierarchy provides a model for managing SQL Server. This model greatly simplifies the management of SQL Server by organizing management functions in terms of the SQL Server Object Model and by providing a single and consistent interface. The primary object is SQL Server, which contains a collection of databases. The Database object contains a collection of Table, View, and StoredProcedure objects. The individual objects contain properties or attributes (that is, SQLServer.Name = "SALESSERVER") and methods or actions (SQLServer.Start or SQLServer.Stop).

In a Visual Basic application, you must create an instance of a DMO automation object before you can navigate the hierarchy or manipulate any of these objects. In the example in following figure, you create an instance of SQL Server from which you then navigate to an object. Use the CreateObject or GetObject functions to instantiate a copy of the object. Usually, you create one copy of the SQL Server object. Using this copy as a starting point, you navigate down the tree until you find the object you want to manipulate.

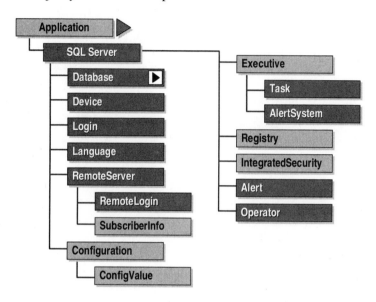

### CreateObject Example

In the following example, a SQL Server object is being created. The *MyServer* variable is used by the controller server to manipulate specific objects, properties, and methods. The Set MyServer command creates an actual SQL Server object.

**Syntax**

CreateObject (class)

**Example**

```
Dim MyServer As Object
Set MyServer = CreateObject ("SqlOle.SQLServer")
MyServer.Connect "sqlimpdev", "sa", ""
```

### GetObject Example

In this example, the controller application is retrieving a SQL Server Table object from SQL Server. The Table object can be manipulated to retrieve table information, to update statistics on the table, or to create an index on the table.

**Syntax**

GetObject ([pathname],[class])

**Example**

```
Dim Mytable As SQLServer.Table
Set Mytable = GetObject (SQLServer.Table)
```

### Navigating the SQL Object Hierarchy

A database object contains other objects that contain or interact with data, such as Table and View (as shown in the following figure) or StoredProcedures. With Visual Basic, you set a variable to point to a particular database object. Once you have a variable that points to an object, it is easy to set and trigger the object's methods.

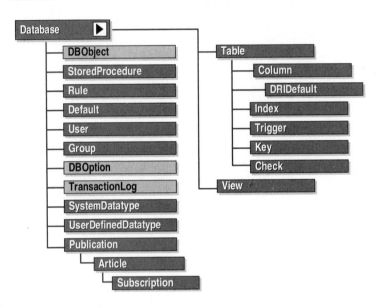

**Example**

```
Dim mydb as Object
Set mydb = SQLServer ("SALESSERVER").Database ("pubs")
```

## Database Object Properties

Object properties are single-named pieces of information that are maintained for an object (for example, Server.Name or Server.Version). Properties are generally simple datatypes. Some of the database objects that you might encounter are listed in the following table.

| Property | Description |
|---|---|
| Application | The application object |
| CreateDate | The date and time the database was created |
| CreateForLoad | Specifies if the database was created with FOR LOAD |
| DataSpaceUsage | Space, in megabytes, used to store data |
| DboLogin | Indicates if login has DBO privileges |
| DBOption | The DBOption object for this database |

Properties are values that you can query and set. For example, the DBOption object has several properties that can be set. In order to refer to an object that exists inside the hierarchy, you must work your way down to the object you want to manipulate first. Once you have a reference to that object, you can set its properties or execute its methods.

In the following example, the SQLServer object contains a collection of servers, and the MYSERVER server is specified. This server object contains a collection of databases, and the *pubs* database is specified. This database object has many other objects, and the DBOption object is the object that will be manipulated. The DBOption object has several properties, and the Single User property is set to True.

**Example**
```
SQLServer ("MYSERVER").Databases("pubs").DBOption.SingleUser=True
```

## Database Object Methods

Object methods are actions that are associated with objects (for example, Server.Start or Server.Stop). Methods are like verbs because they carry out an action. Some of the actions you might take on database objects are listed in the following table.

| Method | Description |
| --- | --- |
| CheckAllocations | Checks internal allocation consistency |
| Check Catalog | Checks consistency of the system tables |
| Checkpoint | Flushes the SQL Server cache |
| Check Tables | Checks consistency of the data and index pages |
| Check TextAllocsFast | Checks allocation consistency of text and image pages |
| Dump | Backs up a database to a backup device |

### Method Implementation

Some Transact-SQL commands and stored procedures map to the functionality of methods. For example, the method Device.Add would be implemented by using the Transact-SQL DISK INIT statement.

The following example updates the *myindex* index on the *authors* table in the *pubs* database.

**Example**
```
SQLServer("SERVER").Databases("pubs").Table("authors").Index("myindex").
UpdateStatistics
```

## Using VBA to Access Information About SQL Server

In this procedure, you run various VBA macros from Microsoft Excel 5.0 to chart the space usage for each database, to list all of the objects, to list column information for a table, to chart CPU usage, and to execute a query.

▶ **To establish a reference to the Microsoft SQLOLE Object library from Microsoft Excel**

In order to access the Microsoft SQLOLE Object library from within the Object Browser in Microsoft Excel, you must establish a reference.

1. Start Microsoft Excel.

2. On the Insert menu, click Macro, and then click Module.

   A new module window appears.

3. On the Tools menu, click References.

   The References dialog box appears.

4. Select the Microsoft SQLOLE Object Library check box.

   If this object library does not appear in your list of available references, choose Browse. Add the following file:

   C:\MSSQL\BINN\SQLOLE65.TLB

5. Click OK.

6. Click OK to exit the References dialog box.

▶ **To access the Object Browser**

You can use the Object Browser to reference the Microsoft SQLOLE object library from within Microsoft Excel. The Object Browser is available only when a module window is open.

1. On the View menu, click Object Browser, or click the Object Browser button on the Visual Basic toolbar.

   The Object Browser dialog box appears.

2. In the Libraries/Workbooks box, select SQLOLE.

   A list of the SQLOLE objects appears on the left. To view the Methods/Properties available for an object, highlight that object.

3. Click Close to exit.

▶ **To chart the space usage for each database**

1. On the File menu, open DB_USE.XLS.

2. Review the file.

3. Edit the VBA Script and replace SERVER_NAME with the name of your SQL Server and log in. For example, if your SQL Server is called MYSQLSERVER, you would replace SERVER_NAME with MYSQLSERVER.

4. On the Run menu, click Start, or click the Run Macro button on the Visual Basic toolbar to run the macro.

5. View the results.

▶ **To list all of the objects in a database**

1. On the File menu, open LISTOBJ.XLS.

2. Review the file.

3. Edit the VBA Script and replace SERVER_NAME with the name of your SQL Server and log in.

4. Run the macro.

5. View the results.

▶ **To list column information for a table**

1. On the File menu, open LISTCOLS.XLS.

2. Review the file.

3. Edit the VBA Script and replace SERVER_NAME with the name of your SQL Server and log in.

4. Run the macro.

5. View the results.

▶ **To chart CPU usage of a process**

1. On the File menu, open CPU_USE.XLS.

2. Review the file.

3. Edit the VBA Script and replace SERVER_NAME with the name of your SQL Server and log in.

4. Run the macro.

5. View the results.

▶ **To execute a query**

1. On the File menu, open EXEC_SQL.XLS.

2. Review the file.

3. Edit the VBA Script and replace SERVER_NAME with the name of your SQL Server, and then log in.

4. Run the macro.

5. View the results.

## Writing a VBA Macro Script

In the following procedures, you write a VBA macro script in Microsoft Excel to update statistics on all of the tables in the *pubs* database.

▶ **To create a new module in Microsoft Excel**

1. On the Insert menu, click Macro, and then click Module.

   A new module window appears.

2. Write a subroutine that:

   ▪ Connects to SQL Server.

   ▪ Iterates through each table in the *library* database.

   ▪ Updates statistics on every table.

   ▪ Does not output any results. See the STATS.XLS file.

3. Run the macro.

▶ **To generate output for update statistics module**

1. Modify the file that you just created to add output capabilities that allow you to view the table names that had statistics updated. See the UPDSTATS.XLS file.

2. Replace all calls to SERVER_NAME with calls to your SQL Server, and then log in.

3. Run the macro.

4. View the results.

5. Close Microsoft Excel.

## Lesson Summary

The OLE programming technology allows applications to share objects for either administration or data access. OLE Automation allows an application to expose objects, properties, and methods to other applications so they can interact. You have to create a DMO automation object before you can manipulate any of the objects. You can use VBA to access information about SQL Server, and you can write VBA macro scripts to update information (for example, from a Microsoft Excel spreadsheet to a SQL Server database).

# Lesson 4: Interfaces for Data Management

Client-side APIs (ODBC and DB-Library) and the server-side API (Open Data Services) play important roles in creating data servers and requesting and receiving connections to information.

## After this lesson you will be able to:

- Describe uses of ODBC.
- Describe some uses of the DB-Library for C.

## Estimated lesson time  20 minutes

## Client-Side and Server-Side APIs

All client applications that access SQL Server do so by making calls using the client-side APIs, which are DB-Library or ODBC.

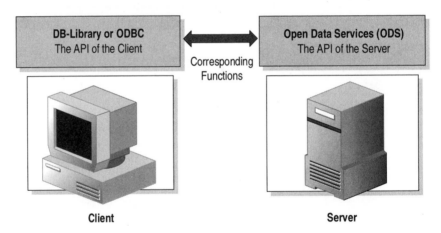

**Client**                                        **Server**

The server-side API, Open Data Services, allows programmers to write their own data servers. For each major function in the DB-Library or ODBC, there is a corresponding function in Open Data Services. For instance, DB-Library or ODBC requests a connection and Open Data Services accepts the request. As another example, the client application makes a DB-Library call to get a data row from the output, and the server application makes a call to Open Data Services. This example adds a row to the results set.

A server application is an application that can:

- Accept connections.
- Interpret ASCII text as commands.
- Provide data requested in one or more relational (rows of columns) results sets.

## Open Data Services—The Server-Side API

Microsoft Open Data Services (ODS) provides a server-based API for creating server-based applications. Another method that SQL Server programmers can use is to write simple applications on top of Open Data Services that distribute data to the outside computing environment.

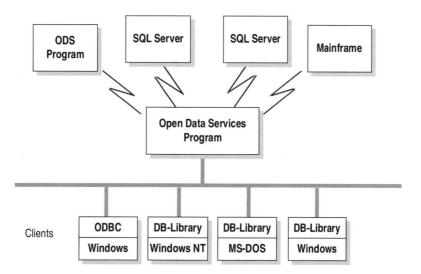

As shown in the preceding figure, applications created with Open Data Services can interact with SQL Server clients, servers, and with any other elements of a network environment that you define.

This interaction allows you to create powerful applications that can:

- Provide extensions to SQL Server by integrating features from your network environment whenever certain events occur within SQL Server.

- Provide gateways to non-SQL Server database environments that allow Open Data Services applications to connect to relational databases or non-relational data sources.

Some applications for Open Data Services might not involve a SQL Server database at all; Open Data Services can be used to build applications that "look like" a SQL Server to a client on the LAN. These applications might do something simple, such as respond to a predetermined procedure call; or they might perform more complex tasks, such as provide a general purpose gateway to another vendor's relational database.

# Open Database Connectivity (ODBC)

ODBC is a client interface for accessing many different databases from Windows-based applications. On a high level, ODBC translates requests for data and services from a client to the target database. You can think of it as a SQL translator and session manager in one. As a translator between client and target databases, a special ODBC driver translates SQL statements sent from a client into the specific SQL language that the target database understands. As a session manager, the driver may act as a mini database engine to exchange data with certain systems, for example xBase files or a spreadsheet. Drivers that translate SQL and act as data brokers are called multiple-tier drivers, such as SQL Server ODBC driver. Drivers that act as database engines are called single-tier drivers, for example xBase.

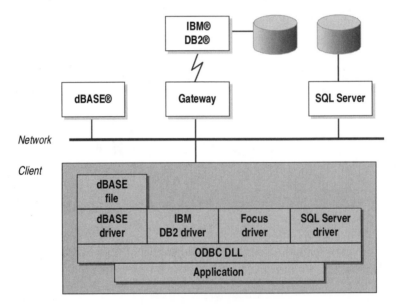

The SQL Server driver enables applications to access data in SQL Server databases through the ODBC interface. The ODBC driver is installed automatically when SQL Server client software is installed on a Windows NT–based, Windows 95-based, or Windows 3.1-based computer.

As shown in the preceding figure, Open Database Connectivity (ODBC) allows you to access many different databases from Windows applications. You can write one application that accesses many different data sources by using different ODBC drivers. If you must migrate the application to use a different data source, recoding is minimal to none.

ODBC is based on the standard defined by the SQL Access Group, and provides most of the functions that are available in SQL Server. While it is used primarily to submit queries and retrieve results sets, it also can be used to trigger database maintenance, perform a bulk copy, and other tasks. Several programming languages and systems use ODBC. Many languages, including Visual Basic and Microsoft Visual C++, provide an object model layer on top of ODBC. This layer allows the programmer to access data using the Data Access Objects (DAO) or remote data objects (RDO) object collections in a way that is consistent with the rest of the programming language. As a result, the programmer does not need to learn ODBC function calls when using these object layers. The latest releases of this interface are extremely fast and efficient. The advantages of being able to change the supporting database system for a front-end application, and the speed that ODBC provides, make it the client API of choice.

## DB-Library

DB-Library is the native programming interface for SQL Server. DB-Library applications can automate data transfer as well as administrative functions in the SQL Sever environment. DB-Library can be used to communicate only with SQL Server databases.

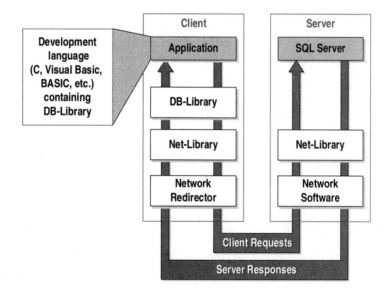

DB-Library consists of C functions and macros that allow an application to interact with SQL Server. Included with DB-Library are functions that send Transact-SQL statements to SQL Server, and functions that process the results of those statements. DB-Library for C offers an extensive set of functions for:

- Opening connections.
- Formatting queries.
- Sending query batches to the server and retrieving the resulting data.
- Using scrollable cursors.
- Bulk-copying data from files or application variables to and from the server.
- Controlling two-phase commit operations between several participating SQL servers.
- Executing stored procedures or remote stored procedures.
- Managing communication between client applications and SQL Server.
- Working with SQL Server and Open Data Services applications, and making all of the server's features available to the client application.

## Lesson Summary

You can use the Open Data Services API to write your own data server. There are corresponding functions in the DB-Library or ODBC to those in the Open Data Services. Open Data Services provides a server-based application programming interface for creating server-based applications.

# Review

The following questions are intended to reinforce key information presented in this chapter. If you are unable to answer a question, review the lesson and then try the question again.

1. You are the administrator of a SQL Server installation. Each day you perform the same types of duties, including backing up the database, tuning indexes, and executing DBCC commands. You would like to create a custom utility to help you manage the databases as well as the SQL Server installation and to present custom graphs of server data. Several skilled programmers are on staff at your company. What tools can you use to build a solution?

\
\
\
\
\
\

2. You want to build an application that executes several predefined queries that are stored on the server. The application also allows the user to build queries on the fly to browse a database. What tools should you use?

\
\
\
\
\
\

# Questions and Answers

Page 969

### Review Questions

1. You are the administrator of a SQL Server installation. Each day you perform the same types of duties, including backing up the database, tuning indexes, and executing DBCC commands. You would like to create a custom utility to help you manage the databases as well as the SQL Server installation and to present custom graphs of server data. Several skilled programmers are on staff at your company. What tools can you use to build a solution?

   **You can build a client front end using Visual Basic, Visual C, Microsoft Excel, or any other development environment that can manipulate OLE automation objects. The client application instantiates and manipulates SQL-DMO objects that in turn program SQL Server. These objects might also return limited amounts of data about particular database and system objects. You can also choose to use Microsoft Excel to present the information in a graphical format.**

2. You want to build an application that executes several predefined queries that are stored on the server. The application also allows the user to build queries on the fly to browse a database. What tools should you use?

   **In this case, several options exist. ODBC or DBLibrary can be used to enable communication between a client application (written in the programming language of your choice) and SQL Server. Both of these APIs are designed to submit queries and return substantial results sets. ODBC offers the added advantage of porting the application to work with a different database back end with little modification to the client-side code.**

APPENDIX A

# A New ERA for Data Modeling

**A philosophical and practical discussion of the nature of good data models. Part 1 of a series on the ERA process.**

by Al Foster

**Al Foster** is a database consultant and principle of Applied Relational Design in Malibu, California

A data model exists not only to implement Dr. Codd's Relational Data Model Version 2, but more fundamentally to provide a logical representation of an organization.

One method for doing this is called Extended Relational Analysis (ERA, a trademark of Relational Systems Corp.), which *DBMS* Magazine will detail in a series of articles. In this, the first of these articles, I'll talk about the basics of the model: how to define entities, relationships, and attributes. Simply put, the ERA modeling process depends on an interview process, and the model that emerges parallels the use of language during those interviews. Entities correspond to nouns, relationships are verbs, and attributes are adjectives, adverbs, or prepositional phrases. ERA combines the words users actually use to describe their enterprise into a sentence; the model represented by that sentence, it turns out, will be a fine fit with the relational model.

Before I get into the mechanics—and believe me, the process I will define is very explicit about the sequence of precise steps to create a model—it will be beneficial to put data modeling into its larger, social context, an aspect few developers consider when designing their relational databases.

## Socializing the Process

Those who use databases and eat sausage would probably be more comfortable if they didn't watch either being made. But if efficiency, clarity, consistency, and quality are the goal—and they are—then end users not only have to watch, they have to help stuff the sausage. When modeling is a social process—that is, when it is an interaction between the modeler and the end users involved rather than something the modeler does in isolation—the chances are much better that a workable model will result.

As a side benefit, the end users may actually acquire a keener grasp of how their business really works. A friend of mine, Miles Coverdale, was doing a modeling session in Toronto, and one of the users said afterwards, "This is the clearest picture of the business I've ever seen. I wish I'd had this when I started."

Remember, too, that quality is in the eye of the beholder: the user community determines the "quality" of the system. If users are involved, they are more likely to like the result.

## A Model Model

Although business communities and the MIS departments often seem to exist in different universes, designing a quality system requires business and data modeling professionals to share a single vision of the system. In general, the visions do not completely merge, so it may pay to spend a moment considering an example where what the modeler intended and what the user perceived are one and the same.

The globe is a model model. Our daughter Jessica, at age 2-and-a-half, used to go to the globe and say, "Dad, show me where Germany is. Show me where Mom is." Young children have a remarkable capacity for conceptualization and abstraction. It was quite clear to Jessica that the orange blob on that strange ball in the library was not really Germany and Mom was not really there. Yet she was convinced that the globe had a one-to-one correlation with the real world and that she could talk about the world and the globe in exactly the same terms.

People do not relate their business to their database with nearly the same confidence that Jessica relates to the globe. That's because many current database designs are about as good as globes of the sixteenth century: they include a lot of Terra Incognita as well as places that are charted but don't really exist.

Just as input from explorers was the crucial factor in helping map makers improve the accuracy of their model, data explorers are the key to more accurate data models. Data explorers are the people who've been out there working with what is being modeled—the business, the enterprise. If the model is to represent the enterprise as a globe does the real world, the crucial factor must be user input and involvement.

The result, if the data model maps the way the enterprise really functions, can be extremely rewarding. I can't tell you how many times I've heard high-level business executives lament, "We know we've got the data, but they tell me they can't get at it. We need a better picture of profitability by product line. We cannot determine our discount position until year end." The problem is mostly a matter of design.

For large companies with large database systems in place this means redesigning the system. That's not to say that much of the existing data and equipment can't be used in the new system. It only means that the system should be properly redesigned first. The developer can then go back and address conversion, data acquisition, and physical implementation issues.

## About the Process

The process  used to get from the verbal description of the situation to an implemented, quality database is the key to how well you do. The quality of a database must be present in its initial design—it cannot be coded in later.

Remember, above all, that the data modelers are not the experts on the business. Their task is to find the experts, including those who have a vision of the future of a business as well as its past. Without continuous feedback on the correctness and clarity of the model, it will reflect the modelers' understanding and interpretation of the business instead of the business itself. Do not change the model without the users' presence, agreement, and understanding.

In short, the data modelers should be more like Peter Falk on "Colombo" than experts from the mountain. They should keep showing up at the door to ask more questions. "Sir, I know I'm a bit slow on this, but I just can't quite seem to get a clear picture. Could we go over that one more time?"

Just as Colombo tries to keep things simple, so should a data modeler. Eschew obfuscation. Keep terminology and jargon to a minimum. The erudition and sophistication of the data modeler are not on trial.

Diagrams and graphics must be clear. Remember the globe example; it could be satisfactorily understood by our 2-and-a-half-year-old with minimal orientation. The world is round like a ball. The big blue areas are the oceans. The different colors are different countries. The letters are the names of places. The Australians use Velcro to hang on. (Well, some of the finer points come later.)

Indeed, one reason the globe model works so well is because it can support increasing levels of understanding—the concept of gravity fits right in. Rotation, inclination, equinoxes, solstices, latitude, and longitude will not require any conceptual backtracking. A data model will exhibit the same attributes if you start by keeping things simple and fundamentally sound.

Sometimes the terminology can get in the way. It's clear, for example, that a data model should never violate the Relational Model and the rules that define normal tables. On the other hand, the term normalization is in some ways unfortunate. It is easy to infer that you start out with tables that are abnormal, and by series of steps render them normal. This is not illogical, but it is anti-social because it encourages data processing personnel to transmogrify the current system into a relational one. The data modeling group is sent off (sometimes even to another state, usually New Jersey) to "build the data model." This proceeds with a minimum of additional input from the users. When the data modelers return, if ever, the procedure is to "present the model to the users" and the goal is to get sign-off, not clarity.

The need for clarity should also dictate the linguistics of the data modeling exercise. The language you use should be applicable to both the real world business and the data model, and, with reasonable advances in the state of the art, the database itself. Yet the definitions and terms necessary to understand should be business terms, not data processing jargon.

Finally, the results should work intuitively. General feelings about such things as the enterprise, navigation, and the meaning of data should not be frequently offended. If your intuition about the business is not consistent with the model, something is wrong. Dave Posey, a friend of mine, was doing a data model for his in-laws at their cattle breeding ranch in Montana. They had just acquired a PC and said, "Can you show us how to use it?" This was their first foray into the world of computers. I am not sure what sort of person attempts to build a data model with his mother-in-law, but when they were done, she was able to easily navigate the database and even write some SQL. This was made considerably easier because the model reflected exactly the way the business was run.

## Extended Relational Analysis

With that prelude as a foundation, let's jump into Extended Relational Analysis.

ERA is a process that moves directly from the business situation at hand to the solution. The process is very explicit about the steps and their sequence in creating a model. ERA unites the language, intuition, and mathematical aspects of data modeling and yields a model that keeps all in sync. It reduces the probability of erring or misidentifying an entity, relationship, or attribute. Think of the ERA modeling process as paralleling language: Identifying words as parts of speech, and then stringing them together into a sentence, as follows.

## 1. Model the Entities

The entities are the nouns of the sentence. They are persons, places, things, or concepts involved in the enterprise.

Modeling the entities is a three-step process: brainstorming what the entities might be, determining whether the results of the brainstorm really fit into the system you're trying to create, and determining a unique way to identify each piece of data (that is, finding the primary key). The end result will be a set of tables, such as those shown in Figure 1.

By the way, if a proposed entity fails to meet any of the following criteria, it needs to be reconsidered. Perhaps it is an attribute (that is, a descriptive word that applies to an entity) rather than an entity in its own right. Or maybe it belongs in another database. The determination of the status of every entity is a collective decision made by the developer and the end users. The best way to proceed in modeling entities is to go through the four steps described below for each proposed entity, one by one, before going on to the next entity.

To determine which pieces of data deserve to be entities having their own table, use the following steps:

**A. Discover an entity.**  The best way to find an entity is to ask the people who operate the business—they have a very specific way of thinking about it. In your discussions with users about their business, entities will be revealed as nouns. In designing a data model for an auto insurance company, for example, such a discussion might produce the results shown in Figure 1. The entities would be the headings on the tables: Claim, Individual, Policy, Rate Category, and Vehicle. Another example of the entities of an enterprise is shown in quiz form in the sidebar entitled "Ma's Health Food."

**B. Determine the scope.**  Next, ask yourself if this entity is within the scope of this project. In Figure 1, a health insurance variable would be outside the scope of the project, which is concerned exclusively with auto insurance. If the modeler and project manager don't control the scope well, they risk modeling too much.

**C. Determine the primary key.**  To find the primary key, ask users how they differentiate between pieces of information. (A claim number, for example, differentiates between claims.) If the differentiating factor is really a basic aspect of the organization of the business, it probably already has a unique identifier. Unique identification is actually as much a business requirement as a mathematical requirement of the relational model (primary keys have to be unique and always available—that is, not null). Businesses have been uniquely identifying things (accounts, vendors, employees, purchase orders, railway cars) since long before computers came into the picture. The primary keys in the example tables are represented by the label PK and are the *CLAIM NUM*, *INDIV NUM*, *POLICY NUM*, *RATE CODE*, and *VEHICLE ID*.

When implementing the database, the primary key of an entity can either be specified by the user or generated by the system. For minor entities—which tend to be things that number far fewer than 100 and don't change much—user-assigned codes tend to already exist. They are easy to remember and meaningful when displayed, so go ahead and use them. Rate category would be an example of a minor entity that gets user-defined keys. Major entities—big, important, numerous, and very dynamic things—are normally identified by system-assigned numbers since user-assigned keys would be difficult to manage and impossible to memorize. A claim is an example of a major entity.

**D. Document the entity in table form.** Draw a table, name it (in user's terms), name the primary key column (using the same unique identifier the user does), for the moment forget about the other columns, and then put in sample data. The sample data should be real data supplied by the users, because their ability to relate to the model is at least as dependent on the sample data as it is on the table structures themselves.

At this stage, the data model is a collection of tables, each with one column—the single unique identifier or primary key—and sample data. Although the relational model is the most flexible database organization and tables can be added over time, a thorough attempt to find all the entities should be made now, because: a (it helps to clarify the discussion, and b) if an entity is missed the next two steps go to hell in a handbasket.

The ERA process reveals omissions better than other modeling processes because of its straightforward graphics and high level of user involvement and understanding.

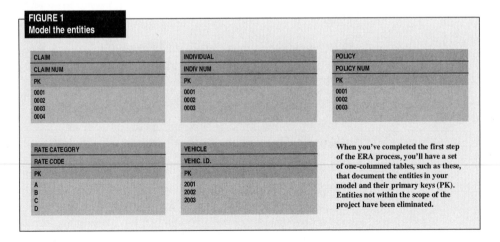

**FIGURE 1**
**Model the entities**

| CLAIM |
| --- |
| CLAIM NUM |
| PK |
| 0001 |
| 0002 |
| 0003 |
| 0004 |

| INDIVIDUAL |
| --- |
| INDIV NUM |
| PK |
| 0001 |
| 0002 |
| 0003 |

| POLICY |
| --- |
| POLICY NUM |
| PK |
| 0001 |
| 0002 |
| 0003 |

| RATE CATEGORY |
| --- |
| RATE CODE |
| PK |
| A |
| B |
| C |
| D |

| VEHICLE |
| --- |
| VEHIC. I.D. |
| PK |
| 2001 |
| 2002 |
| 2003 |

When you've completed the first step of the ERA process, you'll have a set of one-columned tables, such as these, that document the entities in your model and their primary keys (PK). Entities not within the scope of the project have been eliminated.

## 2. Model Relationships

The next step is to model the relationships between the entities. Relationships are the verbs of your data model. Discover the relationship and determine its scope and type for each possible combination of tables in your model, using the fours steps that follow.

Repeat this process until everyone is convinced that no direct relationships (within the scope of the project) exist in the business that have not been documented in the model. It is important that the users try out the model as it is being built. The rule of thumb is that there should be no reasonable activity, transaction, or query within the scope of the project that the model cannot handle.

**A. Discover a relationship.**  For each possible pair of tables, ask if there is a direct relationship. If so, model it by adding a new column to one of the two tables. The new column, usually a foreign key, matches to a unique identifier (primary key) in the other table.

**B. Verify the scope.**  Is this relationship really part of this project, application, or phase?

**C. Determine the type of relationship.**  Is it one-to-one, one-to-many, or many-to-many? This can be determined by asking two questions. The first is: Can the entity in table 1 be linked to more than one of the entities in table 2? The second is: Can the entity in table 2 be linked to more than one of the entities in table 1? If the answer to both questions I no, you have a one-to-one relationship; if the answer to both questions is yes, you have a many-to-many relationship; finally, if the answer to one question is yes and to the other question is no, you have a one-to-many relationship.

For example, consider the table Vehicle and Rates. Can a vehicle be linked to many rates? No. Can a rate be linked to many vehicles? Yes. So what you've got is a one-to-many relationship.

**D. Document the relationship in table form.**  Figure 2 shows the relationships between all the tables in Figure 1, as determined in cooperation with our users. In a one-to-one or one-to-many relationship, a foreign key (FK in the figure) is added to one of the existing tables. For a one-to-one relationship, it doesn't really matter where you place the foreign key. In a one-to-many relationship, you'd put the foreign key on the many side. So in Figure 2, because each policy and each vehicle can have many claims, the foreign key is placed in the Claim table. The fact that one-to-one relationships are symmetrical and one-to-many are asymmetrical is a very easy notion or users to grasp, especially if you are careful to put in sample data.

A many-to-many relationship is modeled by drawing a new table with two columns. Those two columns are foreign keys that match up with the primary keys of the two tables involved in the many-to-many relationship. In Figure 2, there is a many-to-many relationship between policies and individuals and between policies and vehicles. Therefore, I created two new tables, Policy/Individual and Policy/Vehicle. Again, the sample data is important. The users' confidence in and ability to relate to the model will be in proportion to the use of realistic sample data.

Repeat this process until there are no relevant direct relationships that have not been documented in the model.

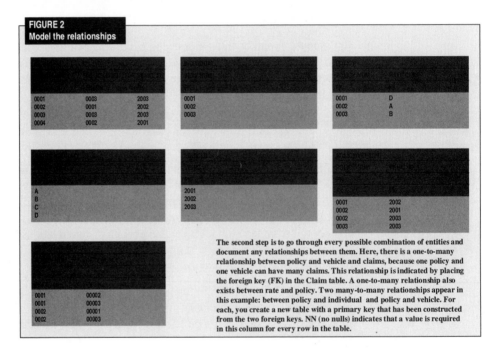

**FIGURE 2**
**Model the relationships**

The second step is to go through every possible combination of entities and document any relationships between them. Here, there is a one-to-many relationship between policy and vehicle and claims, because one policy and one vehicle can have many claims. This relationship is indicated by placing the foreign key (FK) in the Claim table. A one-to-many relationship also exists between rate and policy. Two many-to-many relationships appear in this example: between policy and individual and policy and vehicle. For each, you create a new table with a primary key that has been constructed from the two foreign keys. NN (no nulls) indicates that a value is required in this column for every row in the table.

## 3. Model the Attributes

Attributes are additional qualities users are interested in keeping track of. They're graphically represented as additional columns in the tables. In terms of the language that emerges in the interview process, attributes are adjectives, adverbs or prepositional phrases. (In case you had trouble in English class, adjectives modify nouns, adverbs modify relationships, and prepositional phrases can be used for either.) Figure 3 shows the tables from Figure 2 with attributes added.

As before, there are four steps:

**A. Discover an attribute.**  Is there a quality or characteristic of this entity or this relationship that you would like to keep track of?

**B. Verify the cope.**  Is this attribute relevant or necessary to this phase of the project? Is it derivable? Leave derived data out of the model and obtain it from queries against the model.

**C. Determine the table.**  Pick the table the attribute belongs in. If this is not obvious, you either a) do not understand precisely what the data means, b) overlooked an entity back in the first step, or c) in step two you have missed a relationship, most probably a many-to-many relationship.

The nice thing about saving the attributes for last is that it simplifies the other-wise complex problem of normalization into a intuitive process. If the first two steps have gone well, any attribute will have a table that is quite obviously ready to receive it. In fact, just by using the English language as a guide to describe the attribute ("We need the make of each vehicle" and "We need the name of each individual") you'll find the correct table for all attributes. Moreover, you'll probably discover when you're done that your tables are in proper third normal form even though you've not consciously normalized them.

Although following ERA methodology eliminates the need to worry about it, you may be curious about just what normalization is. Unfortunately (or fortunately, depending on your point of view), an in-depth discussion of normalization is beyond the scope of this article. In a sentence, a table is in third normal form if every field is dependent on the key field and on the key field only.

For more detail, see "A Practical Guide to Normalization" by Tom Kemm from *DBMS* December 1989, which is available on the TelePath BBS (see the letters page for more information about TelePath). Richard Finkelstein also discusses the impact of normalization beginning on page 16 of this issue.

## D. Document the attribute in table form.

Add a column to an existing table. (At this point, a table would be added only if you detected a mistake in step one or two.) Put in sample data and try out the model. Repeat the process until no one can think of any attributes within the scope of this project that you want to keep track of. Trying out the model is very important and at this stage very cheap. If you remember my definition of quality, the model should depict the users' view of the world. If it can not be done with the model while you've got it up on the white board, computerizing the model will not help.

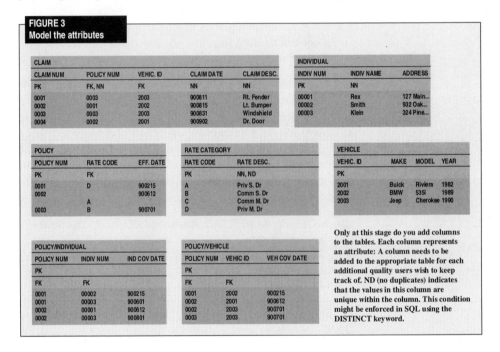

**FIGURE 3**
**Model the attributes**

**CLAIM**

| CLAIM NUM | POLICY NUM | VEHIC. ID | CLAIM DATE | CLAIM DESC. |
|-----------|------------|-----------|------------|-------------|
| PK | FK, NN | FK | NN | NN |
| 0001 | 0003 | 2003 | 900811 | Rt. Fender |
| 0002 | 0001 | 2002 | 900815 | Lt. Bumper |
| 0003 | 0003 | 2003 | 900831 | Windshield |
| 0004 | 0002 | 2001 | 900902 | Dr. Door |

**INDIVIDUAL**

| INDIV NUM | INDIV NAME | ADDRESS |
|-----------|------------|---------|
| PK | NN | |
| 00001 | Rex | 127 Main... |
| 00002 | Smith | 932 Oak... |
| 00003 | Klein | 324 Pine... |

**POLICY**

| POLICY NUM | RATE CODE | EFF. DATE |
|------------|-----------|-----------|
| PK | FK | |
| 0001 | D | 900215 |
| 0002 | | 900612 |
| | A | |
| 0003 | B | 900701 |

**RATE CATEGORY**

| RATE CODE | RATE DESC. |
|-----------|------------|
| PK | NN, ND |
| A | Priv S. Dr |
| B | Comm S. Dr |
| C | Comm M. Dr |
| D | Priv M. Dr |

**VEHICLE**

| VEHIC. ID | MAKE | MODEL | YEAR |
|-----------|------|-------|------|
| PK | | | |
| 2001 | Buick | Riviera | 1982 |
| 2002 | BMW | 535i | 1989 |
| 2003 | Jeep | Cherokee | 1990 |

**POLICY/INDIVIDUAL**

| POLICY NUM | INDIV NUM | IND COV DATE |
|------------|-----------|--------------|
| PK | | |
| FK | FK | |
| 0001 | 00002 | 900215 |
| 0001 | 00003 | 900601 |
| 0002 | 00001 | 900612 |
| 0002 | 00003 | 900801 |

**POLICY/VEHICLE**

| POLICY NUM | VEHIC ID | VEH COV DATE |
|------------|----------|--------------|
| PK | | |
| FK | FK | |
| 0001 | 2002 | 900215 |
| 0002 | 2001 | 900612 |
| 0002 | 2003 | 900701 |
| 0003 | 2003 | 900701 |

Only at this stage do you add columns to the tables. Each column represents an attribute: A column needs to be added to the appropriate table for each additional quality users wish to keep track of. ND (no duplicates) indicates that the values in this column are unique within the column. This condition might be enforced in SQL using the DISTINCT keyword.

## A Simple Concept

Is that all there is to it? Well, yes and no.

Once I was teaching a one-day overview of the ERA model and a chap in the back said, "I don't see what's so great about this. This is the way we used to set up tub files years ago." Like him, many developers will find the ERA process obvious because it is simply a structured procedure for a process good developers have been following all along.

And yet things are rarely as simple as a brief introduction might imply. Conversely, they are rarely as complex as some people like to make them.

Next month I'll go beyond the basics of ERA into some potential complications of the entity recognition process.

**An ERA Quiz**

This is an example exercise adapted from a Relational Systems Corp. database design training seminar. During the interview process, part of designing a database for the fictional owners of Ma's Health Food Store, a data modeler obtained the following information. What entities should be captured from this discussion? The answer is shown in Figure 4.

"Well, Pa and I and the other 300 employees have been runnin' this here little health food store just fine without a computer, but we reckon we'd better keep up with the times if we're gonna keep up with the Joneses, know what I mean? Why sure you do. . .

"Anyway, we need to keep track of these different kinds of items—wheat germ, vitamin E, chocolate covered granola (that's a big seller). . .And we need to know which items are sold in which stores, and which aren't. Be nice to know how many each store's got on hand, too. . .

"And we've been growing, too. Did ya know we have stores in three different states now? You betcha. And we're thinking of branching out to other states like Virginny and Alabama before too long . . ."

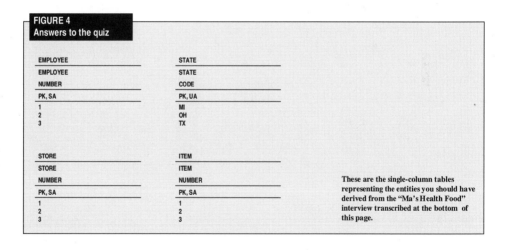

**FIGURE 4**
**Answers to the quiz**

| EMPLOYEE | STATE |
|---|---|
| EMPLOYEE | STATE |
| NUMBER | CODE |
| PK, SA | PK, UA |
| 1 | MI |
| 2 | OH |
| 3 | TX |

| STORE | ITEM |
|---|---|
| STORE | ITEM |
| NUMBER | NUMBER |
| PK, SA | PK, SA |
| 1 | 1 |
| 2 | 2 |
| 3 | 3 |

These are the single-column tables representing the entities you should have derived from the "Ma's Health Food" interview transcribed at the bottom of this page.

## What's a Table?

Tables are the only graphical representation of data used in the ERA process. Users can easily be oriented to tables because everybody is familiar with them. Stock prices and baseball standings, for example, are tabular representations of data The basic rules are:

- Tables are organized in rows and columns and have unique names.
- Columns have unique names (at least within tables) with the same meaning all the way down. They do not have embedded or hidden columns (they are atomic). Their order has no hidden meaning and they refer to unique identifiers (primary keys) that are modeling relationships.
- Rows have unique identifiers and a logical order.

In short, tables are simple, precise, and flexible. Simple means that anyone can read them with minimal orientation. Precise means correct and unambiguous (they are also unambiguous in a business sense). Flexible means that tables show the structure of and the purpose for the data. — A.F.

## APPENDIX B

# System Tables and System Stored Procedures

| System tables | Function | System stored procedures |
|---|---|---|
| *sysalternates* | Has one row for each SQL Server user mapped to a database user | **sp_helpuser** |
| *syscolumns* | Has one row for each column in a table or view, and for each parameter in a stored procedure | **sp_columns** *tablename* or **sp_help** *tablename* |
| *syscomments* | Has one or more rows for each view, rule, default, trigger, and stored procedure with a SQL definition statement | **sp_helptext** *objectname* |
| *sysdepends* | Has one row for each procedure, view, or table that is referenced by a procedure, view, or trigger | **sp_depends** |
| *sysindexes* | Has one row for each clustered index, nonclustered index, and table with no indexes, plus an extra row for each table with text or image data | **sp_helpindex** or **sp_help** |
| *syskeys* | Has one row for each foreign, primary, or common key | **sp_helpkey** |
| *syslogs* | Contains the transaction log | **sp_helpkey** |
| *sysobjects* | Has one row for each table, view, stored procedure, rule, trigger, default, log, and (in *tempdb* only) temporary object | **sp_help** or **sp_tables** |
| *sysprocedures* | Has one row for each view, rule, default, trigger, and stored procedure | **sp_sproc_columns** or **sp_stored_procedures** |
| *sysprotects* | Contains user permissions information | **sp_helpprotect** |
| *syssegments* | Has one row for each segment | **sp_helpsegment** or **sp_helpdb** |
| *systypes* | Has one row for each default system-supplied and user-defined datatype | **sp_help** *typename* **sp_datatype_info** |
| *sysusers* | Has one row for each user allowed in the database | **sp_helpuser** |
| *sysreferences* | Has one row for each reference constraint created | **sp_help** *tablename* |
| *sysconstraints* | Contains information on all constraints created | **sp_helpconstraint** or **sp_help** *tablename* |
| *sysarticles* | Contains article information for each article created for replication | **sp_helparticle** |
| *syspublications* | Contains one row for each publication created | **sp_helppublication** |
| *syssubscriptions* | Contains one row for each subscription from a subscribing server | **sp_helpsubscription** or **sp_helpsubscriberinfo** |
| *syscharsets* | Character set or sort order | **sp_helpsort** |

*(continued)*

| System tables | Function | System stored procedures |
|---|---|---|
| *sysconfigures, syscurconfigs* | Configurable environmental variables | **sp_configure** |
| *sysdatabases* | Databases on SQL Server | **sp_helpdb** or **sp_databases** |
| *sysdevices* | Available database and disk devices | **sp_helpdevice** |
| *syslanguages* | Languages known to the server | **sp_helplanguage** |
| *syslocks* | Active locks | **sp_lock** |
| *syslogins* | User accounts | **sp_helpuser** |
| *sysmessages* | System error messages | **sp_addmessage** or **sp_dropmessage** |
| *sysprocesses* | Ongoing processes | **sp_who** or **sp_processinfo** |
| *sysremotelogins* | Remote user accounts | **sp_helpremotelogin** |
| *sysservers* | Remote servers | **sp_helpserver** |
| *sysusages* | Disk space allocated to each database | **sp_spaceused** |

APPENDIX C

# System Tables Diagram

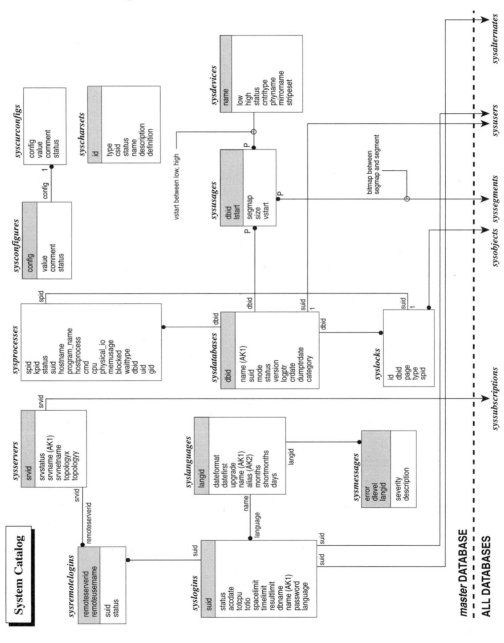

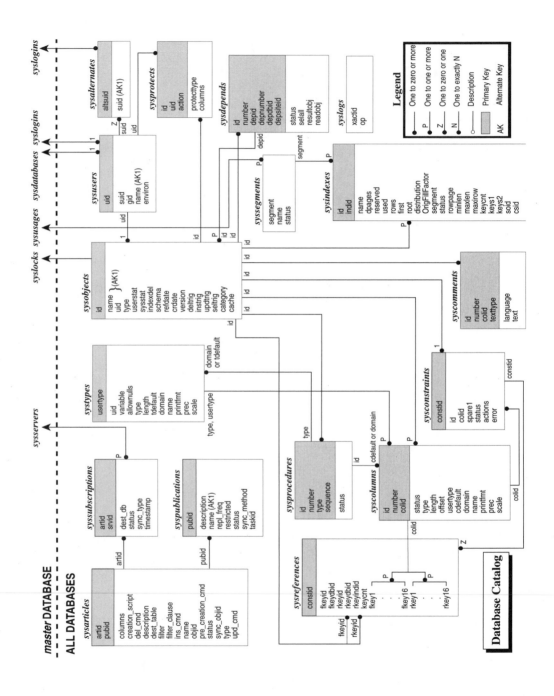

A P P E N D I X   D

# Library Case Study

Throughout this book, the Library Case Study is used to help you complete procedures, understand examples, and execute queries. This appendix introduces you to the Library Case Study and provides you with information about how and why the library's database was designed.

**What do these headings mean?**

Some paragraphs have headings to the left. The headings indicate how the designer can use the information presented to create the database.

## Introduction

The Library Case Study describes an overview of library operations, the book checkout process, the need for historical information, the daily library functions, and the library database design.

# Overview of Library Operations

An interview was conducted with the librarians at West Overshoe Municipal Library. The purpose of the interview was to understand what the library business needs were in order to implement a database strategy that worked for the librarians and the library members. The decisions that the database designer made during the database design process are explained in the following sections. The following figure shows the overall schema of the database that was designed for the library.

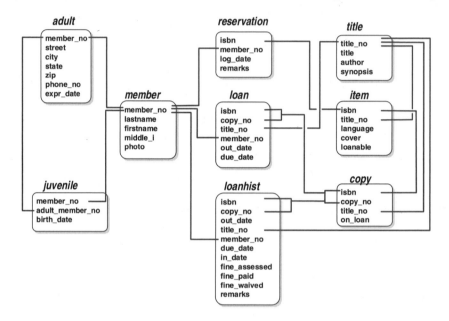

The West Overshoe Municipal Library has approximately 10,000 members, 1,000 titles, and 10,000 volumes (or an average of ten copies per book). About twenty percent of the volumes are out on loan at any one time.

**This request can be fulfilled by a query.**

The librarians are primarily responsible for the book supply. They must try to ensure that the books members want to borrow are available when the members want to borrow them. Also, the librarians must know how many copies of each book are in the library or out on loan at any given time.

**This paragraph indicates several business rules.**

The librarians also keep track of the demand for books. If members want a book that is not currently in the library, the book is placed on reserve for them. When the book arrives, a librarian must notify the member who has been waiting the longest. Members can have as many as four books on reserve at one time.

<table>
<tr><td>

**This paragraph indicates a business rule.**

</td><td>

If a book becomes overdue, the librarians must know which member has which copy of the book. Members are allowed to have only four books out at a time. Members usually return books within twenty days. Most members know that they have a one week grace period before a notice is sent to them, so they try to get the book returned before the grace period ends. Approximately five percent of the members will have to be reminded to return the book. Most overdue books are returned within three months. Approximately one percent of the members will either keep the book for over three months or never return it.

</td></tr>
<tr><td>

**This request can be fulfilled by a query.**

</td><td>

The librarians are interested in who is borrowing books and who is not. One percent of the membership does ten percent of the borrowing, and ten percent of the membership does forty percent of the borrowing. Another ten percent of the membership never borrows a book. This ratio seems to be the same for both adults and for children.

</td></tr>
<tr><td>

**This paragraph indicates a business rule.**

</td><td>

In order to become a member of the library, members must give the librarians their mailing addresses and telephone numbers. The librarians then issue the members a numbered, machine-readable card with their photo on it. This card is valid for one year. A month before the cards expire, the librarian must send a notice to the members reminding them to renew their membership.

</td></tr>
<tr><td>

**This paragraph indicates a business rule.**

</td><td>

Juveniles are also considered members, but they must have an adult member sign for them when they become a member of the library. Therefore, a juvenile's card is good only until the adult's card expires. At West Overshoe Municipal Library, approximately one-half of the members are juveniles. The only information the library keeps on juveniles are their names and dates of birth. If the library has any problems with a juvenile's membership, the librarian contacts that juvenile through the responsible adult.

</td></tr>
<tr><td>

**This request can be fulfilled by a trigger.**

</td><td>

The library needs a system that can detect when juveniles become of age, and then automatically convert their juvenile memberships to adult memberships.

The library does not lend some books—such as reference books and rare books. The librarians must differentiate between books that are lent and those that are not lent. In addition, the librarians have a list of some books they are interested in acquiring but cannot obtain, such as rare or out-of-print books and books that were lost or destroyed but have not yet been replaced. The librarians must have a system that keeps track of books that are not lent, as well as books that they are interested in acquiring.

</td></tr>
</table>

**This request can be fulfilled by a query.**

For each title in the library, a synopsis exists that ranges from one sentence to several pages. The librarians want to access those synopses if members request to know about a book.

Some books may have the same title; therefore, the title can't be used as a means of identification. The librarians call books "items." Items are identified by the ISBN, a unique universal product code. Two books with the same title can have different ISBN numbers if they are in different languages, have different bindings (hard cover or soft cover), or if one can be lent and the other cannot be lent.

## Information Needs

The following table shows some examples of the kind of information that is needed.

### Examples of expiring cards

| | |
|---|---|
| Name | Chen, Sue |
| Address | Kent |
| Expiration Date | Dec 31 1992 |
| | |
| Name | Karns, K.D. |
| Address | Des Moines |
| Expiration Date | Dec 31 1992 |
| | |
| Name | Zucker, Tim |
| Address | Juanita |
| Expiration Date | Dec 31 1992 |

### Examples of overdue books

| | |
|---|---|
| Title | Gone With the Wind |
| Date Out | Feb 20 1992 |
| Borrower | Chen, Sue |
| Address | Kent |
| Phone | (206) 555–4567 |
| | |
| Title | Roots |
| Date Out | Feb 20 1992 |
| Borrower | Chen, Sue |
| Address | Kent |
| Phone | (206) 555–4567 |
| | |
| Title | Hotel |
| Date Out | Feb 20 1992 |
| Borrower | Maki, Ed |
| Address | Bellevue |
| Phone | (206) 555–6543 |

# The Book Checkout Process

This section describes the book checkout process at the West Overshoe Municipal Library.

Once a member locates the books he wants to check out, he takes them to the checkout desk. The librarian then runs the member's card through a magnetic reader, which reads the card numbers. A checkout terminal's screen displays information about the member's account, such as his name, addresses, telephone numbers, and the card's expiration dates Ideally, the librarian would see highlighting or something that indicates if the card is about to expire or has expired.

The checkout terminal's screen should also display information about any outstanding loans that the member currently has, including the title, the date that the book was checked out, and the date that it is due to be returned. Ideally, this information would be presented in a chronological sequence, with the most overdue loan appearing first and the most recent loan appearing last. This is another example where highlighting would be ideal to indicate those loans that were overdue or about to become overdue.

If everything is in order with the member's account, the librarian checks out the books. They would like to check out the books by running a scanner down the spines of the books, as the ISBN and the copy number are encoded on the spines. The ISBN, title, and author information then appears on the computer screen. If the books are not loanable, a warning message appears on the checkout terminal's screen.

Occasionally, when a book is overdue, members sneak the book back onto the shelves to avoid an overdue fee. If a member tries to check out a book that, according to the database, is already checked out, the librarians need to be able to access the checkout information, including the member's name, the last checkout date, and the due date. If a book that is still officially checked out is presented at the front desk for checkout, a message should appear that alerts the librarians that the book is already checked out. By forcing the librarians to clear the previous loan before continuing with the book check out, they would update their records immediately.

Overall, for book check out, the librarians need to know who has the book, when it was checked out, and when it is due to be returned.

## Historical Information Requirements

Occasionally the librarians must locate historical information, mostly for the Town Council and the Planning Commission. These groups always want to know the volume of circulation, the popularity of various books, the reliability of return, and the average length of a borrowing term. Therefore, the librarians need to quickly prepare summaries of these types of information.

The types of information that are frequently requested include the following:

- How many loans did the library do last year?
- What percentage of the membership borrowed at least one book?
- How many books were borrowed by the member who borrowed the most books?
- What percentage of the books were loaned out at least once last year?
- What percentage of all loans eventually become overdue?
- What is the average length of a loan?
- What are the library's peak hours for loans?

These groups request a different type of information than what the members request. The members mostly want to know about book availability; usually by either title or author.

## Daily Library Functions

Stored procedures can be written to fulfill many daily library functions. For the library to run efficiently, the most important daily functions are as follows:

1. Checking out books.
2. Inquiring about book availability by either title or author.
3. Enrolling new members.
4. Inquiring about historical usage based on either book criteria or member criteria.
5. Returning books.
6. Notifying members about books on reserve.
7. Running batch reports, such as generating a list of best sellers that are not checked out or a list of all overdue books.
8. Adding new book titles to the database.

# Library Database Design

Based on the information presented by the librarians, the database designer on this project decided to implement the entities from the preceding scenario in three groups of tables. The first group models the two kinds of people who check out books from the West Overshoe Municipal Library. As shown in the following figure, the first group comprises three tables: *member*, *adult*, and *juvenile*.

### member

| member_no | lastname | firstname | middle_i | photo |
|-----------|----------|-----------|----------|-------|
| PK | NN | NN | | |
| 1 | Anderson | Andrew | A | ~~~ |
| 2 | Barr | Andrew | R | ~~~ |
| 3 | Barr | Bill | NULL | ~~~ |
| 4 | Anderson | Bill | B | |
| 5 | Anderson | Sally | A | ~~~ |
| 6 | Henson | Jack | NULL | ~~~ |

### adult

| member_no | street | city | state | zip | phone_no | expr_date |
|-----------|--------|------|-------|-----|----------|-----------|
| PK, FK | NN | NN | NN | NN | | NN |
| 1 | Elm St | Seattle | WA | 98022 | NULL | Jun 06 1992 |
| 2 | Bowery Ave | Seattle | WA | 98022 | (206)555-1212 | Aug 07 1992 |
| 6 | Bowery Ave | Kent | WA | 98206 | NULL | Mar 03 1993 |

### juvenile

| member_no | adult_member_no | birth_date |
|-----------|-----------------|------------|
| PK, FK | FK, NN | NN |
| 3 | 2 | Jun 01 1980 |
| 4 | 1 | Mar 01 1978 |
| 5 | 1 | Nov 05 1982 |

In this example, the *member* table is the master table, while *adult* and *juvenile* are subcomponents. These entities could have been modeled in several different ways, including using either a single table, a member and juvenile table, or even multiple tables. If a single table had been used for all of the members, many addresses would have been duplicated because children in this model have the same address as their parents. The redundant address information can be reduced by splitting the membership information into several tables. The librarians need to track birth dates of juveniles only, so splitting the membership information into several tables eliminates the NULLs or blank column entries that would have resulted for the birth dates of adults. These tables have been structured to contain some redundant data in order to make querying more efficient. Dividing the tables in this fashion also models the scenario in a way that reflects the membership of the library. In this group of tables, member-to-adult is a one-to-one relationship; adult-to-juvenile is a one-to-many relationship.

All three of the tables shown in the preceding figure use the *member_no* column as a primary key. Because the value in this column is different for each member and uniquely identifies each row of information, the *member_no* column is a good choice for a primary key.

The *title, item,* and *copy* tables logically form a second group, and are shown in the following figure. The key table of this group is *title* table. For each listing in the *title* table, one or more entries exist in the *item* table because a book may be available in several languages, be available in softback or hardback, or be loanable or unloanable. Title-to-item is a one-to-many relationship. For each listing in the *item* table, one or more copies of that item can exist. Therefore, item-to-copy is a one-to-many relationship.

**title**

| title_no | title | author | synopsis |
|----------|-------|--------|----------|
| PK | NN | NN | |
| 1 | Gone With the Wind | Mitchell | ~~~ |
| 2 | Color Purple | Walker | ~~~ |
| 3 | Hotel | Hailey | |
| 4 | Winnie the Pooh | Milne | ~~~ |

**item**

| isbn | title_no | language | cover | loanable |
|------|----------|----------|-------|----------|
| PK | FK, NN | | | |
| 1 | 1 | English | softback | Y |
| 2 | 2 | French | NULL | N |
| 3 | 3 | French | hardback | Y |
| 4 | 4 | NULL | hardback | NULL |
| 5 | 2 | English | softback | Y |

**copy**

| isbn | copy_no | title_no | on_loan |
|------|---------|----------|---------|
| PK, FK | PK | FK, NN | NN |
| 1 | 1 | 1 | Y |
| 1 | 2 | 1 | Y |
| 2 | 1 | 2 | N |
| 3 | 1 | 3 | Y |
| 4 | 1 | 4 | Y |
| 4 | 2 | 4 | Y |

The *item* table has a column titled *loanable.* Rather than putting the information from this column in the *copy* table, the database designer assumes that all copies of a particular item are either loanable or not loanable.

Notice that the *copy* table has a primary key made up of two columns. This type of primary key is called a *composite key.* The combination of *isbn* and *copy_no* uniquely identifies each row in the table. SQL Server allows up to 16 columns in a composite key.

The *copy* table contains a duplicate *title_no* column. This group of tables has been denormalized in order to reduce the number of joins (the linking of two or more tables) needed to retrieve information. Additionally, the *on_loan* column is *derived data*. In other words, the information in the *on_loan* column could be generated with a query each time the information is needed, but the information is kept in the table in order to make it readily available and to reduce the number of calculations that must be performed. Derived data columns also help concurrency. The *on_loan* column is populated using information from the *loan* table, as shown in the following figure. Because the *loan* table is changed frequently, locks could prevent a user from getting this information. The *copy* table is more likely to be used in a read-only fashion, so it would not be necessary to prevent users from accessing information stored there.

---

**Note**   In the following figure, FK1 implies a composite foreign key. FK defines a single column FK.

---

**reservation**

| isbn | member_no | log_date | remarks |
|------|-----------|----------|---------|
| PK, FK | PK, FK | | |
| 1 | 2 | Mar 17 1992 | ~~~ |
| 1 | 3 | NULL | NULL |
| 4 | 3 | Mar 18 1992 | ~~~ |

**loan**

| isbn | copy_no | title_no | member_no | out_date | due_date |
|------|---------|----------|-----------|----------|----------|
| PK, FK1 | PK, FK1 | FK, NN | FK, NN | NN | NN |
| 1 | 1 | 1 | 1 | Mar 15 1992 | Mar 29 1992 |
| 4 | 1 | 4 | 1 | Mar 15 1992 | Mar 29 1992 |
| 4 | 2 | 4 | 2 | Mar 17 1992 | Apr 01 1992 |
| 3 | 1 | 3 | 3 | Mar 18 1992 | Apr 02 1992 |
| 1 | 2 | 1 | 1 | Mar 15 1992 | Mar 29 1992 |

| *loanhist* | | | | | | |
|---|---|---|---|---|---|---|
| *isbn* | *copy_no* | *out_date* | *title_no* | *member_no* | *due_date* | *in_date* |
| PK, FK1 | PK, FK1 | PK | FK, NN | FK, NN | | |
| 1 | 1 | Oct 13 1991 | 1 | 4 | Oct 27 1991 | Oct 26 1991 |
| 2 | 1 | Jul 07 1991 | 2 | 2 | Jul 21 1991 | NULL |
| 2 | 1 | Oct 13 1991 | 2 | 4 | Oct 27 1991 | Oct 28 1991 |
| 1 | 2 | Nov 06 1991 | 1 | 3 | Nov 20 1991 | Nov 14 1991 |
| 1 | 1 | Oct 30 1991 | 1 | 1 | Nov 13 1991 | Nov 15 1991 |

| *loanhist (cont)* | | | |
|---|---|---|---|
| *fine_assessed* | *fine_paid* | *fine_waived* | *remarks* |
| | | | |
| 0.00 | 0.00 | 0.00 | ~~~ |
| 0.10 | 0.10 | 0.00 | ~~~ |
| 0.00 | 0.00 | 0.00 | ~~~ |
| 0.20 | 0.00 | 0.20 | |

Each table has a distinct purpose. The *reservation* table tracks current reservations for each book, *loan* tracks information on currently-loaned books, while *loanhist* keeps information on books that have been loaned and returned. It is possible to combine the *loan* and *loanhist* tables to reduce duplication, but combining them may create different problems. The *loanhist* table is essentially a history of all loans and could become unwieldy. Over time, the librarians may want to dump information from this table, so it makes sense to keep all of this information in its own table. In addition, this business model requires several queries to be made against the *loanhist* table. These queries would be easier to implement and faster to execute if the history information were kept separately from the loan information.

The *loan* and *loanhist* tables also represent different functions of the application. When checking out a book, an entry is made to the *loan* table. When returning a book, an entry is made to the *loanhist* table. By keeping separate tables for each function and denormalizing the tables, the librarians can access the information more quickly. The tradeoff is that because the tables are denormalized, they require more maintenance. For example, when *item.title_no* is updated, the *title_no* column must be updated in the *loan*, *loanhist*, and *copy* tables. Because updates to the *title_no* column may be infrequent, denormalization may speed up queries.

APPENDIX  E

# Quick Reference for isql

**isql** **/U** *login_id* [**/e**] [**/E**] [**/p**] [**/n**] [**/d** *dbname*] [**/q** *"query"*] [**/Q** *"query"*]
[ **/c** *cmdend*] [ **/h** *headers*] [ **/w** *columnwidth*] [ **/s** *colseparator*]
[ **/t** *timeout*] [ **/m** *errorlevel*] [**/L**] [**/?**] [**r** { **0** | **1** }]
[ **/H** *wksta_name*] [ **/P** *password*]
[**/S** *servername*] [**/i** *inputfile*] [**/o** *outputfile*] [**/a** *packet_size*]

| Command prompt switches | Function |
| --- | --- |
| **/U** *login_id* | Allows the user to specify a login ID. Login IDs are case sensitive. |
| **/e** | Echos input. The editor is defined in the EDITOR environment variable. Default is 'edlin'. |
| **/E** | Uses a trusted connection instead of using a password. |
| **/p** | Prints out performance statistics. |
| **/n** | Removes numbering and the prompt symbol (>) from input lines. |
| **/d** *dbname* | Issues a USE *dbname* statement when **isql** starts. |
| **/q** *"query"* | Executes a query when **isql** starts. (Note that the query statement shouldn't include **'go'**). If you issue a query from a batch file you can use %variables. Environment %variables% also work. Use double straight quotation marks around the query, and single straight quotation marks with anything embedded in the query. |
| **/Q** *"query"* | Executes a query and immediately exits **isql**. Use double straight quotation marks around the query and single straight quotation marks with anything embedded in the query. |
| **/c** *cmdend* | The command terminator. By default, commands are terminated and sent to SQL Server by entering **go** on a line by itself. When you reset the command terminator, do not use SQL reserved words or characters that have special meaning to the operating system, whether preceded by a backslash or not. |
| **/h** *headers* | The number of rows to print between column headings. The default is to print headings only once for each set of query results. |
| **/w** *columnwidth* | Allows the user to set the screen width for output. The default is 80 characters. When an output line has reached it maximum screen width, it is broken into multiple lines. |
| **/s** *colseparator* | The column-separator character is blank by default. To use characters that have special meaning to the operating system, precede them with a backslash (\). |
| **/t** *timeout* | The number of seconds before a command times out. If no timeout is specified, a command runs indefinitely; however, the default timeout for logging in to **isql** is 60 seconds. |

(*continued*)

| Command prompt switches | Function |
| --- | --- |
| /**m** *errorlevel* | Customizes display of error messages. The message number, state, and error level are displayed for errors of the specified severity level or higher. Nothing is displayed for errors of levels lower than the specified level. |
| /**L** | Lists the locally configured servers and the names of the servers broadcasting on the network. |
| [**r** { 0 \| 1}] | Redirects message output to **stderr**. If you don't specify a parameter, or if you specify 0, only error-level message severity (severity 17 or higher) is redirected. If you specify 1, all message output (including "print") is redirected. |
| /**?** | Displays the syntax summary of **isql** switches. |
| /**H** *wksta_name* | A workstation name, changing the value in the dynamic system table *sysprocesses,* if the user logs in on a different computer. If no name is specified, the current computer name is assumed. |
| /**P** *password* | Specifies a password. If the /**P** option is not used, **isql** prompts for one. Passwords are case sensitive. |
| /**S** *servername* | Specifies the name of the SQL Server to connect to. The *servername* is the name of the server computer on the network. |
| /**i** *inputfile* | Specifies the name of the file that contains a batch of SQL statements or stored procedures. The less-than symbol (<) can be used in place of /**I**. |
| /**o** *outputfile* | Specifies the name of the file that receives output from **isql**. The greater-than symbol (>) can be used in place of /**o**. Two greater-than symbols (>>) append the file rather than replace it. |
| /**a** *packet_size* | Allows you to request a different size packet. The valid values for *packet_size* are 512 through 65535. The default value for the Windows NT–based version of **isql** is 8192; otherwise the default value is 512 for MS-DOS, although larger sizes can be requested with that version as well. |

# Query Execution

**Interactive mode**  Give the **isql** command (and any of the options) at the operating system prompt. You can read an operating system file into the command buffer with *:r filename*. Do not include a command terminator in the file; enter the terminator interactively once editing is finished.

**Batch mode**  You can read in a file containing a query for execution by **isql** by typing a command similar to this:

   **isql /U alma /P /i stores.qry**

The file must include a command terminator. The results are displayed on the user's workstation.

# Commands to Use with isql

| Commands | Function |
| --- | --- |
| **go** | Executes a command. |
| **reset** | Clears any statements you have entered. |
| **ed** | Calls the editor. |
| *!!command* | Executes an operating system command. |
| **quit** or **exit** | Exits from **isql**. |
| CTRL+C | Terminates a query without exiting from **isql**. |

A P P E N D I X   F

# Bibliography

## SQL Server Resources

### Periodicals

#### *Directions on Microsoft* (formerly *Microsoft Directions*)

A monthly newsletter that reviews and analyzes industry news based on information obtained from sources generally available to the public and from industry contacts. Back issues are available.

Directions on Microsoft
Redmond Communications, Inc.
15127 NE 24th, Suite 293
Redmond, WA 98052-5547
Tel (206) 882-3396     Fax (206) 885-0848

#### *Microsoft Systems Journal*

*Microsoft Systems Journal* (MSJ) is published bimonthly focusing on areas of interest to developers.

Microsoft Systems Journal
PO Box 56621
Boulder, CO 80322-6621
Tel (800) 666-1084
Outside the U.S. call (303) 678-0439
Back issues available call (913) 841-1631

### SQL Forum

SQL Forum is a journal for the international SQL Server Community and is published bimonthly.

SQL Forum
40087 Mission Blvd., Suite 167
Fremont, CA 94539
Tel (800) 943-9300
Tel (206) 672-8870

### Microsoft SQL Server Professional

Pinnacle Publishing, Inc.
PO Box 888
Kent, WA 98035-9912
Tel (800) 788-1900

Internet address: sqlpro@pinpub.com
Web site: http://www.pinpub.com

# Suggested Reading List

### General Database Books

Codd, E. F. *The Relational Model for Database Management: Version 2.* Addison-Wesley Publishing Co., 1990.

Date, C. J. *An Introduction to Database System Volume 1.* Addison-Wesley Publishing Co., 1990.

Date, C. J. *Relational Database: Selected Writings 1985-1989.* Addison-Wesley Publishing Co., 1989.

Elmasri, R. and S. B. Navathe. *Fundamentals of Database Systems.* Benjamin/Cummings, 1989.

Gray, Jim and Andreas Reuter. *Transaction Processing: Concepts and Techniques.* Morgan Kaufmann Publishers, Inc., 1993.

Khanna, Raman, editor. *Distributed Computing, Implementation and Management Strategies.* Prentice Hall, 1994.

Kirkwood, John, editor. *Sysbase Architecture and Administration.* Ellis Horwood Publishers, 1992.

Korth, Henry K. and Abraham Silberschatz. *Database System Concepts*. McGraw-Hill Book Co., 1986.

Shasha, Dennis E. *Database Tuning, A Principled Approach*. Prentice Hall, 1992.

von Halle, Fleming. *Handbook of Relational Database Design*. Addison-Wesley Publishing Co., 1989.

## Microsoft Windows NT Book

Custer, Helen. *Inside Windows NT*, Microsoft Press®, 1993.

## Structured Query Language Books

Bowman, Judith S., Sandra L. Emerson, and Marcy Darnovsky. *The Practical SQL Handbook: Using Structured Query Language*. 2nd Ed. Addison-Wesley Publishing Company, 1993.

Celko, Joe. *Instant SQL Programming*. WROX Press Ltd, 1995.

Celko, Joe. *SQL for Smarties: Advanced SQL Programming*. Morgan Kaufmann Publishers, Inc., 1995.

Chappell, David and J. Harvey Trimble, Jr. *A Visual Introduction to SQL*. Wiley, 1989.

Date, C. J. and Hugh Darwen. *A Guide to the SQL Standard: A User's Guide to the Standard Relational Language SQL* (3rd Ed.). Addison-Wesley Publishing Co., 1993.

Hursch, Carolyn J. and Jack L. Hursch. *SQL the Structured Query Language*. TAB BOOKS Inc., 1988.

Melton, Jim and Alan R. Simon. *Understanding the New SQL: A Complete Guide*. Morgan Kaufmann Publishers, Inc., 1993.

Pascal, Fabian. *SQL and Relational Basics: The Essential Guide to Understanding and Evaluating SQL Databases*. M & T Publishing Co., 1990.

Van der Lans, Rick F. *Introduction to SQL*. Addison-Wesley Publishing Co., 1988.

## SQL Server Books

Garbus, Jeff, Bennet W. McEwan, Ray Rankins, David Solomon, and Daniel Woodbeck. *Microsoft SQL Server 6 Unleashed*. SAMS Publishing, 1996.

Groff, James R. and Paul N. Weinberg. *LAN Times Guide to SQL*. Osborne/Mc Graw-Hill, 1994.

Groff, James R. and Paul N. Weinberg. *Using SQL*. Osborne/Mc Graw-Hill, 1990.

Heng, Tan. *The Visual Basic—SQL Server Primer*. ETN, 1994.

Khoshafian, Setrag, Arvola Chan, Anna Wong, and Harry K.T. Wong. *A Guide to Developing Client/Server SQL Applications*. Morgan Kaufmann Publishers, Inc., 1992.

Mc Goveran, D. and C. J. Date. *A Guide to Sybase and SQL Server.* Addison-Wesley Publishing Co., 1992.

Nath, Aloke. *The Guide to SQL Server.* 2nd Ed., Addison-Wesley Publishing Co., 1994.

Pantajja, Jim, Mary Pantajja, and Bruce Prendergast. *Microsoft SQL Server Survival Guide.* John Wiley and Sons, Inc., 1996.

Sledge, Orryn and Mark Spenik. *Microsoft SQL Server DBA Survival Guide.* SAMS Publishing, 1995.

Vaughn, William R. *Hitchhiker's Guide to Visual Basic and SQL Server.* 4th Ed. Microsoft Press, 1996.

# Suggested Microsoft Official Curriculum

*System Administration for Microsoft SQL Server 6*

This five-day course is intended for system administrators who implement and support Microsoft SQL Server in an enterprise network. At the end of the course, students will be able to install and configure SQL Server version 6; manage the storage requirements of a database; manage user accounts, login security, and database permissions; manage the import, export, and replication of data; and maintain the system and perform day-to-day operations including backing up and restoring a database, recovering from a system disaster, scheduling tasks, setting alerts, monitoring, and tuning performance.

*Implementing a Database Design on Microsoft SQL Server 6*

This five-day course is intended for system engineers and developers who are responsible for implementing Microsoft SQL Server and writing Transact-SQL code. At the end of the course, students will be able to create database devices, databases, user-defined datatypes, and tables; write Transact-SQL statements to query data, manipulate data, and program the server; identify issues to consider when creating indexes; create views, triggers, and stored procedures; enforce data integrity by creation and implementation of constraints, defaults, and rules; describe the two cursor implementations available in SQL Server; determine how distributed data can be implemented; and determine which external components should be incorporated into the server environment.

*Performance Tuning and Optimization of Microsoft SQL Server for Windows NT*

This five-day advanced class is for Microsoft SQL Server database owners, designers, developers, and system administrators who are responsible for diagnosing and tuning Microsoft SQL Server for optimal performance. At the end of the class, students will be able to identify factors that impact performance; configure the server for optimal performance; implement optimal physical database design through the use of segments and indexes; select the best indexes for different types of queries; write better queries based on an understanding of how the query optimizer works; use stored procedures to increase performance; evaluate opportunities for denormalizing logical database design to improve performance; minimize contention and avoid deadlocks; manage ongoing maintenance; and evaluate and solve performance problems using a performance tuning methodology.

# Additional Resources

## Microsoft TechNet

Microsoft TechNet is an information service for support professionals and system administrators. TechNet members receive a monthly compact disc containing extensive technical information. To join TechNet, refer to the TechNet section within Roadmap, or refer to the Microsoft Directory for contact information.

## Microsoft Roadmap

The Microsoft Roadmap to Education and Certification contains complete information about the Microsoft Certified Professional program, Microsoft Official Curriculum, sample exams for the MCP program, and the Microsoft Directory, a worldwide directory of handy Microsoft telephone numbers. The latest version of the Roadmap is available from the following sources:

- Internet: ftp://ftp.microsoft.com/services/msedcert/e&cmap.zip
- MSN, The Microsoft Network online service: Go to Roadfiles
- CompuServe: Go MECFORUM, Library #2, E&CMAP.ZIP
- TechNet: Search for "Roadmap" and install from the built-in setup link.
- Microsoft: Call Microsoft at (800) 636-7544 and ask for the Roadmap. Outside the United States and Canada, contact your local Microsoft subsidiary.

## The Microsoft Developer Network

The Microsoft Developer Network is a technical resource for developers using Microsoft products for development or creating products for the Microsoft Windows operating system. Members receive information on a regular basis through three channels:

The Microsoft Developer Network CD

The Microsoft Developer Network News

The Developer Network Forum on CompuServe

This information includes technical articles written by development experts at Microsoft, documentation for Microsoft development tools, sample code, the latest product specifications, and selected Microsoft Press books. To join the Microsoft Developer Network, refer to the Microsoft Developer Network section within Roadmap, or refer to the Microsoft Directory for contact information.

## CompuServe

CompuServe provides access to technical forums for open discussions and questions about Microsoft products.

## Microsoft World Wide Web Sites

| Site | Description |
| --- | --- |
| www.microsoft.com | Microsoft Corporation's home page. |
| www.microsoft.com/backoffice | The home page for the Microsoft BackOffice suite of products, including Windows NT, SQL Server, Internet Information Server, Microsoft Exchange Server, Systems Management Server, SNA Server, and Microsoft Mail Server. |

# Index

## Q

# Notes

# Notes

# Notes

# Notes

# Notes